Franklin D. Roosevelt and the World Crisis, 1937-1945

PROBLEMS IN
AMERICAN CIVILIZATION

Under the editorial direction of
Edwin C. Rozwenc
Amherst College

Franklin D. Roosevelt and the World Crisis, 1937-1945

Edited and with an introduction by

Warren F. Kimball
Rutgers—The State University of New Jersey
Newark College

D. C. HEATH AND COMPANY
Lexington, Massachusetts Toronto London

To my Mom and Dad

CONTENTS

INTRODUCTION

The fundamental foreign policy questions that found temporary resolution with American intervention in World War II brought on heated debate long before the actual event. Shocked and disillusioned by the failure of World War I to bring on a world of peace and harmony, Americans chose to remain aloof from the everyday activities of international politics during the 1920s, dipping a tentative toe into the troubled waters only when issues of moral leadership or economics were involved. Although the nature and goals of foreign policy in the Republican years (1921–1933) could well be the subject of a separate problem study, most observers agree that virtually all Americans opposed open, power-politics–style intervention on the world scene. Thus, in one sense, the argument over intervention by the United States in what was to be World War II took place when Americans avoided collective security and the League of Nations, expressed concern over the slow but steady deterioration and collapse of democratic government in Germany (the Weimar Republic), and demonstrated concern and shock over Japan's military actions in Manchuria in 1931.

By the time of Franklin Roosevelt's first inauguration as President in March, 1933, Americans found themselves deeply disturbed by the overall international situation. Although the domestic economic crisis of the depression remained uppermost in the public mind, American leaders saw the entire interwar system collapsing around them. Unconsciously and haphazardly begun at the Paris Peace Conference after World War I and renewed at such gatherings as the Washington Naval Conference of 1921, the system aimed at the preservation of the status quo—the standard goal of the victors. Three major nations were excluded from the system: Germany, as the major loser in the war; Soviet Russia, as both a collaborator with the enemy and a social outcast whose avowed goals were the destruction of the existing social and economic order; and China, torn by internal dissension and offered as the ransom required to bring Japan into the system. American participation in the system was extensive, though sharply delimited. Political leadership in European and colonial affairs rested with Britain and France, while in the Pacific area, American leaders agreed only to talk. The Nine-Power Treaty, negotiated during the Washington Naval Conference, consisted largely of a genuflection in the direction of the Open Door in China plus reassuring phrases about that nation's territorial integrity. The basic foundation of the international system in East Asia was the Four-Power Treaty of 1922, which provided for consultations between the major powers—Britain, France, Japan, and the United States—thus eliminating China and Russia from what was intended to be the real power structure. Since private American funds provided much of the system's economic base, both in Europe and Asia, even such limited participation by the United States in political affairs seemed the equivalent of a *nihil obstat.* The Washington Treaties, American approval of the Locarno Agreements, the Kellogg-Briand Peace Pact, and "observing" at the League of Nations all implied American support for the system. The fundamental boundary of this participation was the American policy of avoiding prior commitments requiring the use of military or economic force (sanctions). In spite of almost constant disarmament talks from 1919 through 1933, the United States proved as reluctant to disarm as did the other major powers. But even though they had the arms, American leaders, strongly supported by the public, refused to commit the nation to military defense of the international system.

Not surprisingly, that system—under enormous strain because of the Great Depression—came under direct attack by the three outcasts. The first major challenge came when Chinese nationalism, long ignored and trampled on by the Western powers, provided the impetus for opposition to Japan's dominance in Manchuria. When Chinese opposition reached a level dangerous to Japanese interests, Japan's military leaders responded with quick and brutal force. Americans were appalled. They had long been suspicious of Japanese expansion in East Asia as a challenge to American economic and emotional commitments in China, and the use of military force convinced Americans that Japan could not be trusted. A few, notably Secretary of State Henry Stimson, suggested the use of economic sanctions to pressure Japan to withdraw, but they were quickly overruled by President Herbert Hoover who fully reflected the general American reluctance to guarantee the political status quo by force. Ironically, the United States ended up going to war with a nation which was only trying to maintain the same international system that both countries had helped establish. By American standards Japan had gone outside the pale by resorting to naked force; but Japan saw its action as merely the same thing the Europeans had always done in China. By 1941 the image of Japan in the United States was that of a nation trying to destroy international order and Western civilization, yet in reality the struggle was one of classic power politics with raw materials and economic interests in East Asia the prize.

The second outcast power, the Soviet Union, adopted policies that both frightened and confused the great powers. As Germany became increasingly belligerent under Hitler, the Russians realized that participation in the system that had defeated and controlled Germany would benefit her own security. American diplomatic recognition of the Soviet regime in Russia in 1933, though prompted largely by hopes of improved trade as well as Franklin Roosevelt's belief that nonrecognition of a fact was rather silly, also aimed at using Soviet strength in Siberia as a psychological check upon Japanese expansion in northern China. Nonetheless, the Soviet Union could not join the system in Europe without making economic and political concessions which would jeopardize the ideological structure of the Russian Revolution and the position of leaders in the Kremlin, and that they refused to do. The final result was the Nazi-Soviet Pact of 1939, which collapsed two years later under the pressure of each nation's greed for domination of Eastern Europe. Ultimately, the Soviet Union allied with the Western power system during World War II, but on its own terms and in a spirit of mutual need.

The last of the outcasts, Germany, proved to be the greatest tragedy and the greatest threat to the system. The Allied powers destroyed much of the German political structure in 1919 but then, on the excuse of not interfering in the democratic process, permitted Germany to slide into political chaos. With the French interested only in reparations for reasons of both security and economics, the United

States concerned almost exclusively in capital investment without political strings, and the British combining the two, it became possible for nationalistic demagogues who promised a rebirth of both prosperity and self-respect to gain the support of the German people. For reasons not particularly relevant to this study, Adolf Hitler and the Nazi movement won out against Communists, the militarist/monarchists, and similar groups, all outside the limits of traditional Western liberalism.

Thus, when Franklin Roosevelt became President of the United States in 1933, the general international system threatened to collapse both politically and economically. Although the Great Depression and the military/political challenges posed by Germany and Japan were not intrinsically related, American foreign policy had to deal with both simultaneously. Not surprisingly, the newly inaugurated President concentrated on attempting to restore economic prosperity, since the political aspects of the international situation did not pose immediate threats to American interests or security. Nevertheless, foreign policy matters during Roosevelt's first term (March, 1933–January, 1937) did concern the President and his advisors. In addition to responding to the problems raised by the three outcasts (Japan having displaced China in that role by virtue of using military force, which was moralistically labeled as aggression by the other major powers), Roosevelt also had to make decisions regarding the international economic scene.

In general, historians have claimed that Roosevelt followed a policy of economic nationalism and political isolationism before 1937 either out of personal conviction or because of the pressure of American public opinion, though alternative explanations are possible. The major foreign policy and foreign economic issues of the period certainly did find the United States flatly refusing to commit either political or economic forces to the maintenance of the system. The London Economic Conference of 1933, arranged by the Hoover Administration in harmony with its belief that the roots of the depression lay outside the United States, collapsed when Roosevelt refused to cooperate with various schemes designed to commit American financial strength to the support of British and French currency. On the surface such action appeared to be blatant economic nationalism and thus merely an economic variation of isolationism. However, it is possible to view Roosevelt's decision as an eminently practical one if he honestly believed that such a stabilization scheme simply would not work. In 1936, when the French monetary system seemed on the verge of complete disaster, the Roosevelt Administration worked out an agreement with France and Great Britain that staved off such financial collapse. Not only did Roosevelt believe such action would benefit the American economy in 1936, but he and his advisors also wished to prevent Germany from taking advantage of any economic confusion in France.

So, too, the political crises of the pre-1937 period are open to various interpretations. The slow but steady development of an aggressive and threatening Nazi policy initially caught the great powers with their hypocrisy showing. Revisionist historians and political economists writing in the 1920s and 1930s had left many leaders and large segments of the public in the United States and Europe convinced that Germany had been unjustly persecuted after World War I. Thus Hitler's actions before 1938 could be cast in the light of rewriting the Treaty of Versailles rather than the nightmare of world conquest pictured by later propaganda. Germany walked out of the disarmament conference (by 1933 a *pro forma* facade) and the League of Nations, claiming that the Allies had reneged on their promise to disarm while simultaneously demanding that Germany comply with the highly restrictive disarmament provisions of the Versailles Treaty. In 1935 Germany announced full rearmament and a few months later signed a naval agreement with Great Britain— an action that seemingly gave great-power approval to the German decision to rebuild its military strength. The remilitarization of the Rhineland in 1936 (a move forbidden by the Versailles Treaty) seemed only fair since no one else in Europe had unfortified frontiers, and even German occupation and annexation of Austria (*Anschluss*) in March, 1938, only fulfilled a long-standing recommendation of leading economists that Austria needed to combine with someone in order to be economically viable. No one liked Hitler's style or domestic policies, but persecution of Jews was as old as Christianity. Soviet repression of religion seemed far more immoral than Hitler's campaign against the churches, but no one advocated an invasion of Russia. The notion of intervening to protect minority groups in a country raised challenges to the status quo that no nation could or would even think about. Thus, even as late as 1938 and the famous Munich agreements where Great Britain and France willingly

sacrificed the territorial integrity of Czechoslovakia to German expansion, the great powers could find little justification—either in
terms of practical politics or international "law"—for the use of
strong military or economic sanctions against Hitler.

On the surface, American foreign policy appeared dominated by
a desire to avoid any involvement with either the increasingly tense
European situation or the Japanese *fait accompli* in Manchuria. This
attitude took on concrete form when Congress passed a series of
bills designed to prevent the type of economic commitment to Europe
which many thought had brought America into World War I. Beginning with the Johnson Debt-Default Act of 1934 (which forbade
private loans to nations that had defaulted on their war debts), and
peaking with the neutrality legislation of 1935–1936 (which prohibited
travel by Americans on belligerent ships and virtually eliminated
trade with nations at war), American foreign policy in the mid-1930s
gave the appearance of isolation and refusal to recognize the political
facts of life. At another level, however, the Roosevelt Administration
indicated its awareness of the seriousness of the problem. When the
Italians under Mussolini, lured by fanciful dreams of a new Roman
Empire, went to war with Ethiopia, the United States applied the
Neutrality Laws but simultaneously indicated its willingness to cooperate with any sanctions that the League and the major powers
imposed on Italy. Similarly, during the Spanish Civil War, which
broke out in 1936 and quickly saw the Italians and Germans giving
support to Francisco Franco's rebel forces, American policy was to
go along with any joint European action against the Fascist trio.
In each case, Britain and France refused to take the lead. The Tripartite Monetary Agreement of 1936, mentioned above, again indicated the desire of the Roosevelt Administration to shore up Britain
and France against Germany. In short, the United States under President Franklin Roosevelt seems to have been afraid to lead for fear
that no one would follow. Put another way, it seemed foolish to try
to save Britain and France, particularly in view of American domestic
politics, until Britain and France wanted to be saved.

The year 1937 provided the events that shifted the Roosevelt
foreign policy, slowly but steadily, from passive following to active
leadership. That change is the basic subject matter of this book.
Readers looking in this introduction for a summary of the selections

that follow will be disappointed, for the readings speak for themselves. The various excerpts will not prove anything; rather they will confuse and anger the reader, and—hopefully—stimulate him to further research and thought. The real purpose is to illuminate the major ways in which the Roosevelt foreign policy can be interpreted. Readers should be aware that interpretations usually reflect the background and biases of the authors, though that does not necessarily mean they are wrong.

There are two glaring gaps in this study that demand explanation. First is the complete lack of any coverage regarding American policy toward Latin America—the so-called Good Neighbor Policy. There is no question of the importance of Franklin Roosevelt's policy toward America's hemisphere neighbors, but that policy was initially unrelated, except by the accident of time and space, to the world crisis that engulfed Europe and Asia. In addition, as German and Japanese expansion increasingly occupied American policy-makers, Latin American problems lost their significance, except where they touched directly on the larger struggle (for example, German economic and political infiltration in Argentina and Brazil). In other words, between 1937 and 1945, Roosevelt sought to relate Latin America to the world crisis, making his foreign policy in the Americas largely a function of European and even East Asian politics.

A second gap is the failure of any of the selections to examine adequately the sources of German and, more particularly, Japanese conduct. The policies of those two countries did not develop in a vacuum, and some understanding of their motives and aspirations is essential to an understanding of America's response.[1] Although Americans frequently see themselves as free agents, capable of acting or not acting according to their own desires, that is simply not the case.

Another editorial decision requires comment. This study is titled *Franklin D. Roosevelt and the World Crisis* precisely because it does center on Roosevelt's foreign policy, leadership, and overall ideas. There are many reasons for this choice. One is that the Constitution and the Supreme Court have given the President extensive freedom

---

[1] A good starting point for a study of these questions are two problem studies: Ivan Morris (ed.), *Japan 1931–1945: Militarism, Fascism, Japanism?* (Boston: D. C. Heath and Company, 1963), and John L. Snell and Allan Mitchell (eds.), *The Nazi Revolution,* 2nd ed. (Lexington, Mass.: D. C. Heath and Company, 1973).

of action in foreign policy. More importantly, what makes American foreign policy from 1937 through 1945 hang together is Franklin D. Roosevelt's conception of what its goals and methods should be. Although he has been justly accused of procrastination, a refusal to develop a well-formulated long-term policy, and frequent changes of mind—nevertheless it was to Roosevelt that the public and government officials turned for the final, crucial decisions. To a great degree Roosevelt's critics gave him this point, for most, though not all, attacks on United States policy were directed against the President, often at a personal level.

On July 7, 1937, the smoldering Sino-Japanese conflict once again burst into flames with open warfare between Chinese and Japanese armies in Peking, spreading quickly to Shanghai and other major Chinese cities. From that point on the Roosevelt Administration faced a series of growing crises, ultimately ending with American entry into World War II. The famous "Quarantine Speech" of October 5, 1937, in which the President suggested that international lawbreakers be quarantined, indicated an awareness of the increasing tension, though historians disagree substantially as to whether or not Roosevelt actually had any concrete steps in mind. In that same year Congress, with the support of the Administration, revised the neutrality legislation so that nonarmaments could be sold to belligerents, but only if they paid cash and transported them on their own vessels (the "cash and carry" provision). This permitted the United States to reap profits while avoiding close involvement, though it also made it possible for much of America's economic power to line up behind the French and British.

In Europe, the final breach of the system occurred somewhat later. Although the Munich agreements frightened many, Roosevelt and the leaders in France and Britain wishfully convinced themselves that with most of the claimed injustices of Versailles corrected, Hitler would thereafter concentrate on domestic affairs. The debate over this so-called appeasement policy has been protracted, but in examining it one must not expect Allied leaders to have seen into the future. The death camps, which provided an irrefutable moral imperative for war against Hitler, were not established until the 1940s; nor could the Allies foresee the blitzkrieg into Poland and the Low Countries, followed by the Battle of London and Operation Bar-

barossa (the invasion of Russia). The eventual American position was the moral one, as outlined in Davis and Lindley's *How War Came,* a book written with the encouragement of the Roosevelt Administration.[2] The dilemma of such moral diplomacy, however, is that intervention in the name of righteousness is endless, since it involves imposing one nation's ethical code upon another nation. It was that dilemma which historian Charles A. Beard pointed to time and again between 1937 and 1941, as he repeatedly attacked Roosevelt for leading the United States toward war.

The historical debate over American intervention in both Europe and Asia in 1941 needs some explanation. As the German threat to the system increased, the Roosevelt Administration moved toward deeper involvement by providing sharply increased military aid to Britain and France. When war began with the German attack on Poland (September 1, 1939), Roosevelt quickly initiated a change in the Neutrality Laws to permit the sale to belligerents of war goods —though still on a strict cash-and-carry basis. As the situation deteriorated further in Europe with the fall of the Low Countries and then, by June, 1940, the collapse of French resistance, American aid to Britain, in fact and rhetoric, continued to grow. From that point on American entry into the war against Hitler proceeded in a seemingly mechanical step-by-step progression; the destroyers-for-bases deal, Lend-Lease aid which solved Britain's financial problem, convoying by American warships, the inevitable incident at sea, and then the declaration of war. The last step actually came when the Germans, in an inexplicable afterthought to the Japanese attack on Pearl Harbor, gratuitously declared war on the United States. Whether the public outcry after the "sneak" attack by Japan would have permitted Roosevelt to declare war on the greater military threat, Germany, is a moot point, thanks to Hitler's decision to take the initiative. The Roosevelt Administration claimed that, although Britain's survival was essential to American security, their expanding program of aid held open the possibility that Great Britain could win without any commitment of American ground forces. It is interesting to note that President Roosevelt, in a scenario he personally drew up in January, 1941, envisaged use of American air and naval forces in Europe, but not ground troops.

---

[2] See *Suggestions for Additional Reading* for full references to books mentioned in this introduction.

The contemporary critics of Roosevelt's foreign policies came from two directions. On the Left, people like Beard feared Roosevelt would sacrifice New Deal domestic reform for endless intervention in defense of the old system of power politics and economic imperialism. On the Right stood an array of critics who began with staunch opposition to the same New Deal reforms that so pleased the Left. Since they often tended to personalize their views, as opposed to the Left which leaned more toward historical determinism (i.e., stressing the importance of forces rather than people), conservatives slipped easily from attacks on Roosevelt's domestic programs to a critique of his foreign policy. Strengthened by a sizeable number of Anglophobes, these so-called isolationists formed the core of anti-interventionst groups like the America First and No Foreign Wars committees. Both the Left and the Right believed that America could and should stand alone, a policy more accurately called unilateralism, or what Beard called "Fortress America." Though each segment held a radically different image of the proper domestic system for America, each denied the need for collective security.

The argument began anew among historians after the end of World War II. Republican politicians publicly accused the Roosevelt Administration of either conscious treason or unconscious malfeasance in permitting the Japanese to attack the fleet in Pearl Harbor. The congressional hearings that followed provided the stimulus and some evidence for renewed historical debate. The dispute boiled down to two essential positions: the majority of historians defended Roosevelt's intentions and basic policy, though they often quarreled with specifics. These historians, often referred to today as traditionalists, took their cue from a detailed and extensively researched narrative by William Langer and S. Everett Gleason, both in government service during the war, which studied American foreign policy, 1937–1941. Although these men and most who wrote during the late 1940s and the 1950s often accused Roosevelt of inconsistency and some degree of deception, they essentially presented the coming of war in both Europe and Asia as a function of German and Japanese policies.

The most vociferous critique of the Roosevelt foreign policy came from the Right. Obviously influenced by their belief that Roosevelt had "sold out" to the Russians and communism at conferences like Teheran and Yalta, they accused the President of having set up the fleet in Pearl Harbor so as to provoke war in Asia, with Roosevelt's real goal being to end the impasse at home caused by isolationist opposition to American intervention against Germany. Thus Charles C. Tansill titled his study of Roosevelt's foreign policy, *The Back Door to War.*

Left-wing critics, who proceeded from both pacifism and a desire for domestic reform, proved strikingly impotent during the first score of years following the close of World War II. Men like Harry Elmer Barnes, virtually obsessed by their hatred of Roosevelt, endorsed almost any attack on the President's reputation, ruining their own in the process, though Charles Beard did put together a bitter though effective critique which essentially accused the Roosevelt Administration of lying America into war.

Although recent studies have effectively destroyed the thesis put forth by the conspiracy school, its influence on at least three generations of historians proved extensive. Until the mid-1960s most students of the period concentrated on defending the Roosevelt Administration against such charges, and only in recent years has there been any attempt to again criticize Roosevelt's prewar European policy from a left-wing point of view. Another factor which contributed to the failure of the Left to develop a full-fledged critique of Roosevelt's policy toward the crisis in Europe was that any attack seemingly sympathized with the unsavory Nazi regime. The readings (second section of Part II) provide examples of the current status of historical interpretations regarding Roosevelt's European policies, though a more sophisticated left-wing critique has begun and may develop as diplomatic historians find themselves less preoccupied by the cold war and more exciting contemporary issues.

The question of Japanese-American relations prior to Pearl Harbor is both connected and separate from the European crisis. Although the Roosevelt Administration saw Germany and Japan as a joint threat, particularly after the Tripartite Pact of September, 1940, between Germany, Japan, and Italy, historians have steadily moved in the direction of viewing the two conflicts as only accidentally and incidentally connected. A radical-left analysis would see the Pacific war as merely another example of capitalist imperialism and historical inevitability, but most historians fall into one of three other categories. Those who sadly bemoan the mistaken foundations of America's East Asian policies, claiming that the United States confused sentimental ties and economic hopes in China with reality, clearly constitute a growing and probably dominant portion of historians. Some of these analysts proceed from a position that emphasizes economic motives arising out of the nature of American society (institutional necessity), while others concern themselves primarily with a critique of unrealistic and naive policies, that is, Roosevelt's failure to understand the real nature of East Asian relations and his inability to comprehend and rise above the mistakes of his predecessors. Although these arguments usually comprise two separate and distinct groups, in this case their proponents tend to give each other their arguments or else combine the two points of view themselves, as, for instance, in the case of William Neumann. The second category contains those historians who see the United States essentially as the prisoner of aggressive Japanese policies. Although they often criticize the day-by-day details of the Roosevelt foreign policy in East Asia, these writers appear satisfied with the overall righteousness of American motives. A third group, small but persistent, finds American policy foolish insofar as it stemmed from emotional or unrealistic appraisals of economics and politics in China and the Pacific, but ultimately defends action against Japan as necessary to the maintenance of a balance of power with which the United States could live comfortably. While the last two groups emphasize the unity of the two threats, Germany and Japan, the majority of American historians seem to view the Pacific war as one which could and should have been avoided without jeopardizing the war against Hitler.

For almost two years Great Britain had fought virtually alone, but not unaided, against Hitler's Germany. Then, in 1941, the situation changed. Hitler's greatest gamble, the invasion of Russia, began in June, 1941, and by the close of the year the United States was fighting against both Germany and Japan. By the end of the war in 1945, the two late arrivals stood in the seemingly contradictory positions of victorious allies and bitter, paranoid enemies. How the United States and the Union of Soviet Socialist Republics arrived at that juncture is a main theme of any study of Roosevelt's diplomacy, though not the only question of import. The intense interest of students and scholars in the origins of the cold war is reflected in the selections that follow, though some of the other themes that warrant further study do appear. Issues such as Anglo-American tension over foreign trade, American policy toward nationalism in the colonial empires, and the reconstruction of Germany and Japan, all posed problems which existed independently of the Soviet-American equation during World War II, though such independence rarely lasted beyond 1946 under the pressures of the cold war.

The details of international diplomacy during World War II are far too complex to recount here; in fact, students should be familiar with those details before reading further. Rather, the purpose of this book is to examine the style and goals of Roosevelt's leadership. Each of the selections in Part III utilizes a different grouping of events and issues to illustrate its point, but the evaluation each makes of Roosevelt would apply to the President's overall wartime diplomacy. Although most critiques of American wartime foreign policy began either as simplistic attacks on Roosevelt's naiveté in trying to cooperate with Russia or as defenses of American attempts to preserve the wartime spirit of cooperation, a few perceptive critics saw beneath the surface to more basic problems. Walter Lippmann refused to accept the notion that power politics is dead, and recommended that the United States recognize the inevitable and probably valid desires of Russia for secure spheres of influence. Others, like Under Secretary of State Sumner Welles, though solidly within the mainstream of traditional liberalism in America, foreshadowed the later left-revisionist critique by criticizing Roosevelt's failure to establish a truly cooperative political relationship with Russia early in the war.

In the nearly thirty years that have elapsed since the end of World War II, a complicated and intense historical debate has developed over the question of both the methods and goals of Roosevelt's diplomacy. The arguments have usually centered upon specific issues, of which there are an almost endless number. The decision to postpone territorial settlements until late in the war has been condemned for handing Eastern Europe to Russia, praised as a gallant if foolhardy attempt to avoid old-style power politics, and attacked as adding to justified Soviet distrust of American wartime goals. The unconditional surrender doctrine, proclaimed at the Casablanca Conference between Roosevelt and British Prime Minister Winston Churchill, is simultaneously seen as forcing Germany and Japan to fight on to the bitter end and therefore giving Soviet military forces more time to gain more territory, and as the apogee of meaningful Soviet-American trust. One group criticizes Roosevelt for concentrating on military victory to the point of ignoring equally important political matters, while others assert that political matters, particularly anti-Soviet policies and repression of the Left, remained uppermost in his mind. The decisions of the conferences at Teheran and Yalta, held between Roosevelt, Churchill, and Soviet Premier Joseph Stalin, are alternately praised as the best Roosevelt could do given the realities of the Soviet presence in Europe and the need for aid against Japan, castigated as virtual sellouts to Soviet imperialism, or interpreted as relatively reasonable settlements with Russia, which either Russia or the United States (depending upon your point of view) quickly violated. Most historians do agree that Roosevelt conducted foreign policy within the framework of certain personal idiosyncrasies that often affected the events. The President consistently deferred to domestic political necessities (for example, his comment to Stalin about the Polish-American vote) and also desperately tried to avoid unpleasant decisions. He seems to have confided regularly in no one, though some claim that the resulting gap in our knowledge of his long-term goals comes from Roosevelt's refusal to frame them even in his own mind. At the personal level, Roosevelt remains enigmatic. His policies, however, have been studied intensively, and though each student offers his or her own interpretation, some basic approaches have emerged.

The critique from the Right has largely been rejected by most scholars and students, though it offers valuable insights and poses questions that remain unanswered. Current scholarship tends to emphasize the anti-Soviet activities of American policy-makers, but a small group of scholars like Anthony Kubek have maintained the old conspiracy notions. Popular during the era of Senator Joseph McCarthy, and still supported by a steady stream of publications issued by the Senate Internal Security Subcommittee, their basic thesis is that Franklin Roosevelt foolishly believed that Russia could be trusted and was therefore easily deceived by a small but well-placed coterie of conscious agents of the Communist conspiracy. Such critiques, though often a by-product of partisan politics, had great influence upon students of the 1940s and early 1950s. The actual influence of Russian agents within the United States government has never been determined, nor is it likely to be unless Soviet intelligence records are thrown open to researchers—an unlikely prospect. Although that question remains unanswered, these critics did offer some stimulating suggestions about the relationship of foreign policy and the bureaucracy. Convinced that American foreign policy had been too soft on the Soviets, they claimed that the bureaucracy had become virtually independent of any real democratic (congressional) controls and operated almost without restraints.

Such concern for the structural or institutional pressures behind American foreign policy forms an integral part of any left-revisionist critique, though for different reasons. A distinguishing characteristic of most left-revisionist history is the belief that American foreign policy has sprung from a set of economic and political imperatives that have been present since colonial days. Placing heavy emphasis upon the way in which capitalist economics influenced the development of social and political institutions, these historians usually seek to place American foreign policy during World War II in that broad theoretical framework. Nonetheless, there are very significant differences among the various left-revisionist critics. Some, like Gabriel Kolko, virtually depersonalize history, believing that American foreign policy is essentially deterministic; that is, it follows guidelines made necessary by our economic, political, and social system. Others, like Lloyd Gardner and Diane Clemens, recognize the pressures of American institutions, but maintain that American leaders, and particularly Roosevelt, made conscious decisions and choices that determined the nature and structure of the cold war.

There remain those who, like the defenders of Roosevelt's pre-war policies, criticize the President for tactical errors and specific miscalculations, but support his overall goals and methods. To a great degree these historians see American policy hemmed in by the realities of international power politics. They defended the Roosevelt Administration against charges of selling out to the Russians in Eastern Europe by pointing out that the Red Army decided the issue —not the diplomats. And they defended the Roosevelt Administration against charges of anti-Soviet actions by claiming that Russian paranoia and intransigence prevented the development of any relationship based upon mutual trust.

The historical debate over Roosevelt's foreign policy during World War II has become increasingly sophisticated, and the selections in Part III make evident the fact that scholars have regularly borrowed from the arguments of their opponents. Still, basic philosophical differences continue to underlie their points of view. The last section of readings illustrates the three major interpretations of Franklin D. Roosevelt as foreign policy maker. All three authors see Roosevelt as archetypical of the true nature of American society; whether that be the idealism of moral leadership in the world, the consistent and persistent attempts to extend the scope of our system throughout the world (the Open Door), or a simple practicality often cloaked in idealistic rhetoric.

For a little over twelve years, Franklin D. Roosevelt held the power of ultimate decisions for the foreign policy of the United States. Elected as a domestic leader who promised to bring the nation out of a frightening depression, from 1937 until his death in April, 1945, he found his main energies taken up with two great world crises: the challenge to the international system posed by Germany and Japan, and then the development of what promised to be an equally dangerous challenge from Soviet Russia to the American concept of a proper international society. The great irony of the Roosevelt foreign policy is that the very solution to the first crisis stimulated the second.

I CRISIS DIPLOMACY, 1937-1941

The Contemporary View

Forrest Davis and Ernest K. Lindley
AMERICA—DEFENDER OF CIVILIZATION

Both Forrest Davis and Ernest K. Lindley were journalists whom Franklin Roosevelt frequently favored with exclusive interviews. Such privileges suited all concerned; Davis and Lindley gained wealth and status within their profession, while the President used such occasions to float trial balloons and to "educate" the public. Lindley also wrote three books about Roosevelt, all essentially in the genre of campaign literature. In writing How War Came, *from which the following selection is taken, Davis and Lindley had the full cooperation of the State Department and faithfully reproduced the attitudes of the administration toward Germany and Japan. To them the war was simply a battle between good and evil. Their book was, in the fullest meaning of the word, "official" history.*

In June, 1940, the United States with its tempting wealth, its hemispheric commitments, and its profound stake in the survival of the classical, Christian, liberal tradition of the West, found itself in grave peril. France, a cornerstone of the West, lay crushed. Of the Continental powers only Russia stood erect, her position anomalous. The citadel of England remained untaken, yet her capacity to resist all-out war from the air was as yet untried. Who could be sure that we might not soon be left to fight in the Atlantic area a last-ditch war of survival? Mr. Roosevelt, addressing the Pan-American Scientific Congress which met in Washington while Panzer divisions swept through the Low Countries, accepted as a "dim and unpleasant possibility . . . that the Americans might have to become the guardians of Western culture, the protectors of Christian civilization. Today that fear has become a fact."

To the westward lay dangers equally great. In 1940, Japan was coiled to strike whenever the distraction of the West afforded hope of success. With England subdued, with Germany in command of

From Forrest Davis and Ernest K. Lindley, *How War Came: An American White Paper; From the Fall of France to Pearl Harbor* (New York: Simon and Schuster, 1942).

3

the Atlantic coasts of Europe, and with the American fleet withdrawn to the Atlantic, nothing would stand between Japan and hegemony over eastern Asia, the Indies, and, in all likelihood, Australia, New Zealand, and India. The vast dreams of the samurai military state would then be realizable. Moreover, the other great Pacific power, Russia, was an enigmatic quantity. Only China, shut off from effective use of the sea, inhibited by lack of industrial power, fighting a defensive war with pathetic, persistent gallantry, blocked Japan's career of conquest in Asia. The United States, as the great American power-philosopher, Alfred Thayer Mahan, had disclosed a half century ago (and as the Axis powers have made evident since December 7), was an island, open to attack from all quarters.

In such swift, broad strokes was the strategical situation sketched in June, 1940, by the leaders of this government. The United States faced isolation in a hostile world; not the self-sufficient, negative isolation advocated by the Continental school of American historians and the politicians who vulgarized them, but a sinister condition flanked by formidable enemies. Unless we intelligently resisted we stood in danger of losing our national identity, our character as a free society, and our political independence. To the men who principally shaped American foreign policy, a half dozen, headed by the President and the Secretary of State, this country's potential isolation was real in June, 1940. Cables that hourly streamed into the State Department's decoding room confirmed and emphasized it.

Increasingly in the years preceding 1940, America had been conditioned by the behavior of the aggressors. This country had not rested easy since the rape of Ethiopia and the "China incident" of 1937. Spain, Austria, Czechoslovakia impinged with mounting intensity on our thought, our sympathies, our economy and political relationships. The European war, opening in September, 1939, with the advance into Poland, produced an immediate reaction in favor of England, France, and their allies. The President and the Congress promptly abandoned a Chinese-wall type of neutrality, saddled on the country by influences both parochial-minded and fearful, and prepared to assist our friends of the West.

*   *   *

Before the *Reichswehr* swept, in Churchill's phrase, like a "sharp scythe" through the Low Countries, bringing a foreshadowing disaster to the French at Sedan, Mr. Roosevelt and his circle had not contemplated a swift German victory in the West. The President, as he confesses, was slow to see the immediacy of our defense problem. Like so many Americans, he relied on the Maginot Line, the highly regarded French Army, and the British fleet. True the Nazis had air superiority but that, provided the Maginot Line and the British fleet held, could be overcome by time and the industrial output of the Atlantic powers. In the spring of 1940 this seemed to the President a satisfactory formula for the restraint of nazism in Europe: a trinity of French land power, British sea power, and American industrial power, expressed chiefly in terms of aircraft reinforcement of the European Allies. Three contingencies dominated administration anticipations: (1) allied victory, (2) stalemate, and (3) a slow beating back of the Allies by the Germans, retarded enough to allow this country's industrial assistance finally to turn the scale.

A fourth alternative, a prompt German victory in the West, failed to impress itself on the President and his associates. In the light of Welles' interview with Hitler, during which the Führer boasted of victory in the West by July, and the weight of intelligence reports on the mechanized might of the German land and air forces, the administration's blind spot toward this fourth alternative must be put down to that wishful thinking which persistently underappraised the naked power of the evil forces besetting the democracies in 1940.

Whatever the precise reasons, the fact of present significance is that the blitzkrieg of May, 1940, wrought an instant transformation in American attitudes toward the war, introducing, as the second phase of American participation, a year and a half during which American energy increasingly became absorbed in defense of the country and hemisphere. Gradually, the United States was to evolve into the role of nonbelligerent ally of the peoples resisting aggression. At first, emphasis centered on our own neglected defenses. That was the period of conscription and of appropriation bills that poured billions into the task. Slowly, with many slips and halts, this country began to forge a modern war machine. Then, as the British bulwark held, the Royal Air Force repelling the Luftwaffe, the effort broadened.

By the end of 1940, with the development of Lend-Lease and the open acknowledgment that America had a stake in World War II wherever fought, this country became, in the President's words, the "arsenal of democracy." It had grown apparent to a substantial majority of Americans that their prestige, well-being, and survival depended upon activity that might not stop short of war. In the hot fires of a historic American debate, ranging across the country, often reckless but essentially democratic, the issue had been resolved long before Pearl Harbor in favor of global defense—of defense at a distance. Meanwhile, the men charged with executing national policy abroad had gone steadily forward, fending off hostilities, actuating alliances, acquiring bases, furthering American interest in the remotest islands of the seas, and, above all, "purchasing time" during which the giant forces of the country might be mobilized for its military defense.

* * *

In 1939, when the West responded to Hitler's challenge, the great powers of the Atlantic basin stood erect, although enfeebled by the undigested, badly administered victory of 1918 and by a crisis in their traditional economic system. Great Britain was a sea power, France was amphibian, and the United States, unchallenged in its hemisphere, stood in relation to the outside world as a sea power.

Of the three other great powers of 1939, one was in Europe, one in Asia, and one lay astride both continents. Japan, a samurai state, which had imperfectly applied the political and social lessons of the West, was rapidly returning to *Bushido,* the way of the warrior. Primarily a sea power, Japan also was based on the continent of Asia in Korea, Manchuria, and occupied China. Russia's taproots ran not to the West, but to Byzantium. Since 1917 that great, diversified world of its own known as the Soviet Union had been transforming itself from the absolutism imposed by czarism into a new kind of absolutism arising from below, a huge, all-embracing state organism. The "rights of man" revolution never had gained sway in Russia, which remained in 1917 the most backward of the great powers, and the Revolution of that year abandoned the political democracy of the West in favor of the Marxian dogma of the dictatorship of the proletariat. Russia and Germany, both continental powers, had surpassed the sea powers in their development of military aviation.

But Germany was also a special case ideologically, having roots in the West but also in the Teutoburger Forest. Germany never had foresworn her pagan heritage. Incompletely developed, according to the political standards of the West, the German people did not achieve national unity and the modern concept of the nation until 1870. And in 1933, the Nazi party under the zealot Hitler rejected Western culture and tried to bring the German *Volk* back to the atavistic mores of the Saxon tribes.

On the one hand, the laws of geography, strategical necessity, and economic survival still dictate national behavior. On the other hand, civilization is the product not only of material conditions, but also of ideas, and different concepts of civilization created the great divisions of the wartime world of 1940. The West behaved in one way, Japan in another, Germany and Russia in still others. What do we mean by the West? The phrase applies to the civilization descended from Greek rationalism and Roman law, modified by Western Christianity and developing through the "social contract" revolutions of the eighteenth and nineteenth centuries into the generally humane, politically free, and socially elastic regimes prevailing in the countries bordering the Atlantic. But in 1939 it seemed that an organic civilization, which recognized certain eternal noral values, had lost its proselytizing, dynamic character. Nevertheless, its inertia in the face of the rude assertiveness of fascism was not complete enough to justify the epithetical charges of degeneracy hurled from Berlin and Rome.

The primary custodians of that civilization were the Atlantic powers, France, Great Britain, the United States, the Scandinavian countries, Holland, Belgium, the republics of Latin America, and the British Dominions. Italy had forsaken its Western tradition, but all these other peoples professed political democracy and the common religion of the West, whether derived from Rome, Geneva, Canterbury, or Wittenberg; they used the same cultural language and their values were, generally speaking, interchangeable. A certain unity, therefore, linked the Atlantic peoples, a broad harmony of outlook and interest observed years ago by Thomas Jefferson and Simon Bolivar and finally defined in 1906 by Henry Adams as "the Atlantic system."

When sharply challenged, the towering values of the West regained their positive qualities. The free man in the free state, the sovereignty that resides in the citizen, political democracy as the best of social compromises that permits the easy, bloodless play of forces and interests within the state—these things came back into their own. The West took the counteroffensive sometime about 1940.

With liberty perishing in wide areas of Europe, with Asia under the heel of reactionary and despotic conquerors, the simple concept of the dignity of the individual which once moved our ancestors stood forth again in its original luster. It is this pattern of civilization to which this book refers when it speaks of the West; it is this to which Mr. Roosevelt and other leaders of the American people appeal in public utterance.

These values are by no means confined to the Atlantic basin. It simply happens that in the Atlantic nations, the civilization of the West has had its freest development and its longest sway, but the ideas informing it have permeated most of Europe, including the Balkan states, where they are again flourishing. In Poland also, which accepted the lessons imperfectly, the ideals of the West have a new meaning. And in Asia, the national state of China, drawing its wisdom and strength from a civilization far older than our own, finds at this moment of its ordeal a far deeper affinity with the civilization of the West than with that of its unneighborly neighbor, Japan. In all countries of all continents, men who prefer liberty to subjection belong to the Western cause.

Charles A. Beard

AMERICA—ON THE VERGE OF ENDLESS INTERVENTION

Charles A. Beard began his career as one of the proponents of the "new history," which demanded that scholarship serve a useful social purpose. Convinced that economically favored elites had long exercised undue influence on the development of the American nation, Beard published a series of books which posited just that thesis. In 1934 he published a full-scale study of the development of American foreign policy, The Idea of National Interest, *in which he put forth many of the ideas later adopted by the "left-revisionists" of the 1960s and 1970s. Beard asserted that American leaders had followed a false idea of national interest—one that emphasized economics and the expansion of overseas markets. A strong supporter of Franklin Roosevelt's New Deal, Beard believed that the President's early moves away from such overseas economic goals gave way in the late 1930s to the same old selfishness. Bitter that Roosevelt had deceived him, Beard wrote two studies after World War II in which he essentially compared the rhetoric of the administration regarding peace and neutrality with the fact of ever-increasing American involvement in Europe and Asia:* American Foreign Policy in the Making, 1932–1940 *(1946) and* President Roosevelt and the Coming of the War, 1941 *(1948). In the selection below, taken from Beard's testimony in 1941 before the Senate Foreign Relations Committee on the Lend-Lease bill, he places the entire aid-to-Britain program in the broad framework of a "left-progressive" critique. The hard question he asks— where does intervention in the affairs of others end?—is yet to be answered.*

It is in this spirit, I must beg you to believe, gentlemen of the committee, that I approach the issue before us. There is no question here of sympathy for Britain; this nation is almost unanimous in its sympathy. There is no question here of aid to Britain; the Nation is agreed on that. Our immediate task is to analyze the meaning of the language employed in this bill, and to calculate as far as may be humanly possible the consequences for our country that are likely to flow from its enactment into law—to rend, if we can, some corner of the dark veil that hides the future from our vision. . . .

Unless this bill is to be regarded as a mere rhetorical flourish— and respect for its authors precludes the thought of such frivol-

From U.S. Senate, Committee on Foreign Relations, 77th Cong., 1st Sess., *Hearings on S. 275 (H.R. 1776): A Bill Further to Promote the Defense of the United States, and for Other Purposes* (Washington: U.S. Government Printing Office, 1941).

ity—then, I submit, it is a bill for waging an undeclared war. We should entertain no delusions on this point. We should now face frankly and with such knowledge and intelligence as we may have the nature and probable consequences of that war. Without indulging in recriminations, we are bound to consider that fateful prospect.

The contention that this is a war measure has been, I know, hotly denied. The bill has been called a bill to keep the United States out of war. It has been said that we are "buying peace" for ourselves, while others are fighting our war for democracy and defense. I invite your special attention to this line of argument. I confess, gentlemen of the committee, an utter inability to understand the reasoning and morals of those who use this formula. My code of honor may be antiquated, but under it I am bound to say that if this is our war for democracy and if foreign soldiers are now fighting and dying for the defense of the United States, then it is shameful for us to be buying peace with gold, when we should be offering our bodies as living sacrifices. As I am given to see things, buying peace for ourselves, if this is our war, buying it with money renders us contemptible in the eyes of the world and, if I understand the spirit of America, contemptible in our own eyes. However, that may be, there is no guaranty that this bill will buy peace and keep us out of war, despite professions to that effect.

If the bill is enacted into law and efficiently carried into execution, it will engage our government in war activities, involve us officially in the conflicts of Europe and Asia, and place in jeopardy everything we cherish in the United States. It is true that some Americans doubt this risk. They appear to be confident that they can divine the future in Europe and Asia infallibly. They seem to believe that the United States can determine the destiny of those continents without incurring the peril of war and ruin for the American people. But I am not one of those astrologers. My knowledge of Europe and Asia is less extensive than theirs. I am merely certain that Europe is old, that Asia is old; that the peoples and nations of Europe and Asia have their respective traditions, institutions, forms of government, and systems of economy; and that Europe and Asia have been torn by wars, waged under various symbols and slogans, since the dawn of recorded history.

The history of Europe and Asia is long and violent. Tenacious emotions and habits are associated with it. Can the American people, great and ingenious though they be, transform those traditions, institutions, systems, emotions, and habits by employing treasure, arms, propaganda, and diplomatic lectures? Can they, by any means at their disposal, make over Europe and Asia, provide democracy, a bill of rights, and economic security for everybody, everywhere, in the world? With all due respect for those Americans who clamor that this is the mission of the United States, I am compelled to say that, in my opinion, their exuberance is on a par with the childish exuberance of the Bolshevik internationalists who preach the gospel of one model for the whole world. And I am bound to say, furthermore, that it is an exuberance more likely to bring disasters upon our own country than to carry happiness and security to the earth's weary multitudes.

Against embarking on such a crusade, surely we are put on our guard by the history of the last World War. For public consumption and partly with a view to influencing American public opinion, several European belligerents put forth numerous formulations of war origins and war aims. Later, unexpected revolutions in Russia, Germany, and Austria ripped open the diplomatic archives of those countries. Then were revealed to us the maneuvers, negotiations, and secret treaties spread over many years, which preceded and accompanied that World War. I have spent many weary months studying these documents, and I will say, gentlemen of the committee, that these documents do not show that the European conflict was, in the aims of the great powers, a war for democracy, or for the defense of the United States, or had anything to do with protecting the interests of the United States.

And to state the case mildly, those secret agreements among the powers do not exactly square with the public statements of the belligerents respecting the origins and aims of that war. Nor indeed did the so-called settlement at Paris, in 1919, exactly square with the declared war aims of President Wilson.

This is not to say that the present war is identical with the last war or to recite that false phrase, "History repeats itself"—for it never does. Yet we do know that the present war did not spring out of a vacuum, nor merely out of the Versailles Treaty. Its origins, nature, and course are rooted in the long history of the Old World

The Smoke Screen

FIGURE 1. Internationalism used to hide domestic failure (1940). (*New York Tribune Inc.*)

and the long conflicts of the great powers. In the light of that long history and those long conflicts, a discussion of their mere war aims shrivels into futility.

We, however, poised now on the brink of the fateful decision respecting ourselves, are under positive obligation to discuss the aims of the government of the United States in the activities which would be let loose under this bill, if enacted. Indeed it becomes the solemn duty of all members of Congress to do this. If they are not to vote thoughtlessly and recklessly, they will ask themselves certain grave questions before they vote. And I may say, gentlemen of the committee, I do not envy you that solemn task that falls upon you. Congress cannot in truth escape these questions, for it will be answering them if it passes this bill—answering them conceivably in a manner fraught with infinite tragedy for the United States.

Here are the questions:

Does Congress intend to guarantee the present extent, economic resources, and economic methods of the British Empire forever to the government of Great Britain by placing the unlimited resources of the United States forever at the disposal of the British government, however constituted?

Does Congress intend to supply money, ships, and commodities of war until the French Republic is restored? Until the integrity of its empire is assured? Until all the lands run over by Hitler are once more vested with full sovereignty? Until Russia has returned to Finland and Poland the territories wrested from them? Until democracy is reestablished in Greece? Until the King of Albania has recovered his throne?

Is Congress prepared to pour out American wealth until the Chungking government in China has conquered the Nanking government? Until Japan is expelled from the continent? Until Chinese Communists are finally suppressed? And until Soviet Russia is pushed back within the old Russian borders?

And if European or Asiatic powers should propose to make settlements without providing democracy, a bill of rights, and economic security for everybody, everywhere, will Congress insist that they keep on fighting until the President of the United States is satisfied with the results? If none of the countries deemed under the terms of this bill to be defending the United States succeeds in defeating its enemy with the material aid rendered by the United States, will Congress throw millions of boys after the billions in dollars?

Two more crucial questions are before our Nation in council. After Europe has been turned into flaming shambles, with resolutions exploding right and left, will this Congress be able to supply the men, money, and talents necessary to reestablish and maintain order and security there? Are the members of Congress absolutely sure, as they think about this bill, that the flames of war and civil commotion will not spread to our country? That when the war boom of fools' gold has burst with terrific force, Congress will be able to cope at home with the problems of unemployment and debts with which it had wrestled for years prior to this present false prosperity by borrowing money to meet the needs of distressed farmers, distressed industries, the distressed third of the nation?

As a nation in council, we should not mislead ourselves by phrases and phantoms. The present business of our Congress, it seems to me, is not to split hairs over the mere language of this bill or to try to restrict its consequences to one or two years of presidential experimentation. The present business of Congress is to decide now, in voting on this bill, whether it is prepared on a showdown to carry our country into the war in Europe and Asia, and thus set the whole world on fire, or whether it is resolved, on a showdown, to stay out to the last ditch and preserve one stronghold of order and sanity even against the gates of hell. Here, on this continent, I believe we may be secure and should make ourselves secure from the kind of conflict and terrorism in which the old worlds have indulged for such long ages of time.

The Historical Debate

Thomas A. Bailey

FDR—THE PRIMACY OF PUBLIC OPINION

Thomas A. Bailey, Professor Emeritus at Stanford University, is one of America's most prolific and respected diplomatic historians. His publications have dealt with the entire range of American foreign policy including such books as Woodrow Wilson and the Lost Peace *(1944) and* The Art of Diplomacy *(1968). It is not his imposing list of publications but rather his textbook,* A Diplomatic History of the American People, *which has made him one of the most influential historians of our time. First published in 1940, that text has gone through eight editions and is still the most widely used diplomatic history text in the United States. With the possible exception of George F. Kennan's study of American diplomacy between 1900 and 1950, Bailey's text is probably the most widely read book on American foreign policy among college students of the 1940s, 1950s, and 1960s. Bailey strongly emphasizes the governing influence of public opinion, condemns the isolationist tradition, and sees American policy in the Roosevelt Administration as one of response to the challenge of fascism and militarism.*

In 1937, after more mature reflection and in the face of the deepening crisis in Europe, Congress enacted "permanent neutrality." The revamped law, which also applied to civil conflict, reaffirmed the main provisions of the act of 1936 regarding the nonsale and nonexport of munitions, the extension of loans, and the exemption for Latin America. Travel on belligerent ships was now made unlawful, not just at the passenger's risk.

The question arose as to what should be done about raw materials like copper and oil, which were as vital to war-making as munitions themselves. Profit-conscious America, though wedded to neutrality, was unwilling to deny herself all such trade. As a compromise, the law provided that the President could list certain commodities, and these would have to be paid for upon delivery and taken away in the

From Thomas A. Bailey, *A Diplomatic History of the American People* (8th ed.; New York, 1969). Reprinted by permission of Appleton-Century-Crofts, Educational Division, Meredith Corporation. Footnotes omitted.

ships of the buyer. This so-called cash-and-carry provision was limited to two years.

The Neutrality Act of 1937, although eliminating some of the dangers that had drawn America into World War I, was highly vulnerable to criticism. It was hardly true neutrality, for it extended favored treatment to Latin America and to those sea-controlled nations, like Britain, that could take full advantage of the cash-and-carry provision. While not abandoning freedom of the seas, the United States served notice that it would not fight in all cases to uphold its historic policy. It would safeguard its rights by refusing to exercise them. Instead of employing its vast power to support the democracies against aggression, and thus control events in its own interests, it would permit itself to be tossed about at the mercy of events.

The storm-cellar legislation of the 1930s presumably encouraged the dictators by serving notice that their victims could expect no aid from the rich Uncle Sam. But the extent of such encouragement has probably been exaggerated. One did not have to know much about American government to realize that what Congress passes, Congress can also repeal.

In retrospect, the United States was one war too late in its attempt to legislate itself into neutrality. Such legislation might have prevented embroilment in World War I. But timed as it was, it tended to accelerate World War II, into which the United States was ultimately sucked. . . .

An ugly turn for the worse came on July 7, 1937, when fighting broke out at the Marco Polo Bridge between Chinese troops and a Japanese detachment stationed near Peiping. Reinforcements poured into North China from Japan. Formal declarations of war had gone out of style with the Kellogg-Briand Peace Pact, and this conflict, known as the "China Incident" or the "China Affair," was not officially declared for four-and-one-half years.

The next month, August, 1937, heavy fighting erupted at Shanghai, again with frightful loss of life among the teeming population. As in 1932, the American public was appalled by the slaughter of civilians, and its heart went out to the Chinese underdog. After the incidental killing or injuring of several American citizens on American ships, a strong demand arose in the United States for complete withdrawal from the danger zones.

President Roosevelt, though morally bound to do so, declined to invoke the Neutrality Act of 1937 in the "China Incident." Technically he was justified, for there had been no formal declaration of war. But his real reason was that both he and the American people were warmly pro-Chinese. The application of the neutrality law to both the aggressor and his victim would work greater hardship on China, even though Japanese imports from the United States were much larger than the trickle flowing to China.

But Roosevelt finally took a strong verbal stand in his sensational "Quarantine Speech," delivered on October 5, 1937 at Chicago, the so-called isolationist capital of America. Deploring the recent outburst of "international lawlessness" in China as threatening to involve the United States in a world war, he proposed that those nations stirring up "international anarchy" be quarantined. As he declared in denouncing the dictators:

> The peace, the freedom, and the security of 90 percent of the population of the world is being jeopardized by the remaining 10 percent, who are threatening a breakdown of all international order and law. Surely the 90 percent who want to live in peace under law and in accordance with moral standards that have received almost universal acceptance through the centuries, can and must find some way to make their will prevail. . . . There must be positive endeavors to preserve peace.

The phrase "positive endeavors" indicated that Roosevelt was ready to impose economic sanctions on Japan. Advocates of collective security, both at home and abroad, applauded. But a wild outcry arose from the isolationists against involving the nation in broils with which it had no direct concern. This outburst, though a minority view, evidently caused Roosevelt to soft-pedal his idea of "quarantining." Any attempt at drastic measures without popular support would rip the nation wide apart. Yet a large number of American citizens privately instituted anti-Japanese boycotts, which put a partial pinch on Japan.

In November, 1937, the month after the backfiring "Quarantine Speech," an eighteen-power conference met at Brussels, Belgium, to grapple with the Far Eastern hornet's nest. The United States accepted full membership, but Germany refused to attend and Japan declined to be haled into court. The conclave was thus foredoomed to failure. Japan apparently could be stopped only by force, and neither Britain nor America, the two greatest naval powers, was willing to use force.

The Japanese invasion of China was meanwhile degenerating into an orgy of lust and loot. At various times American citizens, male and female, were subjected to slapping and stripping by arrogant Nipponese soldiers. Some American schools and hospitals were damaged by aerial bombers, despite the huge American flags painted on their roofs.

The most sensational incident of all came on December 12, 1937, when Japanese aviators bombed and sank a United States gunboat, the *Panay,* on the Yangtze River in broad daylight. Two men were killed and some thirty wounded; escaping survivors were repeatedly machine-gunned. The vessel was so plainly marked and the visibility was so clear that the incident could hardly have resulted from mistaken identity. One plausible explanation was that hot-headed Japanese officers, defying the Tokyo government, had thus vented their contempt for Yankees.

The American people were shocked by this wanton attack, which also involved the destruction of three Standard Oil tankers. Cartoonists represented the Japanese ambassador as saying, "So sorry—excuse please," while the bodies of mangled American sailors lay about. Washington promptly demanded apologies, reparation, and adequate precautions against the repetition of such an outrage.

The Tokyo Foreign Office, put in a bad light by irresponsible military men, made haste to tender the most profound apologies and pay full monetary reparation—$2,214,007.36. Thousands of Japanese subjects attempted to make amends through private gifts. In these circumstances, the crisis quickly blew over.

The American public viewed the entire *Panay* incident with surprising calm, quite in contrast with their reaction to the destruction of the *Maine* in 1898. The Far East was on the other side of the world; Americans had already been killed there incidentally; America was being plunged deeper into the depression; and many citizens felt keenly that they should not be inveigled into fighting China's battles.

The strength of the peace-at-any-price feeling was reflected in congressional action on the proposed Ludlow Amendment, which would require a nationwide referendum on a declaration of war, except for actual invasion. Shortly after the *Panay* bombing, and under great pressure from President Roosevelt, the proposal was shelved in the House of Representatives by the shockingly narrow vote of 209 to 188.

As the "China Incident" dragged on, the Open Door became more and more bullet pocked. Little was achieved in 1938 when Washington, with some slight success, imposed a "moral embargo" on the sale of aircraft to Japan. In response to vigorous protests from the State Department against repeated violations of American rights, Tokyo took the position, late in 1938, that new circumstances had rendered old principles void. In short, the Open Door and the treaties that buttressed it were dead. But if the United States would recognize this changed era, and cooperate with Japan's New Order for East Asia, Americans might hope for a larger volume of trade than they had enjoyed under the chaotic and unprosperous old order. Unwilling either to cooperate or to fight—"to shut up or put up"—Washington could do little more than reserve American rights and arrange for a loan of $25 million to the Chinese government through the Export-Import Bank.

Continued flouting of Western rights in China by the Japanese invader finally brought more resolute action by Washington. In July, 1939, out of a clear sky, the State Department gave Tokyo the necessary six-months' notice for the termination of the existing commercial treaty of 1911. This stroke was obviously designed to bring pressure on Japan by clearing the way for an embargo on war supplies. The effect on Tokyo was sobering. The next month, August, 1939, Russia and Germany stunned the democratic world by signing their fateful nonaggression pact. Russia was thus left with a freer hand to deal with the Far East, and her strengthened position evidently caused the Japanese to adopt a more conciliatory tone in their dealings with Washington.

A world already ablaze in the Far East was further inflamed by the fanaticism of Adolf Hitler in Germany. Elbowing his way into power as Chancellor in 1933, he inaugurated an era of sadistic anti-Jewish persecutions, which attained a new ferocity in 1938. The American public, including Jewish citizens in the metropolitan centers, reacted indignantly and urged Washington to protest. Technically speaking, the abuse of Jews in Germany, like that of Negroes in America, was a purely domestic problem, and the State Department was hardly in a position to remonstrate effectively. President Roosevelt and prominent members of his administration nevertheless expressed emphatic disapproval. Among them were the acid-tongued Secretary of the Interior Ickes, who openly condemned Hitler as a "brutal dictator."

Suddenly, in March, 1938, Hitler bloodlessly seized and annexed German-speaking Austria. The democratic powers, wringing their hands in an agony of indecision, prayed that this grab would be his last.

But in the autumn of that same year, 1938, Hitler provoked the most dangerous postwar crisis to date. His bullying demand was for the Sudetenland—the German-inhabited portion of his eastern neighbor, Czechoslovakia. The Czechs, who stood firm during this "war of nerves," mobilized their respectable army and counted on their defensive alliance with France and Russia. Hitler was determined to attack, even though his troops were not yet ready for a full-scale invasion. The nations of Europe seemed to be trembling on the brink of World War II, with Hitler's Germany and Mussolini's Italy arrayed against Czechoslovakia, France, Russia, and Britain.

President Roosevelt, fearing that a general flare-up would jeopardize the United States, kept the wires to Europe hot. Late in September, 1938, he cabled two desperate, last-minute appeals to Hitler and one to Mussolini. The Italian dictator called Hitler on the telephone, and the latter agreed, whether as a result of Roosevelt's intervention or not, to discuss the dispute at Munich. Probably an appeal from London contributed more to this momentous decision.

The conclave at Munich did its melancholy work in two days, September 29–30, 1938. Present were the two strutting dictators, Hitler and Mussolini, and the nerve-shattered premiers of Britain and France. The Soviet Union, although vitally interested in the fate of Czechoslovakia, was not invited—and this snub by the democracies tended to drive Moscow closer toward the embrace of Hitler. The British and French, fearful that their undefended cities would be gutted by Germany's powerful bombing fleets, induced Czechoslovakia to yield the Sudetenland to Hitler, and thus avert a global holocaust. The Czechs were thus sold down the Danube River to purchase an uneasy peace.

The word "Munich" forthwith became the synonym for "appeasement"—the practice of trying to "appease" the insatiable power-lust of the dictators by giving them by degrees what they demanded. Prime Minister Chamberlain, caricatured with an umbrella, returned to London wishfully declaring that he had brought back "peace in our time." Hitler, to be sure, had stated at Munich that the Sudetenland "is the last territorial claim which I have to make in Europe." But the sequel was to prove that both statements were tragically incorrect: Munich was merely surrender on the installment plan.

The Roosevelt administration was evidently moving toward more active support of the democracies against the dictators in the months after Munich. In his message to Congress of January 4, 1939, the President strongly hinted at the desirability of boycotting the "aggressor governments." Rumors that Washington was selling the most modern types of American aircraft to the French spurred rumors of a secret military alliance. The isolationists and other foes of the administration emitted a roar of protest, which increased in intensity when the President was alleged to have said in private, "The frontier of the United States is in France." Isolationist fears were not completely quieted when Roosevelt insisted that some "boob" had invented that "deliberate lie."

Hitler waved another lighted torch over the European powder magazine, in March, 1939, when he forcibly absorbed what was left of mutilated Czechoslovakia. The hollow mockery of appeasement at Munich became transparently clear. The State Department vigorously but vainly condemned in public this act "of wanton lawlessness and arbitrary force."

With Europe teetering on the brink of catastrophe, Roosevelt urged Congress to revise the Neutrality Act of 1937. His aim was to discourage the saber-rattling dictators by serving notice on them that in the event of war the munitions factories of America would be available to the democracies—France and Britain. But a determined isolationist bloc in Congress, strongly supported by proneutrality sentiment throughout the country, stymied all efforts at revision.

Hitler, his appetite increased by appeasement, had meanwhile stepped up his demands upon Poland for the Polish Corridor and Danzig. Both of these German-inhabited areas had been torn from the side of Germany by the Treaty of Versailles. The Poles, stiffened by their Western allies, France and Britain, resolutely resisted these demands, and insisted upon peaceful negotiation.

The key to the diplomatic puzzle was dictator Joseph Stalin, the Sphinx of the Kremlin. Fearful of Hitler's aggressions, he was attempting in the summer of 1939 to negotiate a defensive alliance with Britain and France. When the two Western democracies tried to drive too hard a bargain, Stalin went behind their backs. To the amazement and consternation of the outside world, he concluded with Hitler, on August 23, 1939, a nonaggression pact. A secret agreement at the same time assured Stalin of his share of Poland when the imminent partitioning took place.

The Russo-German pact in effect gave Hitler a green light for the invasion of Poland and the starting of World War II. There had been much loose talk in the Western democracies of egging Hitler on Stalin so that the twin menaces would bleed each other white in the vastnesses of Russia, while the democracies remained secure. Stalin now cleverly contrived to turn Hitler against the democracies in the expectation that they would bleed one another white, while he emerged supreme.

Hitler was now unrestrainable. With Poland deprived of any possible Russian assistance, and with her French and British allies far distant, he pressed his advantage to the hilt. The Poles, unwilling to be the victims of another bloodless bargain, refused to budge. While Hitler insisted on either his terms or war, the urgent appeals of President Roosevelt fell on deaf ears. On that memorable September 1, 1939, Hitler, unable to bluff the Poles and impatient of further parley, gave the fateful orders, and the mechanized German hosts burst into Poland.

Britain and France both honored their alliance with the Poles. After Hitler had spurned their demands to withdraw, they declared war on Germany, September 3, 1939. Two days later President Roosevelt issued the routine proclamations of neutrality and invoked the strait-jacket Neutrality Act of 1937. The long-dreaded and long-prophesied World War II had at last erupted.

*   *   *

When Hitler unleashed the dogs of war in 1939, the American people had already taken their stand. An overwhelming majority wanted to stay out of the conflict, but a large body, which grew into a strong majority, feared that America would be unable to do so. Approximately 90 percent of the American people distrusted Hitler and hoped that the allied democracies—France, Britain, and Poland—would win. Unlike 1914, there was no pro-German element worthy of the name.

Foreign propaganda, unlike 1914–1917, was of little significance. The Germans made some effort to cultivate American sympathy, but their seeds fell on barren ground. The Allies, generally speaking, refrained from large-scale propaganda activity. One does not waste money and energy in assaulting a fortress already won.

The most effective propaganda work, as in 1914–1917, was done by volunteer groups in America. As the lines were drawn by 1940, the most vocal noninterventionist organization was the America First Committee, with its center in isolationist Chicago and its leading orator the famed aviator, Colonel Charles A. Lindbergh. The leading interventionist organization was the Committee to Defend America by Aiding the Allies, with the noted journalist William Allen White as its first head. Its avowed objective was to keep America out of the war by giving the Allies enough material aid so that they could defeat the Axis menace. "The Yanks are not coming" ought to be, avowed White, the unofficial slogan of his committee. But as the war ground on, the organization became more openly interventionist, and White dropped out.

Momentous changes had occurred in the standards of intenational conduct since 1914. The naked aggressions of the dictators in the 1930s had caused the aerial bombing of civilian centers to become recognized as a new refinement of "civilized warfare." Treaties had become whole wastebaskets full of paper; nonaggression pacts were made to lull the prospective victim into a false sense of security. Unoffending neighbors were assaulted with devastating suddenness. International law—one-way international law—was cynically used by the dictators to justify prior violations of international law and to prevent weak nations from joining effectively in their own defense. Hitler, who commanded the most terrifying striking power yet amassed, had little respect for the force of world opinion. The only language he really understood was the language of superior force.

The unvarnished truth is that by the late spring of 1940, if not earlier, Hitler had virtually abolished neutral rights and unofficially declared war on all the democracies—including the United States. The rape of Czechoslovakia, Poland, Norway, Denmark, Holland, Belgium, and Luxemburg should have provided adequate warning. But the American people were reluctant to recognize Hitler's challenge. Many disillusioned souls lamented the blunder of having entered World War I. Others, remembering the munitions scandals uncovered by the Nye Senate Committee, steeled themselves against being gulled again by the munitioneer, the profiteer, the financier, and the sloganeer. Immense numbers of America Firsters regarded this conflict as just another European war of imperialism. Five years of neutrality debate and legislation had not only strengthened the isolationists, but had developed a neutrality-at-any-price complex.

*   *   *

The existing Neutrality Act of 1937 flew in the face of two basic American desires: to stay out of the war and to help the democracies win it. The Allies, although assaulted by a Germany armed to the teeth, could not legally buy a single cartridge in the United States. The cash-and-carry clause of the Neutrality Act of 1937, valid for only two years, had expired in May, 1939. American merchantmen, laden with the vital raw materials of war like copper and oil, were now free to steam into the submarine-infested combat zones. Dangerous incidents, like those of 1917, seemed bound to drag America into the conflict.

Keenly aware of the need to revamp the Neutrality Act Roosevelt called Congress into special session less than two weeks after Hitler's invasion of Poland. To help the democracies resist aggression—although he did not put it that baldly—he recommended a repeal of the arms embargo. To insulate the United States against the conflict, he urged a reenactment of the expired cash-and-carry safeguard and a restriction against American ships and citizens sailing into the danger zones.

The ensuing debate, in Congress and out, was one of the most stormy and momentous in American history. Noninterventionists insisted that a repeal of the arms embargo was unneutral, because it would change the rules after the game had begun so as to help one side against the other. They further argued that the United States, after again developing a huge vested interest in the munitions business, would slither into the conflict.

The repealists, for their part, declared that the existing straight-jacket legislation was basically unneutral. It merely served to throw American influence on the side of the "aggressors." Hitler, they argued, would never have attacked Poland if he had been assured that his victims could secure weapons from the United States. But some of the repealists were candid enough to point squarely to self-interest: America's defenses would be bolstered by a victory for the democracies.

The question of setting up danger zones into which American ships could not sail aroused violent controversy. The noninterventionists believed that any other course would lead directly to shooting. The interventionists feared that such a prohibition would leave small neutrals like Norway completely at the mercy of Hitler, and would be an abdication of America's sacred principle—freedom of the seas.

Both the friends and foes of repeal had one thing in common: they professed a desire to keep America out of the war. Those citizens opposing repeal would insure neutrality by ignoring the conflict; those favoring repeal would ensure neutrality by helping the Allies keep the fight on the other side of the Atlantic.

The Fourth Neutrality Act—that of 1939—was finally approved by comfortable majorities in both houses during November, 1939. Despite loud outcries from Berlin, the arms embargo was lifted and American ships were forbidden to enter the danger zones. But the Allied purchasers of war materials would have to operate on a "come-and-get-it" and "cash-on-the-barrelhead" basis.

The revised law was basically a compromise. The noninterventionists gave up the arms embargo in order to get the danger zone; the repealists accepted the danger zone in order to get a repeal of the arms embargo. The new act of 1939, though losing most of the old teeth, retained certain restrictions of the former law, notably those regarding loans to warring nations and travel on belligerent ships. The preamble specifically stated that the United States, while declining to exercise certain of its "rights or privileges," was not abandoning them. Thus Congress made one final but futile attempt at "storm-cellar" neutrality. . . .

The so-called phony war came to an abrupt end in the spring of 1940, when the German armies suddenly engulfed both Denmark and Norway, without warning and without a declaration of war. In May, 1940, also without warning and in violation of solemn nonaggression pledges, Hitler assaulted neutral Belgium, Holland, and Luxemburg. Within twenty days the British armies were driven out of France, and but for the so-called miracle of Dunkirk would have been annihilated. Early in June, 1940, Mussolini, coveting a jackal's share of France's carcass, pounced upon his neighbor from the rear.

In desperation, France appealed to Roosevelt for "clouds of

planes." But the President, who was fully aware of isolationist sentiment and the sole power of Congress to declare war, found his hands
tied. He could do no more than extend his "utmost sympathy" and
promise all the arms that America could spare—without military
commitments.

Prostrate France, her "impregnable" Maginot Line flanked, signed
an armistice with her conqueror, on June 22, 1940. Hitler staged the
ceremony, with a gleeful eye on the ironies of history, in the same
railway car on the same spot in the same forest where the Armistice
of 1918 had been concluded.

These six weeks that shook the world shook the American "Maginot minds" out of their complacency. Britain, the last bastion of
democracy in all Europe, might go under at any moment. A woefully
unprepared United States would, in this event, be forced to defend
the Americas against a ruthless dictator who would have the economic and military power of Europe behind him—and perhaps the
British navy as well.

The panicky feeling that swept the United States was best reflected in a sudden upsurge of preparedness activity. Under the
driving leadership of Roosevelt, Congress voted nearly $18 billion
in a relatively few weeks. But drafting manpower proved to be more
difficult than appropriating money. Not until September, 1940, and
only after vehement opposition from the isolationists, did Congress
pass a conscription law. This measure authorized the first peacetime
draft in American history.

The fall of France also forced the United States to abandon its
technical neutrality toward Britain in favor of an unneutrality that
would bail out Britain. In April, 1940, following Hitler's assaults on
Denmark and Norway, Washington "froze" the assets of those two
countries in America so that such funds would not be available to
the aggressor. These were the first in a long series of "freezings."
Every major aggressive move by the dictators elicited condemnation
from Washington, and in several cases promises of help for the victims. The State Department consistently refused to recognize the
fruits of aggression, and maintained formal diplomatic relations with
a number of governments-in-exile. In a memorable speech on the day
Italy entered the war against France, Roosevelt proclaimed with
startling directness that "the hand that held the dagger had struck
it into the back of its neighbor."

Unneutral deeds followed unneutral words. In June, 1940, Washington worked out a clever trade-in scheme, under an almost forgotten law of 1917. The government would turn over to the American airplane manufacturer a number of planes already constructed, to be replaced by more recent models being built. The private manufacturer would then transfer the older craft to the British. Washington also sold to private concerns a vast amount of old military equipment, with the understanding that it would be resold to the British. This process involved about 600,000 rifles and 800 cannons, as well as huge stocks of machine guns, mortars, and ammunition, all of which proved a godsend to Britain. These transactions in their final stages did not involve the United States government, and technically Washington kept its skirts clean as far as international law was concerned.

As time passed, these transparent subterfuges were largely dropped. Washington ruled that American airplanes could be flown directly to Canada, without having to stop at the border to be pulled or pushed across. It allowed thousands of British pilots to train in Florida, where flying conditions were better than in Canada. It permitted damaged British warships to undergo extensive repairs in American shipyards. All such activity, of course, was not neutrality. But this was a war in which Hitler, by brazenly assaulting neutrals, had rendered neutrality meaningless and dangerous. America preferred to bolster Britain, at the cost of neutrality, rather than let Britain collapse and then have to face the fury of Hitler alone.

In the summer of 1940, while Hitler was vainly trying to bomb Britain into submission, American interventionists increased their clamor for large-scale assistance. Many of them harped on the theme that the United States Navy had left over from World War I some fifty overage, four-funnelled destroyers. These craft were of no immediate use to the United States, but they might prove the salvation of Britain in combating Germany's submarine blockade and in repelling invasion by Hitler's mechanized armies.

Responding to such pressures, Washington announced the momentous destroyer-base deal, on September 3, 1940. Roosevelt, in an executive agreement, promised to turn over the fifty vessels directly to Britain. The British, for their part, made outright gifts of sites for bases on Newfoundland and Bermuda for ninety-nine years. At the same time, they granted rent-free leases, for ninety-nine years, on six additional sites ranging from the Bahamas to British Guiana. Almost

A REPORT FROM THE OLD DOMINION

FIGURE 2. FDR and the problem of public opinion (1941). *(Richmond Times-Dispatch)*

simultaneously, but not as a formal part of the deal, Downing Street quieted fears that Hitler might use the fifty destroyers against America when it gave a formal pledge never to sink or surrender the British fleet.

The destroyer-base deal soon touched off a furious debate in the United States. Few discerning citizens questioned the value of these potential bases, for with air power growing in destructiveness the sites could be used to fend off or forestall possible German attacks on the United States. Few thoughtful Americans could deny the usefulness of the destroyers to Britain. But many Americans sharply challenged the way in which the transaction was carried through— by a simple executive agreement, without the advice and consent of the Senate. The noninterventionists in particular were up in arms. "The United States," declared the New York Daily News, "has one foot in the war and the other on a banana peel."

President Roosevelt's coup was clearly vulnerable to criticism. The transfer of fifty warships from the navy of the United States to that of a belligerent was not only a gross violation of neutrality, but also of pre-Hitler international law. Berlin could have found complete justification in this act for a declaration of war. The disposal of public property in such a fashion presumably violated a domestic law as well. But Roosevelt's attorney general prepared a labored defense, much of which hinged on the placement of a comma—"the Battle of the Comma." As for the President's not seeking the prior approval of Congress, the stock answer was that Congress was slow and windy, and that by the time the isolationists had all had their say, Britain might have been knocked out. Public opinion on the whole acquiesced in the deal, despite the bitterness of the noninterventionists and many partisan Republicans. Congress finally and indirectly put the seal of approval on the transaction when it voted money for the development of the ninety-nine year bases.

With the destroyer deal consummated, the United States virtually abandoned any remaining pretense of neutrality. The American people refused to sit on the side lines, shackled by neutrality and international law, while Hitler rode roughshod over neutrality and international law. They were determined, by an overwhelming majority, to stay out of the war. But they were no less determined to lend unneutral assistance to a fellow democracy—again "the world's last hope"—in its desperate struggle for survival. The old concepts of neutrality thus went out the window in favor of self-interest.

In 1940, as in the Wilson-Hughes campaign of 1916, American diplomacy felt the paralysis of a Presidential campaign. President Roosevelt had to move cautiously in his program of aid to the Allies, because the isolationists opposed that policy, and because the Republicans opposed the administration.

Roosevelt finally consented to accept the nomination for an unprecedented third term. He explained that he could not withhold his experienced hand in this grave crisis, despite his personal desire to return to private life. His critics hotly charged that, drunk with power, he really wanted to hang on, and that he had arranged to have himself "drafted." The Democratic platform pledged abstention from "foreign wars" and promised aid to nations resisting aggression. The Republicans nominated the dynamic and tousle-haired Wendell Willkie, an interventionist who had rocketed from political nothingness within a few short weeks. Their platform likewise pledged aid to peoples resisting aggression and proclaimed opposition to "a foreign war."

In foreign affairs there was little to choose between the platforms and speeches of the two candidates. Both Roosevelt and Willkie promised aid to the Allies; both promised to bolster the nation's defenses; both promised to keep the nation out of war. Roosevelt was later embarrassed by some of his ringing declarations, particularly the one at Boston, where he proclaimed, "I have said this before, but I shall say it again and again and again. Your boys are not going to be sent into any foreign wars."

Willkie deserves immense credit for his role as one of the founding fathers of a bipartisan foreign policy. He might have convulsed the country, and weakened the hand of the President abroad, by loudly condemning the drift toward interventionism. But favoring the cause of the Allies, and putting patriotism above partisanship, he helped save both military conscription and the destroyer deal, although objecting to the "dictatorial action" involved in the latter transaction.

In ordinary times the Republicans might have been able to defeat Roosevelt by their charge that junking the two-term tradition was the entering wedge for a dictatorship. But these were no ordinary times. One of the most effective arguments used by the Democrats was that Hitler and his fellow dictators hoped for the defeat of Roosevelt. Many voters believed that Roosevelt's experience was needed in this crisis; that he would prove more effective than Willkie in achieving preparedness; that one should not "swap horses in mid stream"; and that Roosevelt would be a more inspiring war leader should the United States be sucked into the abyss. "Better a third term than a third rater" was a Democratic rallying cry.

The nation tramped to the polls in November, 1940. Roosevelt won by a landslide in the electoral college, although his opponent polled an impressive popular vote. There was no rejoicing in Berlin or Rome or Tokyo.

His hands freed by the election, Roosevelt could now turn to the task of rendering large-scale assistance to beleaguered Britain. The British were rapidly reaching the end of their financial tether. But to lend them billions of dollars would produce economic dislocations at home and abroad, and inevitable postwar friction over repayment. With a keen memory of the defunct Allied war debts, Roosevelt declared that he was going to get rid of the "silly, foolish old dollar sign." He used the analogy of lending garden hose to a neighbor, whose burning house endangers one's own, and then expecting it back when the fire is out. Similarly, Roosevelt would lend arms and other assistance directly to those nations resisting aggression, and expect a return of this equipment or replacements for it when the fire was out. Such was his historic lend-lease scheme.

The Lend-Lease Bill, symbolically numbered 1776, was introduced into Congress in January, 1941, and rather misleadingly named, "An Act Further to Promote the Defense of the United States." The ensuing debate compared in bitterness and volume with that over the repeal of the arms embargo in 1939. The Aid-the-Allies group warmly backed Lend-Lease as a "defense" measure that would help Britain defeat the European aggressors and at the same time keep America out of the conflict. The America First zealots denounced this "blank-check bill"—this "Dictator, War, Bankruptcy Bill"—as a sure guarantee of war. Mothers kneeling on the steps of the capitol exhibited the sign:

Kill Bill 1776
Not Our Boys

Republican Senator Taft of Ohio, a leading isolationist, scoffed that

"Lending war equipment is a good deal like lending chewing gum. You don't want it back." Isolationist Senator Wheeler of Montana, referring to the earlier plowing under of surplus crops, branded the scheme as one designed "to plow under every fourth American boy."

Despite vehement opposition, the Lend-Lease Bill carried. American public opinion rather strongly favored it as a means of fending off the war. But if the people could have foreseen that it would lead to involvement by gradual steps, they no doubt would have been less enthusiastic. The final vote was 60 yeas and 31 nays in the Senate; 317 yeas and 71 nays in the House. Thus the United States formally pleaded itself, to the limit of its enormous industrial and financial resources, to lend "defense articles" to those governments "whose defense the President deems vital to the defense of the United States."

The Lend-Lease Act, which sanctioned the expenditure of an ultimate $50 billion, must take high rank among the most momentous laws ever passed by Congress. It was more than an abandonment of neutrality, because neutrality had already been abandoned. It was an unofficial declaration of war on the war-mad dictators—or rather a belated acceptance of the fact that the dictators had already unofficially declared war on all the democracies, including the United States. The Lend-Lease law proclaimed a tacit, nonshooting alliance with Britain and other nations whose resistance to aggression merited American support. Militarily and diplomatically this "aid-to-democracies-bill," which greatly boosted British morale, was one of the grand climaxes of the war.

Unlike the destroyer deal, lend-lease was no simple executive agreement cooked up behind drawn curtains. It was debated "over every cracker barrel in the land," supported by a respectable majority of the voters, and passed by wide margins in Congress. The American people, through their regularly elected representatives, had spoken. They still hoped to stay out of a "shooting war," but they were willing to stake the democracies to victory even at the risk of involving themselves.

The American occupation of Denmark's Greenland, in April, 1941, proved to be another long stride toward an undeclared war with Germany. A German lodgment in this area would constitute an intolerable threat to the mainland of the United States and to the lend-lease lifeline to Britain. The State Department entered into negotiations with the Danish minister in Washington, Henrik Kauffmann, for Denmark's motherless colony. Acting solely on his own responsibility, he signed an agreement permitting the United States to occupy Greenland during the emergency for defensive purposes and without detriment to Danish sovereignty.

Diplomatic complications speedily ensued. The Hitler-dominated government in Copenhagen promptly disavowed the Greenland deal, and forthwith recalled Kauffmann. Secretary Hull refused to recognize the recall, while continuing to regard Kauffmann as the regularly accredited minister. The United States, in dealing with an unprincipled adversary, was thus forced to fight the devil with fire. As a step toward hemispheric defense, and as a means of bolstering the Monroe Doctrine, the occupation of Greenland was completely in line with the recommendations approved by the American foreign ministers in Havana in the summer of 1940.

Relations with Berlin meanwhile continued to deteriorate. Following a brutal German attack on the neutral Egyptain steamer *Zam Zam,* in May, 1941, with injury to several Americans, Congress authorized the seizure of scores of foreign ships, many Axis owned or controlled, immobilized in United States ports. Many of them were transferred to the British flag. Later that same month President Roosevelt startled the nation with a proclamation of unlimited national emergency.

Then, on May 21, 1941, the American merchantman *Robin Moor* was torpedoed and shelled in the South Atlantic by a German submarine. This was the first United States vessel of any kind to be deliberately sunk by German hands, either in or out of the war zones. American public opinion was shocked and angered, even though no lives were lost. Senator Carter Glass of Virginia expressed the views of countless interventionists when he cried, "I think we ought to go over there and shoot hell out of every U-boat."

Hitler's spokesmen defended the sinking by alleging that the *Robin Moor* was carrying contraband of war to Britain's South Africa. Yet the Germans, in forcing the passengers and crew into small boats hundreds of miles from land, had not made provision for their safety in accordance with international law and the London protocol of 1936, which Berlin had freely signed. Roosevelt angrily denounced this act of "piracy," but Germany rejected his claims for damages. Washington in retaliation "froze" all German and Italian assets in the United States, and ordered all German and Italian consulates, as hotbeds of subversive activity, to be closed. Berlin and Rome retaliated in kind.

The *Robin Moor* opened a new chapter in German-American relations. Until then, Washington had little justification for complaint against the Germans, as far as America's specific rights were concerned. But it had much reason to complain of Hitler's ruthless attacks on the community of nations, of which the United States was a leading member. On purely legalistic grounds, Berlin had much better grounds for protest against America's unneutral aid to the Allies than America had for complaint against Germany's infractions of America's rights. The Lend-Lease Act widened the breach irreparably. The United States was now a virtual cobelligerent of the Allies. Hitler, with bitter memories of America's role in terminating World War I, did not wish to provoke a showdown yet. But henceforth the German submarine commanders, pursuant to orders, could hardly be expected to refrain from defending themselves against American destroyers escorting Lend-Lease supplies to Britain.

Bruce M. Russett

FDR—UNNECESSARY INTERVENTION AND DECEPTION

Charles A. Beard did not teach graduate students for the last three decades of his career and hence had no opportunity to train a "school" of supporters. His ideas were often too facilely lumped together with the vitriolic, ad hominem *attacks written by right revisionists like Charles Tansill and Frederic Sanborn and were long dismissed as unscholarly. Recently, Beard's basic arguments have been revived by Bruce M. Russett, a member of the political science department at Yale University and author of a number of studies on international relations. Admittedly influenced by the questions raised by American intervention in Vietnam, Russett argues in* No Clear and Present Danger *that American national security did not require military intervention either in Europe or Asia. Unlike Beard, however, Russett grants that the survival of Great Britain was essential to the security of the United States which places him in the position of arguing that a negotiated settlement with Hitler was both possible and practical.*

Nonbelligerent Assistance

In retrospect, the fear that America would be left alone in the world against two great victorious empires in Europe and Asia seems terribly exaggerated. Clear-cut victory was not in prospect for either, nor does the assumption that they could long have maintained a close alliance seem especially plausible. The critical American mistake may well have been in backing the Japanese into a corner, for without war in the Pacific the American conflict with Germany very possibly could have been held to limited naval engagements, but no clash of ground troops. In short, we might at most have fought a limited war.

These conclusions are highly speculative; the situation of the time cannot be reproduced for another run, searching for an alternate future. Perhaps I underestimated the risks that an American determination to avoid war would have entailed. On the other hand, the proposition that the war was unnecessary—in a real sense premature, fought before the need was sufficiently clearly established, though the need might well have become apparent later—is worth considering. Just possibly the isolationists were right in their essential perspective.

This last may be unpalatable, especially because the intellectual company of some of the most famous isolationists—William Borah, Hiram Johnson, and Burton Wheeler—is not very distinguished. Others like Father Coughlin were home-grown fascists, or, like Charles Lindbergh, are remembered as naive admirers of Germany. But once more, I do not imagine that the United States should have carried on blithely in 1941 as though nothing were happening elsewhere in the world. Complete isolation would have been much worse than intervention. All Americans would agree that American strategic interests required substantial assistance to the belligerents against Germany. Both Britain and Russia had to be preserved as independent and powerful states. With a little less certainty I would also grant the need to keep a significant portion of China viable.

It seems, however, that those goals could have been achieved by the belligerents themselves, with great American economic and noncombatant military aid. As insurance, American rearmament had to go on. A sustained defense effort not less than what was later accepted during the Cold War would have been required. That would imply 10 percent of the American GNP devoted to military purposes, as compared with about that amount actually expended in 1941 and a mere 1.5 percent in 1939. That much, incidentally, would with Lend-Lease have been quite enough to revive the economy from the depression and assuredly does not imply idle resources.

With this prescription I find myself at odds with the extreme critics of Roosevelt's policy, men who spoke at that time and again, briefly, after the war. Most of the President's military and economic acts seem appropriate and, indeed, necessary. I have no quarrel with the decisions for rearmament or to institute Selective Service, with revision of the Neutrality Act to permit "cash-and-carry" by belligerents (effectively by the Allies only), with the destroyers-for-bases exchange, with Lend-Lease, or with the decision to convoy American vessels as far as Iceland. Even the famous "shoot-on-sight" order, even as interpreted to allow American destroyers to seek out the sight of U-boats, seems necessary if the convoys were to be protected on the first stage of the critical lifeline to Britain. I do have some serious reservations about the way in which those decisions were publicly justified, a matter for discussion below. But the content of those decisions seems fully defensible. And irritating as they surely were, Hitler would probably have continued to tolerate them in preference to more active American involvement.

Only two major exceptions to the content of American policy in 1941 appear worth registering. One is the vote by Congress in mid-November 1941, at the President's behest, removing nearly all the remaining restrictions of the Neutrality Act. It permitted American ships to carry supplies all the way across the Atlantic, instead of merely as far as Iceland. This almost certainly would have been too much for Hitler to bear. Had he allowed American ships to claim the benefits of neutrality and arrive unmolested in Britain, his entire effort to force British capitulation by naval warfare would have collapsed. The more American, rather than British, vessels carried cargoes the more ineffective the submarine campaign would have become. The situation would have required great self-restraint—a trait for which Hitler was not noted—and a willingness on all sides to envision a compromise peace as the outcome. Probably that willingness could not have emerged so quickly. More likely Hitler would have felt obliged to order his submarine commanders to attack all American shipping, instead of merely replying if attacked by American escort ships. The change would have precipitated heavy American merchant losses rather than just the occasional incident, usually involving warships, implied by the previous policy. That in turn might well have demanded more self-restraint by Roosevelt than was possible in the American political system, even if he had wanted very badly to avoid war. In short, the new American policy probably would have led in a few months to open, declared conflict. But as to whether that final step was necessary, as part of a plan to preserve an independent Britain for an ultimate negotiated settlement, I remain unconvinced.

The other and more serious exception I take is with President Roosevelt's policy toward Japan . . . . It was neither necessary nor desirable for him to have insisted on a Japanese withdrawal from China. An agreement for a standstill would have been enough, and he did not make an honest diplomatic attempt to achieve it. He refused to meet Prince Konoye in the Pacific to work out a compromise, and after Konoye's fall he rejected, on Hull's advice, a draft proposal that could have served as a basis for compromise with the Japanese. We have no guarantee that agreement could have been reached, but there was at least some chance and the effort was not made.

Worst Case Analysis

Several very serious objections to my view of a viable American policy can still be offered. The first is that I have minimized the dangers that would have been implied by a successful American effort to stay out of the war. My reply is essentially that the fundamental power balance in the world was more stable than many thought it to be. More generally, the argument could be extended to the cold war period, when I think we often took on the Chicken Little syndrome, exaggerating the threat to that stability in the face of every immediate crisis, coup, or distant war. ("The sky is falling! Run and tell the President!") Roosevelt's own words, though exaggerated, may have even more value than he thought: "We have nothing to fear but fear itself."

Cold war, and especially overt international violence, provides a condition of heightened fears, a fog of war in which everyone is especially likely to overrate the threat an enemy constitutes. At the beginning of World War II, for instance, British and American intelligence estimates of German war production were exaggerated by 50 to 100 percent.

In 1941 perhaps any possibility, however slim, of a true German *victory* was so undesirable as to justify intervention. Neither that nightmare, nor the retrospective chance of a Nazi government equipped with nuclear weapons, is one with which Americans could rest complacently. But we must always weigh possible outcomes by what we think is the probability that they will occur. Otherwise we fall victim to "worst case analysis," always trying desperately to avoid the worst regardless of how unlikely it is to happen even without our efforts. Death or mangling in a traffic accident is a possibility every time we step into an automobile. Most of us are nevertheless usually willing to take that risk rather than accept the far more likely losses to be incurred by giving up normal mobility for business and pleasure. Yet in analyzing international politics we sometimes forget this lesson.

During the past decade, members of the administration in Washington decided that if a Viet Cong government ever took power in Saigon it might well set in motion a row of falling dominoes throughout Southeast Asia, as one non-Communist government after another tumbled. Before long the result might have been a set of Chinese or Russian-dominated governments, hostile to American interests, in the entire area. To avoid such an undesirable outcome they introduced a massive American military force. What was perhaps not asked, however, was whether another outcome which even they would consider nearly as undesirable—the quagmire—was even more likely to happen in the event of intervention than was the fall of dominoes in the absence of American military action. Thus by seeking to foreclose one very bad but improbable outcome in Asia, the United States government made another one much more likely. Such action was probably encouraged by a simple-minded, and erroneous, use of the game theory principle of "minimax." That principle advises one to choose a strategy so as to minimize the chance of getting the outcome you regard as worst—but properly understood it does not mean bending all efforts to avoid very bad but very improbable events.

What is more, no comprehensive analysis of the broader costs and gains of fighting in Vietnam seems to have been made anywhere in the government. Narrow quantitative studies of body counts and controlled hamlets, made by systems analysts in the Pentagon, have been much blamed for the Vietnam fiasco. True, they often were naive or based on fabricated "information." Yet in a myopic perspective of systems analysis the Vietnam war can be considered something of a success. The minimal goal, to maintain an anti-Communist government in Saigon, has been met for a decade despite the incompetence and unpopularity of that government. A *narrow* analysis of military and political conditions necessary to achieve such an outcome would not deal with the broader political, economic, and moral costs of the war, to Vietnam and to the United States. It is the job of analysts elsewhere in the decision-making system—in the White House, the State Department, even Congress and the academic community—to measure those broader costs and to weigh their acceptability. But of course that broader evaluation was never properly undertaken either by policy-makers or by social scientists. Nor indeed was anything like such an analysis undertaken at the time of American entry into World War II. Strategic and political assumptions about the postwar world were left for improvisation or retrospective rancor.

Naval action in the North Atlantic, with American destroyers dropping depth-charges on German submarines and receiving torpedoes in turn, constituted America's first limited war. Another objection is that such a war could not, politically, have long continued. No doctrine for fighting limited war existed. Americans thought peace and war to be antithetical. Woodrow Wilson had felt impelled, despite his preferences, to declare war on Germany in 1917 over the issue of unrestricted submarine warfare. Very possibly it would have proved politically impossible to sustain long a policy of limited war in 1941 and 1942. The experience of the 1950s in which Americans did fight such a war against hundreds of thousands of Chinese troops, was still in the future—though it was to demonstrate how a conflict could be controlled if the will was there. The scenario I have put forth for the 1940s, one of rearmament, assistance, but careful avoidance of belligerency barring a true collapse of one of the major allies, would have required enormous political skill and possibly a quality of political support that did not exist in the country. Perhaps any idea of "fighting to the last ally" would have been too "cynical" to survive public debate. A few isolationists opposed both rearmament and aid to the allies, both of which were essential pillars in the policy I suggest. This last difficulty particularly demanded a candid discussion of foreign policy options, a discussion that Roosevelt never really led.

A Broad Coalition

Nevertheless, it is a mistake to lump all "isolationists" together as uniform advocates of a single policy. The opponents of American participation in the war included such a diverse lot as Oswald Garrison Villard, Socialist leader Norman Thomas, economist Stuart Chase, University of Chicago President Robert Hutchins, progressive Senators Borah, Johnson, LaFollette, and Wheeler, United Mine Workers leader John L. Lewis, former President Hoover, and conservative Senators like Robert A. Taft and Arthur Vandenberg. (The breadth of the anti-interventionist coalition in 1940 suggests the possibility of a similar broad-based coalition, including many from the right, emerging against intervention in the 1970s.) Certainly they all shared the view that Germany and Japan did not constitute a clear and present military danger to the United States. But many "isolationists" supported most or all of the proposed military buildup; the others offered no substantial opposition. Lindbergh wanted to "arm to the teeth." As one historian has told us:

> Isolationists displayed no unanimity in their stand on specific defense measures. They made no concerted effort to block expansion of America's armed forces, however. Many isolationists, in fact, became ardent champions of the strongest possible defense and, occasionally, outdid the Administration in their efforts to improve America's military capabilities.

With a single exception to be explained shortly, during the years 1939–1941 army and navy appropriations passed virtually unanimously, despite the numerical strength of those in Congress who opposed entry into the war. Most isolationists even were willing to give some aid to Britain. They opposed Lend-Lease, but proposed instead a two-billion dollar loan to help British war effort, as a less sweeping commitment. A financial loan would not give the President power, as Lend-Lease did, to integrate the American economy with the British war effort, nor would it tempt him to act with American naval forces so as to insure the safe arrival of actual goods to be lent or leased. Whether the substitute represented a deep-seated willingness to maintain Britain, or merely a political response from a desire to appear positive, is unimportant. The necessary political base for some substantial assistance to the British and later the Russians was there. And from many quarters Roosevelt heard the advice that while doing so, and fortifying the Western Hemisphere, he should allow Germany and Russia to exhaust each other.

Only two kinds of preparedness measures proposed by the administration were fought by many isolationists; some naval construction, and Selective Service. The opposition to certain naval expenditures came early, in 1938, and faded thereafter. It stemmed from fears that a big navy would only be used to involve the United States in a distant war. This in turn was rooted in a long-term suspicion by many liberal isolationists of foreign trade and investments as a source of danger. Charles Beard saw the United States as potentially able to achieve economic near-sufficiency; he feared a big navy would be demanded to defend trade and therefore wanted trade reduced to a minimum. Similarly, the Naval Construction Bill of 1939 initially included appropriations for developing the base on Guam. The isolationists feared such an act would antagonize the Japanese—but they did not oppose similar funds for projects on Wake and Midway Islands, closer to the United States. They wanted a navy capable of protecting the Western Hemisphere, but not able to embark on further adventures. Opposition to renewal of Selective Service in 1941 centered less on the draft than on the possibility that conscripts might be sent overseas.

Thus the political climate was not nearly so hostile to rearmament and aid short of war as we may imagine. The same can be said of the public at large. As early as January 1939, a Gallup poll found 65 percent of the population anxious to spend more for defense. Throughout 1941 approximately the same proportion consistently, in repeated polls, were solidly in favor of aid to Britain. In fact, they declared it was "more important to help England than to keep out of war." Almost every survey found more than half the population approving Roosevelt's actions in helping Britain; another 20 percent felt he had not gone far enough. Franklin Roosevelt therefore was pursuing a policy that was both politically viable and sufficient to keep the Allies in the war. Only toward the end of 1941, in dealing with both Germany and Japan, did his decisions lead inevitably to war. . . .

Power and Candor

The years 1940 and 1941 marked the first great exercise of a President's powers as commander-in-chief during peacetime. They represent a period when secret military planning with the British became extremely close, and when American naval forces were committed to actions that were sure to involve them in hostilities. Restraints on the President's execution of foreign policy loosened and have never been restored. A good deal of controversy over Roosevelt's intention's raged during the 1940s, and still has not entirely abated. Some extreme revisionists who published immediately after the war accused him of *seeking* war with Germany and Japan, and of deliberately inviting the Japanese attack on Pearl Harbor.

Most historians reject these extreme interpretations. Such charges about intentions probably can never be substantiated or conclusively disproved, and they have distracted us from more important questions like the one posed in this essay—regardless of intentions, was the conflict in fact necessary? One standard interpretation seems to be that Roosevelt decided at some point, perhaps several years before Pearl Harbor, that the United States would have to go to war. But isolationist sentiment was so powerful that he felt unable to present the issue squarely to the people, and so proceeded cautiously, step-by-step, to help the Allies as much as Congress and the electorate would permit. According to this interpretation he is to be faulted for never having frankly discussed his private conviction that the United States should go to war to prevent Axis domination, and the implications of his policy.

Some aspects of his leadership seem chillingly familiar to those of us who have since listened to Lyndon Johnson, Robert McNamara, and Dean Rusk discuss their intentions in Vietnam. The most famous incident occurred in FDR's October 30 campaign address to an Irish-American audience in Boston, when he declared, "I have said this before, but I shall say it again, and again, and again. Your boys are not going to be sent into any foreign wars." At the time he did worry a bit whether he could keep this promise, but decided that the phrase "foreign wars" was too ambiguous to bind him. To his speechwriter he remarked, "If we're attacked it's no longer a foreign war."

Even so, we cannot judge Roosevelt guilty of duplicity on this evidence. Most observers feel that he still did not believe his assistance to Britain would lead to all-out war, but rather continued to hope that British resistance, sustained by America, would be enough to hold Hitler back. One historian who has carefully considered the question remarks about Lend-Lease, despite its almost unprecedentedly nonneutral nature:

> The president felt with great sincerity that this policy would not lead to American involvement but to a British victory that alone would keep the nation out of war. . . . His own personal hatred of war was deep and genuine, and it was this conviction that set him apart from men like Stimson and Morgenthau, who decided that American participation was necessary in the spring of 1941. . . . It is quite possible that Roosevelt never fully committed himself to American involvement prior to Pearl Harbor.

But if Roosevelt is acquitted of these charges, it is not possible to let him off so easily for his acts on two other occasions. He certainly was not above manipulating the facts about naval incidents in the North Atlantic, in a way that provided a perfect precedent for his successor a generation later. In September 1941, a German submarine fired two torpedoes, both missing, at the American destroyer *Greer*. President Roosevelt responded, in a radio broadcast, with the following description to the event as an act of "piracy": The *Greer*

> was carrying American mail to Iceland. . . . I tell you the blunt fact that the German submarine fired first upon this American destroyer without warning, and with deliberate design to sink her. . . .
> We have sought no shooting war with Hitler. We do not seek it now. But neither do we want peace so much that we are willing to pay for it by permitting him to attack our naval and merchant ships while they are on legitimate business.

It later emerged that the "legitimate business" was that the *Greer* "had been following the U-Boat for more than three hours and had been broadcasting its position to nearby British naval units."

The second incident occurred the following month when the destroyer *Kearny* was torpedoed. Although the ship was not sunk, eleven American sailors were killed. In his subsequent radio address Roosevelt declared:

> We have wished to avoid shooting. But the shooting has started. And history has recorded who fired the first shot. . . .
> America has been attacked. The U.S.S. Kearny is not just a navy ship. She belongs to every man, woman, and child in this Nation. . . . Hitler's torpedo was directed at every American, whether he lives on our seacoast or in the innermost part of the Nation far from the sea and far from the guns and tanks of the marching hordes of would-be-conquerors of the world.
> The purpose of Hitler's attack was to frighten the American people off the high seas—to force us to make a trembling retreat.

What really happened in this incident, where "history has recorded the first shot," was described two days later in a formal report by Secretary of the Navy Knox:

> On the night of October 16–17 the U.S.S. Kearny while escorting a convoy of merchant ships received distress signals from another convoy

A FAIR QUESTION.

FIGURE 3. FDR accused of a lack of candor (1939). *(Kansas City Star)*

which was under attack from several submarines. The U.S.S. Kearny *proceeded to the aid of the attacked convoy. On arriving at the scene of the attack the* U.S.S. Kearny *dropped depth bombs when she sighted a merchant ship under attack by a submarine.*

Compare these statements of Roosevelt with those of President Johnson in August 1964, after two naval incidents in the Tonkin Gulf:

This new act of aggression aimed directly at our forces again brings home to all of us in the United States the importance of the struggle for peace and security in Southeast Asia.

Aggression by terror against peaceful villages of South Vietnam has now been joined by open aggression on the high seas against the United States of America. . . . We Americans know—although others appear to forget—the risk of spreading conflict. We still seek no wider war.

Lyndon Johnson was an avowed admirer of Franklin Roosevelt, and a young New Dealer before the war. Did he, or his speechwriter, consciously draw on the earlier experience? Certainly he failed to mention the clandestine American-sponsored air-attacks and South Vietnamese naval actions against the North Vietnam coast that had been conducted prior to the Tonkin Gulf Resolution. If Hanoi interpreted the American destroyers' presence in the Gulf as part of those actions, then its response was something less than "open aggression." Yet Johnson's reply was a severe air strike, then the pre-drafted Tonkin Gulf Resolution and ultimately full-scale American intervention. In the subsequent election campaign he lashed his opponent's advocacy of a bombing campaign even though his administration had reached a consensus that heavy air attacks on the North would in fact be necessary.

In this context it is worth quoting once again from Charles Beard who, though extreme and sometimes blind in his hatred of Roosevelt, uttered some ringing prophecies. If Roosevelt's acts stand as precedent, he warned,

The President of the United States in a campaign for reelection may publicly promise the people to keep the country out of war and, after victory at the polls, may set out secretly on a course designed or practically certain to bring war upon the country.

He may, to secure legislation in furtherance of his secret designs, misrepresent to Congress and the people both its purport and the policy he intends to pursue under its terms if and when such legislation is enacted. . . .

> *He may publicly represent to Congress and the people that acts of war have been committed against the United States, when in reality the said acts were secretly invited and even initiated by the armed forces of the United States under his secret direction.*

Without accepting the most insidious charges of those who attacked Franklin Roosevelt, it is nevertheless clear that his actions as Commander-in-Chief, for a cause that was generally popular, made similar acts by his successors much easier. Recall again some of his initiatives, not submitted to Congress: the destroyers-for-bases exchange by an executive agreement more important than almost all of the nearly one thousand treaties that have been submitted to the Senate; the order to American forces to occupy Iceland; the order that American warships should convoy British as well as American vessels in the North Atlantic, and later to "shoot on sight"—and to seek out—German submarines. In these interpretations of his power Roosevelt was hardly timid. Even one, like this author, who considers these steps, at least, to have been in the immediate American interest, has some qualms. We can allow one of Roosevelt's firm sympathizers to sum up the argument, though we may reach a different verdict:

> *Franklin Roosevelt repeatedly deceived the American people during the period before Pearl Harbor. . . . He was like the physician who must tell the patient lies for the patient's own good. . . . A president who cannot entrust the people with the truth betrays a certain lack of faith in the basic tenets of democracy. But because the masses are notoriously short-sighted and generally cannot see danger until it is at their throats, our statesmen are forced to deceive them into an awareness of their own long-run interests. This is clearly what Roosevelt had to do, and who shall say that posterity will not thank him for it?*

Roosevelt, like Johnson after him, not only was uncandid, but made his decisions within a small circle of intimate advisers.

Warren F. Kimball

FDR—THE DILEMMA OF DEMOCRACY AND FOREIGN POLICY

Early attacks on President Roosevelt's prewar foreign policy rested largely on the accusation that he consciously deceived the American public about his actual goals. Warren F. Kimball, associate professor at the Newark College of Rutgers University, uses the Lend-Lease Act as a case study in examining that charge. He does not quarrel with Roosevelt's basic assumption—that Germany posed a very real threat to the security of the United States thus justifying unlimited aid to Britain—and generally reflects the traditional view supporting Roosevelt's program of a steady escalation of involvement. He infers an "adversary" system in which the opposition party prevents the party in power from acting without public restraints, but fails to deal with the problem of actions done in secrecy or a bipartisan policy where dissent receives little public attention.

In March, 1941, the British ambassador, Lord Halifax, wrote Churchill concerning his frustrations in trying to deal with the American government. Although he admitted that the United States had made great strides in developing its defenses, he complained that the Roosevelt Administration was disorganized and loaded with loose ends. Trying to deal with them, he commented, "seems like hitting wads of cotton wool."

The Englishman has my belated sympathies, for I find the job of drawing conclusions concerning Roosevelt and his foreign policy just as elusive as the fixed channels of authority Halifax futilely sought to find. Some of the events surrounding the Lend-Lease Act need no conclusions. The initial stimulation of Britain's financial crisis, combined with the President's clear-cut belief that Britain had to be aided against Hitler, slowly but surely forced the Roosevelt Administration to provide financial aid. Once the disillusion following World War I plus the war debts problem were added to the brew, something akin to Lend-Lease became only a matter of time. The steps—from the Pittman Act, to the destroyers-bases deal, to the "fire-hose" analogy, and finally the bill itself—need no further recounting. . . .

From *"The Most Unsordid Act": Lend-Lease, 1939–1941* by Warren F. Kimball, (Baltimore: Johns Hopkins Press, © 1969). Reprinted with permission. Footnotes omitted.

The story of the Lend-Lease Act is a fascinating case study in the legislative process, particularly as it functioned during the Roosevelt Administration. The broad concept was unmistakably Franklin Roosevelt's, but the initiative for the specific legislation remained almost exclusively with Henry Morgenthau, his staff, and the two Englishmen, Arthur Purvis and Sir Frederick Phillips, Although Congress, other Cabinet members, and even the President himself managed to make modifications to the original draft of the act, the basic shape of the powers granted to the executive remained the same as in the first rough proposal worked out by the Treasury and the BPC* on January 2, 1941.

The generally accepted picture of Franklin Roosevelt as a chaotic, haphazard, almost impulsive administrator is largely upheld, but that is not true of his political activities. He waited far too long before he finally proposed the badly needed consolidation of the aid to Britain program which the Lend-Lease Act provided, but the vote the bill received in Congress indicates that his sense of political timing was honed to a fine edge. In addition, his legislative tactics in and around Congress proved virtually errorless. The delay in proposing the Lend-Lease Act stemmed not only from his uncertainty about just how to solve the problem but also from a desire to avoid any large-scale debate over his foreign policy until he felt the time was right. Certainly any attempt to formalize the program of aiding Britain would have brought on just such a debate; thus it was more convenient to leave it in the hands of an informal organization under Henry Morgenthau, who could be trusted to carry out the President's wishes faithfully.

The major controversy that still surrounds the Lend-Lease Act is where the historian begins to hit those "wads of cotton wool." What were the motives of President Franklin D. Roosevelt in proposing and pushing through what was most definitely an extraordinary grant of power to the executive? This is, of course, only part of the broad problem of trying to analyze Roosevelt's entire foreign policy with respect to the European situation, but critic and friend alike agree that the Lend-Lease Act was the most significant of all the steps toward war taken before December 7, 1941.

Even the most ardent supporters of the Lend-Lease Act did not try

---

* British Purchasing Commission.—Ed.

to defend it in terms of traditional interpretations of international law. Cordell Hull, a devoted believer in the value of international law, told the congressional committees during his testimony on the bill that one could not be expected to obey the law rigidly when the opponents of democracy did not. Anyone could see that the act gave Hitler an excuse to declare war on the United States, but that was not the question. The Roosevelt Administration maintained that Hitler had never worried about legitimate excuses for war in the past and assumed that if he wanted war with America he would not hesitate to manufacture a reason. The real question was not whether the Lend-Lease Act was a warlike action in terms of international law, but whether or not it would inevitably involve the sending of American military forces to Europe to fight against Germany.

A more extreme corollary of that problem was the accusation that President Roosevelt consciously devised the Lend-Lease Act as a means of getting America into the war, in spite of public and Congressional objections. The more responsible members of the opposition concentrated on claiming that the legislation would force the United States to enter the war, but they usually stopped just short of actually accusing the President of planning it that way. Senator Arthur Vandenberg, in the privacy of his diary, condemned the bill and claimed it made Roosevelt "the Ace Power Politician of The World," turning the White House into the "G.H.Q. for all the wars of all the world," but he did not flatly assert that the President hoped for war. Henry Stimson, Roosevelt's Secretary of War, told his subordinates that the Lend-Lease Act was taking America into the war, and he may well have hoped for just that, but Stimson was notoriously more of a war-hawk than the President. General George Marshall, in an interview in 1957, admitted that the act made America's entry into the war a probability instead of a mere possibility but maintained that it did not guarantee active hostilities. The Italians seemed the most certain that the bill presaged the sending of United States troops to Europe. They apparently planned to sink a large luxury liner in the Panama Canal if the bill passed, but the scheme was foiled by the United States Coast Guard. The chief adviser in the German Foreign Ministry on American affairs, the perceptive Hans Dieckhoff, was more concerned with the broader scope of United States policy. His analysis was remarkably reasoned and logical and is worth quoting at length:

Essentially the development of public opinion in this matter will depend upon the progress of the war; if Germany succeeds in defeating the English decisively in the near future, then in all probability American public opinion will be in favor of staying out of the war; if the war continues undecided for a considerable time, then there is a considerable danger that public opinion will develop in the direction of a growing willingness to enter the war.

Thus, as the Roosevelt Administration maintained, German actions would be the prime determinant of whether or not America would actively join the fight. Like Stimson, Dieckhoff believed the immediate effect of the Lend-Lease Act would be to boost the morale of the British.

Publicly and privately, as far as can be determined, Roosevelt stoutly maintained that the purpose of Lend-Lease was to keep America out of war, but the question remains, did he really believe that? Certainly he resented Senator Burton Wheeler and the other more caustic critics of the bill. The day after he signed the bill, he sat down after supper with Robert Sherwood and Toie Bachelder, two of his speechwriters, to write an address to be given to the White House Correspondents Association. As Sherwood recalled later, the President dictated "one of the most scathing, most vindictive speeches" the speechwriter had ever heard. He pulled out all the stops in attacking those who had accused him of the basest of motives in proposing the Lend-Lease Bill. Roosevelt never used that draft and was obviously just getting it off his chest, but the depth of his feelings was unmistakable.

The accusation by Senator Wheeler and other contemporaries that the President's true foreign policy was consciously kept hidden from the American people has been echoed by his critics ever since. To charge Franklin Roosevelt with misleading the public during the election of 1940 is to accuse him of doing what virtually every presidential candidate has done since the Constitution went into effect. It is the nature of the system which causes what Winston Churchill so aptly termed America's "quadrennial madness." Like Woodrow Wilson in 1916, Roosevelt too was forced by political exigencies to advocate peace and preparedness, and like Wilson he was convinced that America's national interests were involved in the final outcome of the European struggle. Granted, Wilson firmly believed the United States could stay out of the war since he thought Britain and France could contain if not crush German militarism, whereas Roosevelt was not sure America could avoid the actual fighting—but a rather rational doubt does not indicate a desire. More to the point: must a candidate dwell on the possibility of war when doing so would probably elect people whose policies might, in his view, endanger national security? As much as one sympathizes with Roosevelt's dilemma, the national election is the one time every four years when the President should be obligated by his own conscience and the nature of the American political system to be totally honest and candid with the public. In that sense, democracy may be a suicide pact, which by its nature requires honesty regardless of the possible consequences. The Lend-Lease Act, however, was a postelection issue and thus poses a different set of questions.

Some of Roosevelt's motives in proposing Lend-Lease are obvious. The legislation began as a solution to a financial problem but quickly evolved into a solution for the equally important defense production tangle. Lack of coordination in defense purchasing among the American Army, Navy, and foreign buyers could be largely eliminated by Lend-Lease, and the act had the additional attraction of providing the administration with a means of getting American industry converted more quickly to defense production. Convinced, as were most Americans, that Germany posed a threat to democratic institutions, the administration designed the bill to permit Britain to keep fighting, yet Roosevelt and his Cabinet were determined not to fight the war for British goals. Morgenthau insisted that Britain use every available source of dollars and gold, while Stimson rammed American-type weapons down the throats of the very reluctant British military. Hull maintained to the end that some sort of collateral should be posted by the United Kingdom, while Roosevelt's distrust of the British penchant for power politics and British colonialism has been amply demonstrated elsewhere.

Churchill described the Lend-Lease Act, in a speech before Parliament, as "the most unsordid act in the history of any nation," but not all Englishmen have agreed. The suspicion that the United States was using the United Kingdom's financial crisis as a means of increasing America's share of the world market at Britain's expense lingered on throughout World War II. *The enfant terrible* of English historians, A. J. P. Taylor, bluntly asserted that Britain sacrificed her future in order to save the world. He believed Lend-Lease ruined

Britain as an exporting power and ruthlessly stripped her of her remaining dollars. The British official historians were less harsh in their language and more understanding in their knowledge of the exigencies of American politics, but they nonetheless criticized the nature of the Lend-Lease Act. Although admitting that the Lend-Lease Bill pulled Britain out of absolute poverty, one described the new situation as the "poverty of the poor relation." Writing from hindsight, and obviously influenced by the abrupt termination of Lend-Lease at the end of World War II, they sadly complained that the barrier that existed between the dollar and the pound sterling was a man-made barrier which could have been eliminated had the United States been willing to pool its financial resources with those of Great Britain. Each country could then have met its own expenses with its own currency. As one American student of history and semantics aptly pointed out, the Americans ignored the reality that money was a medium of exchange and instead concentrated on the mistaken notion that money was itself something of value. Even Hitler voiced the accusation that the Americans intended to take advantage of Britain's woes. His public statements to that effect can be dismissed as propaganda, but similar private comments to Spanish and Russian diplomats indicated Hitler honestly believed that the British would have to satisfy America's imperialistic desires as a condition of aid.

It is misleading to state flatly that the American government used England's financial crisis as a means of substituting an American economic empire for the British one. Had this been a conscious policy of the Roosevelt Administration, far heavier pressures would have been applied. Although Morgenthau correctly accused the British of dragging their feet on the sale of British-owned investments in America, by the fall of 1940 the issue was largely forgotten since it would obviously be too late with too little. Morgenthau defended his hard bargaining on the grounds of political necessity, and that claim is partially supported by the fact that the only really strong administration demands for such sales came in connection with the first Lend-Lease appropriation. Roosevelt's emphatic rejection of suggestions that the United States trade credits for British Caribbean islands demonstrates the absence of any ambitions to acquire additional territory, and the periodic references to Britain's extensive economic holdings in Latin America were never coupled with any concrete proposals about how to transfer them to American hands. Individual American businessmen tried to use the wartime situation to force Britain to sell her American holdings at a discount, but the British government usually refused to submit to such blackmail, and the American government made no moves to force the issue. In fact, Morgenthau frequently condemned such actions.

Morgenthau's policy of forcing Great Britain to pay cash right to the end of their dollar resources found ample justification in the Congressional debate over Lend-Lease. The statistical evidence of Britain's dollar shortage overwhelmed opposition claims that the British could continue to fight against Hitler without aid from the United States. Nevertheless, the American belief in the fabled riches of the British Empire persisted. Many Americans, including Cordell Hull and Frank Knox, never really grasped the fact that Britain could run out of dollars without being bankrupt, and there are indications that even President Roosevelt remained skeptical of that fact. In spite of such doubts, the United States did adopt a policy that provided Britain with what was essentially a subsidy, not a loan. Thus, as one recent study of the economic aspects of Roosevelt's foreign policy points out, the nature of the Lend-Lease Act itself demonstrates that America had no intention of stripping England of her economic empire. Although some congressmen may have hoped that reverse Lend-Lease might result in the expansion of American business interests at the expense of British interests, nothing of the sort was ever hinted at by any of the members of the administration.

Unquestionably, the notion of taking advantage of England came to the mind of many Americans. But in spite of the broad opportunities for doing just that, the administration limited itself to occasional snatches of wishful thinking. Possibly Roosevelt and Morgenthau pushed Britain as far as they thought they could without causing the English to consider some sort of arrangement with Hitler, but if so, their success in hiding such a nefarious conspiracy is quite remarkable. If they were subject to such compelling greed, it appears highly un-likely that they would have been able to stop short of forcing Britain to divest herself of virtually all her American holdings. It is far more logical to assert that the hard bargain America drove rose initially out of the image of British opulence and continued because of the need to convince Congress that America had no choice but to provide the subsidy Britain required.

The Germans may have believed that England became a "paid vassal" of the United States with the enactment of Lend-Lease, but neither the British nor the Americans saw it that way. Arthur Purvis, Britain's most successful representative in Washington during this trying time, expressed his heartfelt thoughts in a letter to President Roosevelt shortly after the Lend-Lease bill became law. In a handwritten note of thanks he told Roosevelt: "Apart entirely from what it means for the successful outcome of the struggle, I felt the ring of an understanding of human values—so rare in these days—which gives hope and inspiration for the future of men after the job is done."

The crux of the debate over Roosevelt's foreign policy during this prewar period, including the Lend-Lease Act, is really just another facet of an age-old question that American democracy has never really answered: does the elected official have a responsibility to follow what he believes is desired by the electorate, or must his primary allegiance rest with his own conscience? To put it another way, must the leader in a democratic society first convince the public of the wisdom of his policies by open and above-board methods, or may he embark on a course of action and face the consequences at the next election? Do we trust our elected officials, or must they stand for election on every new policy decision?

A part of that question is answered by merely reading the United States Constitution. In this presidential form of government, no provisions are made for any sort of referendum by the public on major policy decisions. Unlike the parliamentary system, the American electorate is stuck with its choice of president. Thus, in terms of legal responsibility, the public debate over the Lend-Lease Act was interesting but not binding on the President or Congress. But legal responsibility is not what makes a democracy work. Rare indeed is the congressman or President who does not acknowledge, particularly at election time, that his aim is to represent the wishes of the people; thus, when those desires are expressed, most elected officials feel constrained to follow them. The conflict arises when the people indicate a course of action which directly disagrees with a representative's conscience. On many issues he is able to vote with his conscience and still avoid defeat at the polls; at other times resignation may be the only solution (though one rarely resorted to by politicians). To be sure, the promise that he would represent the wishes of the electorate is also an element to be considered by one's conscience, but often the crisis that faces the country will not allow the elected official to ignore his own reason and vote strictly as his constituents demand.

In the case of Franklin Roosevelt and a majority of the members of Congress, the conflict was acute. Roosevelt and most of Congress were convinced that Hitler's Germany was a direct and growing threat to the national security of the United States. The administration believed that the British were fighting America's war, yet right down to the day of Pearl Harbor, American public opinion opposed entering the war. The argument over Roosevelt's foreign policy and more specifically, the Lend-Lease Act, thus revolves around a series of questions. First, was economic warfare with Germany in the national interest of the United States? If we assume that in the presidential system it is the responsibility of the President to make that determination, then the only quarrel is with his judgment. The answer to that question is far beyond the scope of this study, but if we assume that the national interest of the United States was involved, then new problems which are germane to the Lend-Lease Act are raised. A negative response, of course, ends the discussion, for Roosevelt stands condemned as of that point.

If one accepts the position that economic warfare against Germany was necessary, the question of the duties and limits of leadership in a democracy again occurs. This time it can be considered in the more restricted area of foreign policy. Even if one asserts that leadership in a democracy must be open and frank, is it necessary for a democratic nation to put itself at a disadvantage in its dealings with non-democratic nations that are not so limited? If the answer to that question is no, then Roosevelt seemingly worried far too much about public opinion and unanimity. If one carries this ultra-realist viewpoint to its logical conclusion, the President should have used his extensive powers as commander in chief to embroil the United States in the war with Germany as quickly as possible and then relied on wartime patriotism to bring on national unity. On the other hand, if one still believes that the democratic leader should be democratic *so long as national security is not irreparably compromised,* then we can examine events surrounding the passage of the Lend-Lease Act to see if President Roosevelt followed that injunction.

Roosevelt was undoubtedly eager to obtain maximum public and congressional support for the Lend-Lease Act. Since he had just been elected for a four-year term, his concern could hardly have been caused by a fear of defeat at the polls. The only logical assumption is that the President was attempting to work within the democratic structure as fully as he could without endangering American national security. The "dictator" charge is hard to substantiate. Roosevelt, most often accused by his own generation of being "King Franklin" and a potential dictator, actually took more care than any other President in similar circumstances to maintain the proper relationship between the executive and legislative branches. Abraham Lincoln and Woodrow Wilson both acted far more arbitrarily. Roosevelt was very leery of usurping congressional prerogatives during the Lend-Lease debate and worked very closely with the congressional leadership.

The basic criticism lodged against Roosevelt was the nature of the Lend-Lease debate, particularly during the hearings and on the floor of Congress. Charles Beard boiled it down to one bitter sentence: "At what point in time . . . did the President and the Secretary [Hull] decide that the policy of neutrality and isolation . . . was untenable and announce [it] to the public?" Beard naïvely seems to be asking a professional politician openly to affront and insult a large group of voters by bluntly proclaiming that their ideas were totally wrong, yet in essence, that is just what the Roosevelt Administration did. The Lend-Lease debate was long and full. For the opposition to claim that the administration avoided the key issue, namely the long-term implications of the act, is to confess their own inability to persuade the American public and other congressmen that those implications were dangerous to the national security. In a democratic society it is the responsibility of the loyal opposition to point out to the public what it believes to be misguided actions on the part of the majority party. To expect the majority to make predictions that would, by their utterance, jeopardize their program is like demanding that a guilty man plead guilty in a court of law. When the opposition cannot convince the majority of the wisdom of their position and subsequently turns to verbal accusations of foul play and *ad hominem* arguments, one detects the pungent odor of sour grapes, or at the least, party politics.

More importantly, a reading of the printed hearings on the Lend-Lease Bill and the newspaper accounts that dealt extensively with the legislation and its implications indicates without any doubt that nothing was left unsaid about the bill. If, with all the information available, the public could not clearly see the possible and probable results of the Lend-Lease Act, then they were hardly the ones to be trusted with major decisions. Time and again the bill's opponents warned that it meant war, yet Congress overwhelmingly approved it. There was no need for the Roosevelt Administration to point out the dangers and thereby weaken its case; the isolationists took care of that. Right or wrong, the Lend-Lease Act and the nature of the accompanying debate fell well within the basic practice of the American political system. Whether Roosevelt believed Lend-Lease would keep America out of war, or only wishfully hoped for that effect, is essentially a moot point. The legislation was fully discussed and resoundingly approved by Congress and thus, indirectly, by the people. Even so, although few can quarrel with the stated purpose of the Lend-Lease Act, one is still disturbed and even shocked by the lack of candor displayed by the Roosevelt Administration during the evolution of the legislation.

For better or for worse, regardless of the means or purpose, as of March, 1941, the United States of America had made the irrevocable commitment. Although actual war was nine months away, the Lend-Lease Act was a public announcement of the creation of the most productive and cooperative coalition of modern times—the Anglo-American alliance against Nazi Germany.

Sidney Lens

FDR—PRISONER OF CAPITALISM

Doctrinaire, radical left critiques of American society have become far more
frequent as intellectuals have reacted against the Vietnam War. There has
always been, however, a small coterie of men like Sidney Lens who have
consistently viewed American history as a function of the imperatives of its
capitalist economic system. In The Forging of the American Empire, *Lens*
sees American foreign policy since the American Revolution as essentially
the story of ever expanding imperialism. There have been remarkably few
left-revisionist critiques of Roosevelt's prewar policy, possibly because of the
awkwardness of criticizing any sort of anti-Hitler policies, and even so rigid
an ideologue as Lens clearly supports the war against Nazi Germany. What
concerns Lens is the centralization of presidential power and the unspoken
economic motives behind Roosevelt's actions. Like others on the radical left
(e.g., Gabriel Kolko) Lens infers that the United States would have remained
at peace with a Nazi regime which did not threaten the Anglo-American
economic system.

On September 3, 1939, the day Britain and France declared war on
Germany, Franklin Roosevelt told the American people: "I hope the
United States will keep out of this war. I believe that it will. And I
give you assurances that every effort of your government will be
directed toward that end." The Democratic platform on which he ran
for an unprecedented third term was even more forthright: "We will
not participate in foreign wars, and we will not send our Army, naval,
or air forces to fight in foreign lands, outside of the Americas, except
in case of attack. . . . The direction and aim of our foreign policy
has been, and will continue to be, the security and defense of our
own land. . . ." Speaking at Boston during that campaign, Roosevelt
repeated a theme he referred to often: "I have said this before, but
I shall say it again and again and again: Your boys are not going to
be sent into any foreign wars. . . . The purpose of our defense is
defense."

In the light of what happened subsequently some historians have
questioned Roosevelt's sincerity, as they were later to question that
of Lyndon Johnson in respect to the Vietnam War. But there was an

economic and political logic to events that transcended the wishes of mortals—a logic rooted in industrialism, private profit, and competition, which literally drove the great nations against each other, and all of them against the weaker states. The capitalist system subsists on markets and access to raw materals; and if those should be cut off abroad through political or economic manipulation, the home country is enervated by the social diseases of unemployment and economic stagnation. Subsidized competition in Latin America by Germany and Japan, for instance, caused Secretary of the Treasury Henry Morgenthau to record in his diary of December 16, 1937, the alarming possibility that "we're just going to wake up and find inside of a year that Italy, Germany, and Japan have taken over Mexico." Should Germany establish its suzerainty over Europe it would have both the economic and military wherewithal to whittle the U.S. sphere of influence in Latin America toward oblivion; and should Japan forge an empire that included China, Southeast Asia, Singapore, and the Dutch East Indies, half the world's raw materials would become inaccessible to other powers. Disruption of the status quo would have dire economic consequences as well as dire strategic ones for the have nations.

This is not to say that no alternatives to war existed in 1939, that the march toward conflict could not have been slowed down, that a modus vivendi could not have been reached for a few more years. Just prior to Hitler's invasion of Sudetenland, for instance, a group of German generals led by Ludwig Beck and Franz Halder plotted to arrest Hitler and establish a military regime to prevent a general war. Their plot, alas, depended on Britain and France manifesting a will to resist the Fuehrer, and when this failed to eventuate the generals drew back. There were to be other plots in the coming years, and no one can tell for sure what might have happened had the Allies given them more concrete support. Similarly, the government of Japan under Fumimaro Konoye was slightly more tractable than the one that followed his resignation, headed by General Hideki Tojo. Whether judicious concessions to Konoye's regime might have cut the ground out from under the militarists—at least for some years— is one of those historical "if's" whose answer can only be guessed. In either case, however, peace might have been preserved for a period.

But the war did start in 1939 and Roosevelt cast his lot with the nations that were least inimical to the interests of the American establishment, Britain and France, against those most inimical, the Axis powers. Unlike Wilson, who called on his fellow citizens to be "impartial in thought as well as in action," Roosevelt was openly disposed toward the Allies both in spirit and in performance. There were at the time a number of neutrality laws on the books prohibiting sale and transport of munitions to belligerents, or floating loans on their behalf. Within three weeks FDR had called Congress into special session to revise these acts so that the combatants could buy what they wanted as long as they paid cash and carried away the ordnance on their own ships—cash-and-carry, it was called. In theory, both sides could buy in the United States, but in practice, since Britannia ruled the waves, the benefits of the bill were confined to England and France. So blatantly unneutral was FDR's bill that, even though the vast majority of Americans wanted the Allies to win, the debate in Congress lasted six acrimonious weeks.

Concurrent with the lifting of the arms embargo, the Roosevelt Administration prevailed on the Latin American republic to issue the Declaration of Panama, which delineated a "safety belt" around the Americas 300 to 1,000 miles wide. Combatants were warned not to engage in any naval activity in this zone, and the declaration, though it turned out to be a dead letter, was the first of a number of steps toward "regional security" that welded the hemisphere behind Big Brother in the north.

Once again, because of the benevolence of geography, the United States was able, despite its partiality, to stay out of the shooting for a relatively long period—two years and three months—and once again it benefited handsomely while the resources of Britain and France were dissipated. During the depression years, many leading figures had feared that full employment would never again return. Senator Hugo L. Black, a future Supreme Court justice, had thrown a bill into the hopper reducing the work week from forty-eight to thirty hours, so that the permanent army of jobless could be absorbed by sharing the work. Senator James F. Byrnes, a future secretary of state, urged that "we accept the inevitable, that we are now in a new normal" with millions doomed to unemployment to the end of their days. Harry Hopkins, often referred to as the Assistant President, at late as 1937 argued that it was "reasonable to expect a probable minimum of 4 million to 5 million unemployed in future 'prosperity' periods." But as the war orders came in and as Washington itself enlarged its military budget, the 9 to 10 million idle hands, as of 1939, were incorporated into the productive process. In the first two years alone the factories doubled their output, almost 6 million workers were added to the nonagricultural payroll, and exports climbed from $3.2 billion to $5.1 billion. The war put America back to work, where CWA, NRA, PWA, and WPA failed. The cold war that followed kept it at the workbench thereafter.

Had hostilities lapsed into a stalemate, America might have stayed out of the fray even longer. But Germany had perfected a new strategy of warfare—the blitzkrieg, a war of movement in which tanks and planes were used to overrun or encircle enemy positions quickly —that gave Hitler a series of unparalleled victories. In two weeks the 800,000 German invaders, in mechanized divisions, with 1,400 planes at their disposal, decimated a Polish army twice as large and captured 150,000 square miles of territory, including Poland's richest mines, most productive plants, about 22 million of the nation's 35 million population. Simultaneously the Soviets, under the Hitler-Stalin agreements, took the eastern portion of Poland, completing the obliteration of that nation. After this initial thrust came a lull in hostilities while the French army and the British Expeditionary Force sat snugly behind the concrete and steel fortifications called the Maginot Line, and the Germans bivouacked behind their recently finished Siegfried Line, neither side peppering each other with anything more lethal than propaganda leaflets. The only fighting was in Finland, which the Soviet army invaded at the end of November, but this like the subsequent seizures of Latvia, Estonia, Lithuania, Bessarabia, and Bukovina by the Kremlin, were sideshows to the main event. Three months after the onset of war the British had not suffered a single casualty; Senator William Borah called it a "phony war," others called it a "sitzkrieg." Hitler seemed willing to wait, on the theory that his enemies would once again accept a fait accompli and come to terms; the Allies, on the other hand, were now convinced that a settlement was impossible, that a combination of the "impregnable" Maginot Line and the British blockade would bring the Nazis to brook.

Soon, however, the "phony war" became dramatically real again— and American aid began to accelerate in cadence with the Allies' adversity. In April 1940, Hitler's legions occupied Denmark—despite a recently signed nonaggression pact—and marched into Norway, where their Norwegian agent, Vidkun Quisling, had tried to prepare the way. The British mobilized a small force to defend the small state and sent some ships to challenge the invaders, but the German steamroller could not be stopped. In May it rolled into Belgium; neutral Holland was devastated and conquered in five short days. The Maginot Line, behind which the French hoped to wage a "war of position" similar to the type of fighting that prevailed in the First World War, was neutralized by the simple device of sending Panzer divisions around it in the north.

In less than two weeks the German troops were at the English Channel and the British were forced into the humiliating—though successful—evacuation of 338,000 men at Dunkirk. Simultaneously Belgium surrendered, and on June 10, Mussolini, sensing a "quasi-mathematical certainty of winning," declared his nation at war with France. A few days later as the French army continued to reel backward, Paris fell. Thus within a month Hitler had achieved what the Kaiser had been unable to do in four years. The newly installed British Prime Minister, Winston Churchill, pleaded with France to continue fighting and offered political union of the two countries as an incentive, but except for Charles de Gaulle, who preserved the flame of resistance in his London exile, the ancient nation was a psychological shambles. On June 22, 1940, at the Forest of Compiègne, and in the same railway carriage in which Germany had surrendered twenty-two years earlier, Hitler imposed an armistice whereby the Nazis occupied half of France; the other half was left to a puppet regime in Vichy, under Marshall Henri Pétain and Pierre Laval. England was now alone, battered by Goering's Luftwaffe, awaiting an amphibious invasion—if Hitler could assemble the necessary landing craft. "The winter of illusion," as Churchill had called the sitzkrieg, had passed into a summer of furious conquest, with the British leader promising his countrymen nothing but "blood, toil, tears, and sweat" for the immediate future.

"The American people," according to Sherry Mangam in a November 1943 *Fortune* article, "were eased into the war by a process of discreet gradualism and manufactured inevitability. . . . Pearl Harbor merely legalized the accomplished fact." The manufacture of inevitability was accelerated by Roosevelt when the European house of cards began to topple. On May 16, 1940, as he asked for $1.2 billion more in defense money, he drew a harsh picture of what lay in store for the American people. With air power at its present technological levels, he said, the United States was no longer safe behind its two oceans: New England could be attacked from bases in Greenland; New York from airfields in Bermuda; and Seattle from stations in Alaska if the Japanese were to conquer it. To counter such gruesome possibilities he urged that "this nation [be] geared up to the ability to turn out at least 50,000 planes a year."

Three weeks later FDR began to supply England with military equipment in direct contravention of international law, which holds that it is an act of war for a neutral to give weapons to a belligerent. Brushing aside old restrictions on the sale of weapons, he shipped rifles, machine guns, and other matériel to the British. In August he exchanged fifty mothballed destroyers with Britain in return for ninety-nine-year leases on naval and air bases in Newfoundland, Bermuda, the West Indies, and British Guiana. Theoretically such an arrangement required, under the U.S. Constitution, a two-thirds vote of the Senate, but the President took action by executive fiat—a precedent which would become commonplace in the turbulent 1960s. Meanwhile, Roosevelt also asked for, and received, authorization to spend $4 billion more for a two-ocean navy; added two venerable Republicans to his cabinet, Henry M. Stimson and Frank Knox, to give it the flavor of national unity; set up a Joint Board of Defense with Canada, and concluded an agreement with the Latin American nations at a meeting in Havana, affirming that all of them would stand as one to protect "the integrity or political independence of an American state." Most important was the passage of the first Selective Service Act in peacetime history, allowing for the immediate draft of 800,000 men between twenty-one and thirty-five. It was coupled with assurances that it was only for "hemispheric defense," and "your boys are not going to be sent into any foreign wars. They are going into training to form a force so strong that, by its very existence, it will keep the threat of war far away from our shores."

Roosevelt's own steamroller was slow to start but it gained momentum, especially after the 1940 elections, which he won with 449 electoral votes, compared to 82 for Wendell Willkie. America clearly was now in a "war short of war." When Congress convened in January 1941, the President urged it to support all nations which upheld, in his historic phrase, the "Four Freedoms"—freedom of speech, freedom of religion, freedom from want, freedom from fear. And a few days later he proposed a far-reaching and unique method for financing Britain and the various governments in exile—such as de Gaulle's Free French—which was to be five times as costly as the loans made by Uncle Sam in World War I. Under the Lend-Lease Act, passed after bitter debate in March 1941, the chief executive was authorized to "sell, transfer, exchange, lease, lend" any war matériel to any government that "the President deems vital to the defense of the United States." This was without question a flagrant violation of international dictum, but it was approved in spite of bitter debate and strong opposition from Republicans (135 against, 24 for). "Never before," declared antiwar critic Senator Burton K. Wheeler, "has the Congress of the United States been asked by any President to violate international law. Never before has this nation resorted to duplicity in the conduct of its foreign affairs. . . . Never before has a Congress boldly and flatly been asked to abdicate." The bill, he predicted, "will plow under every fourth American boy." Nevertheless it passed, and in the next four and a half years $49.1 billion in munitions, food, goods, and services were doled out to U.S. allies, about three-fifths to Britair and about one-fifth to the Soviet Union, after it was attacked by Hitler. The recipients "paid back" in *reverse* lend-lease about $8 billion; that is, they made available airfields, hospitals, depots, barracks, food, and oil, for America's own armies overseas.

Churchill called America's effort "the most unsordid act in the history of any nation," but it was in truth indispensable for Washington's goals as well. Hundreds of thousands—perhaps millions—of additional American "boys" would have died on the western front if the $11 billion in aid (427,000 trucks, 13,000 combat vehicles, 2,000 locomotives, 11,000 railroad cars, 35,000 motorcycles, 4.5 million tons of food, 4 million pairs of army shoes, tanks, planes, oil, etc.—15 million tons of supplies altogether) had not been delivered to the Soviet Union to help it contain, then roll back, Hitler on the eastern front. Though American goods in each category were ordinarily only 5 to 10 percent of the total used by Stalin's forces, they were a decisive and vital part, without which—locomotives, for instance—Soviet armies would have been too poorly supplied to defeat the Germans. Insofar as Britain was concerned, by December 1940, after paying out $4.5 billion for foreign purchases, mostly American, she was starved for dollars and had to suspend all but a few munitions orders. Without Lend-Lease her effort too would have faltered, again forcing U.S. soldiers eventually to fight more of the war. In effect, the Roosevelt Administration substituted dollars for casualties.

After Lend-Lease there was nothing either discreet or gradual about America's plunge toward the maelstrom. It was no longer a question of whether but of how. Within a few weeks all Axis vessels in American harbors were sequestered for the duration. In April, Greenland was occupied for "hemispheric defense." In May the President ordered fifty oil tankers transferred to British use, and after a freighter had been sunk by a German U-boat, declared a state of "unlimited national emergency." By now Roosevelt was no longer talking about solely defending the United States. "Our Bunker Hill of tomorrow," he said, "will be several thousand miles from Boston," perhaps in Iceland, Greenland, the Azores, or the Cape Verde Islands. In June, Axis consulates in the United States were padlocked and the assets of the three countries—with none of whom America was yet formally at war—frozen. A new selective service bill extended the service of drafted men from a year to eighteen months and removed the limit on the number of men that might be in training at any one time—previously set at 900,000. Despite the popular feeling that America was headed for battle, hostility to conscription was still so great that this bill carried the House by only a single vote.

By the summer of 1941 it was obvious that there were no limits to the war—that the stakes were the whole planet, and that this was, in fact, a Second World War. This was clear not only to the Axis nations, which had joined in a formal Tripartite pact in September 1940 to help each other in case any of them became engaged with the United States, but to Churchill and Roosevelt as well. Even before he became head of the British government, Churchill had cabled FDR: "I am half American, and the natural person to work with you. It is evident we see eye to eye. Were I to become Prime Minister we could control the world." Roosevelt had other ideas on *how* the world should be controlled—with Britain as junior, not senior, partner—but it was evident that the martial confrontation had total, rather than limited, objectives. It became more evident on June 22, 1941, when Hitler turned his Panzers loose on his erstwhile nonaggression partner, the Soviet Union. Taking Stalin completely by surprise, he unleashed 150 divisions and 2,400 planes on the eastern front, and within ten days had temporarily immobilized the Soviet air force and captured 150,000 Russian soldiers. The buffer zone that Stalin had so meticulously established melted like butter before the advance, and by October, as the Nazi legions battered at Moscow itself, the Soviet Union had lost a half million square miles of its richest industrial territory and 1.7 million men. Only the Russian winter, for which the Germans were badly prepared, stalled their drive.

In the face of the attack on the Soviet Union the pace of America's undeclared war became even more feverish. On June 24, Roosevelt announced he was making Lend-Lease supplies available to Moscow. On July 7, Iceland, a Danish colony that had cut loose from its mother country, was occupied by American forces and used as an intermediate base for ships and planes headed for England. This was a major step toward hostilities because Rosevelt simultaneously ordered American destroyers to escort merchantmen carrying Lend-Lease goods as far as the island—where the British would take over —and drop depth charges when they suspected the presence of German submarines. Until then the President had held off on convoying ships because he feared public opinion was not yet ready for what was so patently a war measure. Caution, however, was out of style.

In September, after a German U-boat fired two torpedoes at the U.S.S. *Greer* and two merchantmen were sunk, the chief executive proclaimed a "shoot on sight" policy against enemy submarines. In a Navy Day address that month the President proclaimed that "America has been attacked" by "rattlesnakes of the sea. . . . The shooting war has started." He raised hackles on many skins by stating that he possessed a secret map to prove that the Nazis planned to divide South America into "five vassal states." They were also determined, he said, to "abolish all existing religions." International law was now a dead letter, the only relevant law remaining was that of "self-defense," in whose interests he asked Congress for two major modifications of the Neutrality Laws. One called for putting guns on merchant vessels, the other for lifting the restriction on going into combat zones. "I consider the pending Senate decision," said Senator Arthur Vandenberg, a Republican leader, in discussing the FDR proposals, "as substantially settling the question whether America deliberately and consciously shall go all the way into a

shooting war, probably upon two oceans. The ultimate aknowledg-
ment by Congress of a state of war, I fear, will be a mere formal-
ity. . . ." Nothing more was needed to trigger the explosion but an
"incident" that would unite the American people.

That incident occurred at 7:55 A.M. on Sunday, December 7—
not in Europe or the Atlantic but on the other side of the world,
in the Pacific. The Japanese attacked Pearl Harbor, Hawaii, with
135 bombers and a flotilla of ships, killing 2,403 Americans, destroying 149 planes on the ground, and shattering 6 battleships and
various other vessels in less than two hours. Roosevelt described
the attack as "sudden" and it galvanized the American people behind their government as in no other war. Almost everyone believed
that the Japanese had perpetrated a "sneak" assault, without warning, and many were convinced that had it not been for this treachery
war might have been avoided.

Pearl Harbor, however, was merely the exclamation point to a
very long sentence. In July 1940, Roosevelt cut off the supply of oil,
scrap iron, and aviation gasoline to Japan—all vital to its economy.
The Nipponese responded by moving into Indochina (with the be-
grudging approval of Vichy), consolidating their influence in Thailand, and threatening the Dutch East Indies and Singapore. Washington countered by making some loans to China to buttress its
defense and demanding ever more vigorously that Japan respect the
Open Door. There was no reconciling these two approaches—to expand economically, Japan felt she needed to control additional territory, while the United States opposed further territorial expansion
by anyone since it inevitably would close what might be, or might
become, an Open Door.

Both governments knew, weeks or months before Pearl Harbor,
that they were headed for war. The Japanese had completed their
plans on September 18. Secretary Stimson recorded in his diary for
November 25, 1941, that Hull, Frank Knox, General George Marshall,
Admiral Harold I. Stark, Roosevelt, and himself met at the White
House that day and discussed "how we should maneuver them
[the Japanese] into the position of firing the first shot without allow-
ing too much danger to ourselves." Testifying before a congressional
committee on Pearl Harbor five years later, he reminisced that "one
problem troubled us very much. If you know that your enemy is
going to strike you, it is not usually wise to wait until he gets the

jump on you by taking the initiative. In spite of the risk involved, however, in letting the Japanese fire the first shot, we realized that *in order to have the full support of the American people* it was desirable to make sure that the Japanese be the ones to do this so that there should remain no doubt in anyone's mind as to who were the aggressors." (Emphasis added.)

According to Oliver Lyttelton, British Minister of Production, "Japan was provoked into attacking Pearl Harbor. It is a travesty on history even to say that America was forced into the war. It is incorrect to say that America ever was truly neutral even before America came into the war on an all-out fighting basis." And according to Arthur Sulzberger, publisher of the prowar *New York Times,* "we did not go to war because we were attacked at Pearl Harbor. I hold rather that we were attacked at Pearl Harbor because we had gone to war. . . ." War, in other words, was expected and considered inevitable by both sides; Roosevelt simply wanted the other side to perform the first overt act so that he could consolidate public opinion behind him. That the strategy worked is evident from the vote on the war resolution December 8th—82 to 0 in the Senate, 388 to 1 (Representative Jeanette Rankin of Montana, a pacifist) in the House.

The prologue to Pearl Harbor, apart from indicating the irreconcilable economic and political motives of the belligerents, reveals a key aspect of America's transition to global imperialism—the centralization of power in the presidency.

The Second World War generated only meager opposition—from a few leftist groups such as the Trotskyites (the Stalin Communists, of course, had become the most fervid supporters of the war after Hitler's invasion of Russia), the diehard isolationists, and some small numbers in the German-American and Italian-American communities. Victory was won, despite a high cost in dollars—$330 billion, exclusive of subsequent payments for pensions, veterans' aid, and interest on loans—with a relatively low cost in blood compared to other nations, 292,000 dead in battle, 671,000 wounded (as against 6 million killed and 14 million injured for the Soviet Union). Despite controls on wages, prices, rents, materials, and job transfers, civilian life was disturbed only minimally, and not a single American city or building was touched by a foreign bomb. Under the circumstances there has been little disposition to castigate Roosevelt for transforming a government theoretically based on popular and congressional "consent" to a vassal run by executive fiat. Yet he reshaped the process as no president before him had done, and developed a credibility gap at least as ominous as the one created by Lyndon Johnson a quarter of a century later during the Vietnam War. He made innumerable treaties and arrangements, both for execution of the war and for shaping the postwar world, without seeking approval of the Senate as provided in the Constitution or invoking popular discussion, as provided by a higher concept of democracy. He did not *follow* popular will, but manipulated it toward goals he had already determined on, including entry into the conflagration itself.

Alden Hatch, in his sympathetic book *Franklin D. Roosevelt: An Informal Biography (*1947), asked FDR's closest associates—including Mrs. Roosevelt, Admiral William D. Leahy, Samuel L. Rosenman, Justice Felix Frankfurter, Ernest K. Lindley, and others—"When do you think that the President decided that the United States would probably have to enter the war?" In every instance, he records, "the reply fixed the time within a few weeks" of the Hitler-Stalin Pact. Adolf Berle, Assistant Secretary of State from 1938 to 1944, said in 1946 that "the date when war was considered probable rather than remotely possible was shortly after the Munich conferences. . . ." In his memorial address at Harvard, April 1945, Justice Frankfurter stated that Roosevelt made the decision "for the utter defeat of Nazism" as "essential to the survival of our institutions" not "later than when Mr. Sumner Welles reported on his mission to Europe," in March 1940. For one or two years at least, while the American people were being assured by their President that he was trying with might and main to stay out of war, he had already decided that entry was inevitable—and was proceeding accordingly.

He engaged in a host of actions that were either violations of international law, such as supplying weapons to a belligerent, or violations of the U.S. Constitution, such as failure to seek Senate approval for the agreement exchanging fifty destroyers for British bases, or the occupation of Greenland and Iceland. By misrepresenting what he fully expected he would have to do—go to war—the President was able to acquire authority far beyond what he was entitled under the basic law of the land. Under the Lend-Lease Act he could designate whether a nation was a friend or a foe, and in effect enter into binding war alliances that should have been the prerogative of Congress, or at least a joint prerogative, not an exclusive one of the President's. Whether the American people did or did not want an alliance with Britain or the Soviets is beside the point; what is pertinent here is that Roosevelt accrued to himself the right to determine what his people "wanted" or were entitled to, *without* their actual consent. Roosevelt, to be sure, was an instrument of the social system he served; he moved in accord with the economic and political necessities of that system. But within prescribed limits he could act decisively or phlegmatically, and in this situation his direction was firmly fixed. Each single step he took may not have been conclusive in itself, but cumulatively they headed the nation as inexorably into war as if a favorable vote had been taken in September 1939 rather than December 1941. The logic of each move led to another, so that in reality the decision on war or peace was predetermined. The only real questions were when, where, and under what conditions. It is significant that the war resolution of December 8, 1941, was not on the question of "declaring" war, but simply "recognizing" that a state of war already existed. Having set this precedent it was to be expected that future presidents would similarly bypass the mechanism for "consent of the governed" and catapult the nation into all kinds of adventures about which it was uninformed, unprepared, and unconsulted.

It soon became commonplace for the President to arrive at secret understandings with the heads of foreign governments that were of the utmost significance for the future, and normally should have been placed before Congress. By way of example, in August 1941—four months before the United States formally entered the war—Roosevelt held a historic meeting with Churchill off the coast of Newfoundland, at which the famous Atlantic Charter was drafted. Apart from the fact that it was somewhat unorthodox, as the *Chicago Tribune* observed, for the head of a nation *not* at war to be discussing common strategy with the head of a nation at war, there were other, equally disconcerting, features. On his return Roosevelt told the press that no new commitments had been made, when in fact agreement had been reached on the broad strategy not only for the war in Europe but the impending one in Asia. The two political titans, moreover, had concurred on a number of specific items, ranging from the relatively minor one of occupying the Azores to the grandiose one of setting up, in the future, a machinery for policing the world.

In the subsequent meetings with Churchill and Stalin, especially at Yalta, all kinds of agreements were concluded over the disposition of territory and spheres of influence in Europe and Asia (that Greece, for instance, would be a British sphere, Bulgaria a Russian sphere, or that half of Sakhalin Island would go to the Soviet Union in return for her secret pledge to enter the war against Japan), and all of this without Congress or the American people even knowing about it. Thus in rapid order the mechanism for government by consent of the governed was dismantled in favor of a mechanism by which the executive arrogated the broadest power of peace and war, of life and death, to himself. This helped pave the way for a dramatic transformation not only of the style but of the essence of government.

Roosevelt and Japan

William L. Neumann

A SEPARATE WAR—THE MYTHICAL BASES FOR AMERICAN POLICY

The late William L. Neumann spent most of his academic career analyzing American foreign policy in East Asia. Although he never resorted to personal attacks or insinuations of treason, Neumann consistently viewed the Japanese-American War of 1941–1945 as an avoidable tragedy which came about largely because of America's double standard and misconceived notions about the realities of power in that part of the world. His early criticism of Roosevelt's immediate prewar policies was included in Harry Elmer Barnes' collection of early revisionist essays on the Roosevelt foreign policy, and because it is one of the few in that book which has stood the test of time, it is excerpted below. Neumann wrote a perceptive survey of Japanese-American relations, America Encounters Japan *(1963) as well as* After Victory: Churchill, Roosevelt, Stalin and the Making of the Peace *(1967).*

The war between the United States and Japan was neither, as official and semiofficial histories paint it, a struggle between good and evil nor a contest between a peace-loving nation and an arrogant proponent of aggression and chaos. These are the conventional labels used by nations to describe their enemies. Every victorious power attempts to certify similar interpretations of recent wars as eternal truths. While such moralistic simplifications have their value as nationalist propaganda, they have no place in an honest attempt at an unbiased study of international issues. Righteousness has never been the exclusive preserve of any one nation, nor has virtue been completely wanting among even the most chauvinistic peoples. If the Pacific conflict is to be the subject of moralizing, it might better be described as a tragedy of errors and as the unwanted offspring of false assumptions and follies on both sides of the Pacific.

From William L. Neumann, "How American Policy Toward Japan Contributed to War in the Pacific," in Harry Elmer Barnes, ed., *Perpetual War for Perpetual Peace* (Caldwell, Idaho, 1953). Reprinted by permission of The Caxton Printers, Ltd. Footnotes omitted.

The errors and fallacies of Japanese policy have often been set forth for Americans with a rich collection of assorted invectives. Stripped of all gratuitous adjectives and adverbs, Japan's course is clear and the errors of Japanese assumptions then become patent. An island nation with a growing population, stimulated by Western penetration, found its resources inadequate to achieve its aspirations for a higher standard of living. Following the Western pattern, Japan looked abroad for land, markets, and raw materials. Japan also developed aspirations for the status of a major power, again stimulated by Western influences, particularly by the humiliating experiences of the early post-Perry decades. It was in these formative years that Japan learned how helpless a small power could be in the face of energetic Western imperialism, backed by hostile naval squadrons. These two aspirations combined to create an expansionist movement in Japan which looked primarily to Asia for its fulfillment. When economic penetration of Asia was checked by political obstacles in the form of intransigent Chinese war lords, Japan turned to the ultimate weapon of imperialism, military force.

Japanese expansionism also brought to the fore a chauvinistic group of military leaders who developed a racialist concept of Japan's manifest destiny. They believed that Asia was at last to find peace and economic progress under Japanese leadership in the form of the Greater East Asia Co-Prosperity Sphere. No alien nation, neither Russia nor the United States, was to be permitted to stand in the way of this goal. To this end Japan fought a border war in Manchuria against the Soviet Union from 1937 to 1939. When the United States, from 1931 onward, stood firmly behind the Chinese Nationalist government, Japan's best customer became Japan's enemy. When other methods seemed unavailing, Japan prepared for a trans-Pacific war to remove the American barrier to an area which Japan believed was vital for national security and prosperity. But the willingness of the people of the United States, once attacked, to fight a long and costly war over a cause remote from their shores was not foreseen by Japan's leaders. This was the fatal error of Japanese policy. This was the false assumption which was to bring that nation to defeat and to destroy the accomplishments of two generations of vigorous diplomacy.

Americans have given little attention to the errors of their own

Far Eastern policies. Self-examination is not a characteristic of the victor, even when the fruits of victory prove bitter. Most studies of the coming of the Pacific war by Americans still accept the official assumptions as valid. The United States is seen as a force exerted in behalf of peace and stability in Asia. American attempts to maintain the status quo and uphold the integrity of China are judged wise even though they failed. More important, the basic premise of American policy from 1931 onward—that the United States has a vital national interest in blocking the expansion of Japan in Asia—is seldom questioned. Yet on this premise any justification of the diplomacy of Secretary of State Henry Stimson or of the foreign policy of the Franklin D. Roosevelt Administration must make its case.

* * *

Already it is possible to outline the misconceptions of American policy-makers and to see in what respects they were blinded to basic facts and key relationships in Far Eastern international policies. No consideration was given to the historic ambitions of Russia in Asia nor to the expansionist element in Stalinist Communism. As a result there was a complete disregard for the role which a strong Japan played in the Far Eastern balance of power. Gross errors were also made in calculating that Japan could be coerced by economic pressure and naval force to follow American bidding in its relations with China. The political and economic importance of China for Japan was not grasped, despite the fact that Japanese leaders spoke of it as a national interest to be defended regardless of costs. This blindness to the importance of China for Japan contrasts with the gross overrating of the importance of a Japan-free China for the United States. It was assumed by some key figures in the Roosevelt Administration that this objective was worth the blood and toil which a costly trans-Pacific conflict would entail. Behind this premise was another, equally invalid. This was the assumption that the power relationships of Asia of the 1920s could be maintained—or, after 1931, restored—despite the rising power of Japan and the Soviet Union and the internal political disintegration of the Chinese Nationalist government. The instrument of maintenance or restoration was not to be forces within Asia itself but the pronouncements and threats of American power with its center thousands of miles from

Asia's shores. Faith in the growth of American naval power under the Roosevelt Administration disregarded the strength by which the Japanese navy sought to counter American building.

The history of American policy in the Far East from 1931 onward is largely a story of these blunders and fallacies in the interpretation and implementation of American interests. It was Henry L. Stimson, twice secretary of war, who, as President Hoover's secretary of state, first set the course of American opposition to Japanese expansion. . . .

. . . In justifying his policy Stimson agreed that if the Sino-Japanese conflict had occurred two generations earlier it would have had little meaning for the United States. But in 1931, he said, American economic and political interests in the Far East were "considerable." The United States did have, in 1931, an important and profitable trade with Asia. The chief source of that profit was not China, however, but Japan, where large quantities of American cotton were purchased and paid for by Japanese silk exports to the United States. The total value of American exports and imports to and from Japan in the 1930s was three to four times the value of exports and imports from China. In the peak years, 1927–30, American exports to China never exceeded 4 percent of the total American exports while imports from China were less than 5 percent of the total. Even as late as 1938 American sales to Japan reached over $230 million while China, in the same year, purchased only some $56 million worth of American goods.

American investments in China itself were also relatively small and never reached 2 percent of the total American foreign investment. In 1935 the value of Chinese private securities held by Americans reached only $16.7 million while Americans held over $323 million of Japanese private securities. Of $2.6 billion in foreign investments in China, Japan claimed the larger amount, while most of the remainder was held by Great Britain. As late as 1943 a census of American-owned assets in China totalled only $122 million. It was for this small economic stake in China that the profitable trade relationship with Japan was to be endangered and finally destroyed by the Stimson and Roosevelt policies.

American interests in China were often discussed in future terms rather than in present realities. To some extent this dream was a projection of the past, of the early New England trade with Canton and of the great fortunes made by a few score families from the trade in teas and silks. Roosevelt himself showed signs of this type of thinking. After Stimson, in January, 1933, had won the President-elect's support for his nonrecognition policy, two of Roosevelt's advisers, Raymond Moley and Rexford Tugwell, tried to dissuade him from committing his administration to a policy they considered futile and dangerous. To their plea Roosevelt answered with the remark that his ancestors had traded with China and for this reason he had the deepest sympathy for the Chinese. The President's mother had lived in China as a small girl and the President repeatedly told the story of the business dealings of his family in the China trade of the early nineteenth century.

A less romantic argument for the future economic importance of China and for American prosperity was developed in Marxian terms. Expressed most forcefully by Nathaniel Peffer's *Must We Fight in Asia?*, this line of argument stressed the inevitable collapse of American capitalism if it failed to capture new markets. China with its more than four hundred million potential customers was thus essential to the continuation of the American economic system. War with Japan over China was necessary to preserve a capitalism which could no longer live on its domestic markets. Short of turning the United States into a socialist state and sharing the surplus with the American worker, a war of imperialist powers for China was said to be inevitable—so the argument ran.

Whether the argument was made in present or future terms, phrased in romantic aspirations or Marxian dialectic, the assumption was made by the makers of American policy that this country's economic stake in China, along with the political stake, constituted a vital national interest. Yet six years after the end of the war against Japan, American trade with China had practically disappeared and American investments in China were largely liquidated. Similarly, American political influence within China itself had reached a twentieth-century low. No noticeable damage had been done to the American economy and few would argue that a war to replace the Communist rulers of China by a pro-American regime was essential to American security. Historical developments have thus illustrated the falsity of the Stimson-Roosevelt assumptions.

Arguments were also presented in behalf of American intervention in the Sino-Japanese conflict which went beyond the traditional political and economic concepts of national interest. World peace, in which the United States was said to have a vital stake, was also to be preserved by the Stimson-Roosevelt Far Eastern policy, according to its supporters. Stimson believed that American sponsorship of the Kellogg-Briand antiwar pact called for active steps to maintain peace by opposing Japanese expansionism. Secretary Hull thought along similar lines. In January, 1938, the secretary was asked for statistics by the Senate on American economic interests in China. The secretary replied that there was in China "a broader and much more fundamental interest—which is that orderly processes in international relationships must be maintained." Spokesmen for the Roosevelt Administration frequently made similar claims for their policy's peace-spreading characteristics.

Two assumptions were made in these arguments. The first was that peace between two Asiatic powers was a matter of direct concern for the United States and an important enough national interest to justify the risk of speading the war. The second assumption was again the optimistic one that a third power, far from the seat of conflict, could adjust the differences of the warring powers by supporting the weaker against the stronger. For over a century the American policy of neutrality had been based on the assumption that peace was divisible and that it was to the interest of this country to avoid wars in which national security and national prosperity were not endangered. That policy, dating back to the precepts of George Washington and Thomas Jefferson, was now discarded on the assumption that neutrality was no longer a workable policy and that the use of American political, economic, and military strength could effectively check wars on other continents by exerting pressure on one of the contestants. The validity of these assumptions can most objectively be tested by their results.

*   *   *

After 1938 the increase of Hitler's power in Europe and the fall of Austria and Czechoslovakia made it easier to overcome congressional opposition to naval building and to administration pleas for a two-ocean navy. For the fiscal year of 1939, total arms expenditures mounted to more than twice those of 1935. The Navy also drew on the Treasury for over $670 million in 1939, almost $900 million in 1940, and for over $2 billion in the fiscal year ending in June, 1941.

Authorizations later that year, moved by the fall of France, almost doubled the Navy's building goals.

As the Navy grew larger, there was increasing confidence that American naval power could easily threaten Japan into submission or, if necessary, crush the Japanese forces with a minimum of losses for the United States. There was no expectation that the war would be a long one or a hard one. The American racialist stereotype of the Oriental, assuming basic inferiority on the part of the yellow races, did not permit any consideration of the possibility that the Japanese might be a formidable opponent. The surprise victory of the Japanese over the Russians in 1904–1905 was forgotten, even though it had once raised the stature of Japan in American eyes.

In July, 1937, shortly after Japan renewed its warfare against China, President Roosevelt began work on a plan to force the Japanese into submission by a joint British-American naval blockade to cut off Japanese trade. The opposition of many of the leading admirals to such a bold plan, which they believed meant war, as well as the adverse public reactions to the famous "quarantine speech" in October, 1937, led the President to put his plan aside.

In 1938 a new joint Army-Navy Plan was drafted for use against Japan. It assumed that Japan might begin hostilities against the United States after a period of strained relations and without a formal declaration of war. Among the American fleet's tasks was a westward movement from Pearl Harbor to capture and establish control over the Caroline and Marshall Islands. The Ingersoll conversations in London had already explored the possible use of the new British naval base at Singapore for operations against Japan.

In mid-April, 1939, the United States fleet, which had been moved to the Atlantic three months earlier, was suddenly ordered by the President to return to the Pacific. The Atlantic transfer had been considered as only a temporary one but the fleet was to have remained longer and to have been part of the New York World's Fair. In the fall of 1939, despite the outbreak of war in Europe, reinforcements were also sent to Admiral Hart, commander of the Asiatic Squadron, consisting of a half dozen new submarines and a squadron of planes. Hart had asked for a heavier cruiser squadron because of the increased dangers of operation in the western Pacific, but this much strength could not be spared for the Pacific Fleet.

While in the Pacific, the fleet was based on the California coast.

But in October, 1939, a substantial number of ships—eight heavy cruisers, one aircraft carrier, and eighteen destroyers—were detached from the West Coast and stationed at Pearl Harbor. In April, 1940, the fleet was moved in its entirety to Hawaii for the conduct of the annual maneuvers. Although the fleet's plans called for a return to the West Coast in early May, orders were given to postpone the return for two weeks. Before that period expired, the fleet was assigned to Pearl Harbor for an indefinite period. For two decades, since its assignment to the Pacific in 1920, the fleet had been based on the West Coast. This move, shifting the center of American naval power some 2,500 miles closer to Japan, was a highly significant event in the history of the power relations of the two countries.

In October, 1940, the commander in chief of the fleet outlined a new war plan which aimed at intercepting trade between Japan and the Americas. To achieve this extensive operation, major reinforcements were to be sent to the Asiatic Squadron which would retire to the East Indies area where it would operate in conjunction with British and Dutch naval forces. Another American detachment was to patrol the North Atlantic from Hawaii to the Aleutians, sweeping the sea for Japanese commerce and raiders. The remaining forces would reconnoiter the Caroline and Marshall Islands preliminary to offensive operations against these Japanese outposts.

The naval movements could be interpreted only as efforts to coerce Japan or as preparations for actual hostilities. For the most part the initiative for these movements did not originate in the Navy Department but with the President and the State Department. In the case of the shifting of the fleet base to Pearl Harbor, both the commander in chief of the fleet, Admiral Richardson, and Admiral Stark, chief of naval operations, were in opposition. Richardson was also critical of any stick-waving at Japan which might end in hostilities. He argued that Pearl Harbor was not adequately equipped and that the Japanese knew that the American forces were not sufficiently supported with auxiliary ships to conduct offensive operations. Another factor, generally overlooked, was that, in the 1938 fleet maneuvers, the aircraft carrier *Saratoga* had launched a successful surprise attack on Pearl Harbor from a position only a hundred miles away.

Roosevelt's decision to use the naval power of the United States in an effort to squeeze concessions from Japan, or to engage in war, if necessary, came not only from his own assumptions about American interest and American superiority, but also at the urging of the British government. As early as March, 1939, Lord Halifax, British foreign secretary, was urging that the American fleet be returned to the Pacific and that this step be so timed as to have maximum psychological effect on Japan. The British also assumed that war was likely with the Japanese, but at the same time they were eager to keep most of the strength of the Royal Navy in European waters.

One British objective was to strengthen Singapore with detachments of the American navy. Five days after he became prime minister on May 10, 1940, Churchill sent a personal message to Roosevelt asking for American ships to be dispatched to Singapore. In early October of the same year, after the fall of France had drawn most of Britain's Far Eastern ships to the Mediterranean, Churchill again urged that American power be shifted to the western Pacific. He suggested the reinforcement of the Asiatic Squadron with battleships and once more offered Singapore as a base. In late November, 1940, another request came from London for the division of America's Pacific forces and a greater extension of power west of Hawaii. If war came as a result, Britain's First Sea Lord, Sir Dudley Pound, argued that the Japanese navy could be stopped north of the Dutch East Indies. The British ambassador to Washington told Hull that British naval experts had also figured out that the American fleet, if based at Singapore, could, on the opening of war, reach Japan before the Japanese navy attacked in the South Pacific. This optimism about the ability of the American fleet to move boldly into Japan's home waters was, fortunately, not shared by top American naval commanders. Admiral Leahy, formerly chief of naval operations, told the President in October, 1940, that any reinforcements sent to the Asiatic Squadron would be lost in the event of war. Later it was revealed that the Singapore base lacked the equipment to effect major repairs on capital ships and would have been inadequate as a center of American operations in Far Eastern waters. The November, 1940, request was not filled, but before the year closed some further reinforcements were ordered to Admiral Hart's Far Eastern Squadron.

In Washington the amateur naval strategists not only included President Roosevelt but also Secretary Hull and one of his aides, Stanley Hornbeck, State Department adviser on Far Eastern affairs. Hornbeck, according to Admiral Richardson, was exercising more influence over the disposition of the United States fleet in 1940 than was its commander in chief. When part of the fleet was moved west, to be based in Hawaii in October, 1939, the order was sent with the strong approval of the State Department.

The major decision, the retention of the entire fleet at Pearl Harbor, was apparently made by the President himself. When the fleet commander asked the meaning of this move, he was told by the chief of naval operations that it was to have a "deterrent effect" on Japanese moves into the East Indies. Admiral Richardson doubted, however, whether the intended effect could be obtained. Japanese espionage in Hawaii, he was certain, was effective enough to inform Tokyo that the American fleet had assembled with only an 85 percent complement and without the train of auxiliary ships needed for offensive action west of Hawaii. When the admiral presented this argument to the President in person, he found that Roosevelt was certain that the contrary was true and was determined not to permit a withdrawal to the West Coast bases. Admiral Stark agreed with Richardson on the inadvisability of keeping the fleet at Pearl Harbor.

Several Japanese newspapers pointed out that the decision to move the fleet base was an effort to stop rumored Japanese moves toward the Dutch East Indies. But they also suggested that it would be difficult for the fleet to remain at Pearl Harbor because of limited facilities. The information now available on the formulation of Japanese foreign policy, in 1940, gives no support for the President's belief in the effects of his strategy. Roosevelt admitted some uncertainty about his policy, but held out against the opinion of his two top naval commanders and told Stark that he would "sit tight" on his decision.

As an amateur naval strategist, Roosevelt had other ideas about employing the Navy against Japan. For the most part he vastly underrated the ability and strength of the Japanese navy and expressed overly-optimistic views about the capabilities of the American fleet. In October, 1939, discussing the possibility of Japan's moving into the Dutch East Indies, he said that "we could easily intercept her fleet—an operation which American forces would have had to conduct some five thousand miles from their nearest major base. A year later, in October, 1940, the President's optimism went so far as to touch on the realm of fantasy. At that time he told the secretary of the navy that he was considering shutting off all trade between Japan and the Western Hemisphere if Japan took action against British possessions as a result of the opening of the Burma Road. This blockade could be achieved, thought the President, by a patrol of light ships stretching across the Pacific vastness in two lines. One would run from Hawaii to the Philippines and the other from Samoa to Singapore. Admiral Richardson, when the secretary of the navy told him of the President's plans, said that war would surely result, that the fleet was in no condition to carry out such an operation, and that to attempt it would expose many ships to certain destruction. Richardson's objections "hurt the President's feelings," according to Secretary Knox, and Richardson was shortly after relieved of his post.

Before being relieved of his command, Admiral Richardson drafted a tentative plan for carrying out a limited blockade, based on a more realistic measure of the fleet's limitations. His plan, however, called for the shifting of some ships from the Atlantic to facilitate operations and it never received the President's approval. Richardson was himself doubtful whether any offensive operations could be successfully conducted in Japanese waters without major increases in American strength.

Despite Richardson's doubts, the American public received assurances from many quarters that the Japanese navy was not to be feared. A study of naval power in the Pacific by an American officer, published in May, 1941, stated that a surprise attack on the Pacific Fleet had already been averted. Pearl Harbor was already on a war footing, this authority believed, and, referring to Japan's successful surprise attack on the Russian navy in 1904, he said that there would be "no American Port Arthur." Only a few weeks before December 7, a popular writer on military affairs told a national radio audience that Japan was in no position to fight the United States. The Japanese navy was said to be hopelessly handicapped by lack of air support and Japanese air power was termed "almost nonexistent." Six months earlier, Admiral Turner, director of the War Plans Division, told a British-American staff conference that the American navy could keep Japanese strength at home merely by cruising in mid-Pacific waters.

This myth of overwhelming fighting superiority lulled many Americans into the passive acceptance of the coming conflict. Although it was obvious to many that the Roosevelt Administration was taking a position which would force a military showdown, opposition voices were softened or stilled by a belief in a quick and inexpensive victory. The traditional assumptions of white or Anglo-Saxon superiority made it easy for the public as well as for government leaders to believe that an Oriental nation could not equal or outdo the West in adapting itself to the techniques and machines of modern warfare. It was this belief that also contributed to the unpreparedness of Hawaii and the Philippines.

The underrating of Japanese strength and morale also dominated the last phase of American peacetime relations with Japan. Like the naval program, the Roosevelt Administration's economic program was based on the assumption that threat and pressure would achieve American ends in dealing with Japan.

The first call for the use of economic pressure against Japan followed the issuance of the Stimson doctrine in 1932. Proponents of sanctions advocated striking two blows at the Japanese, one by an embargo on arms and munitions and the other by a boycott on Japanese goods sold in the United States. The latter appealed particularly to the American manufacturing groups who were facing the competition of inexpensive Japanese merchandise which, in the depression years, seemed to be selling widely on the American market. Neither program was successful, however, because of the unwillingness of Congress and of the public to interfere in the Asiatic conflict in the early 1930s.

When Japan struck at China again in 1937, the movement for economic measures was revived with great strength. Former Secretary of State Henry Stimson, now a private citizen, took the lead with a letter to the *New York Times* in October, 1937. Stimson called upon the United States to end the sale of arms to Japan and claimed that in this manner the conflict could be brought to a halt. In contrast to the views later expressed in his memoirs, he argued that aid could be given to China "without serious danger to us." There was no thought of sending troops to participate in the Sino-Japanese conflict, Stimson said. With a rare bit of foresight he wrote that to attempt to send American troops "would do much more harm than good." After repeating the various assumptions about American interests in China (these were also the Roosevelt Administration assumptions), Stimson closed by expressing the hope that the President's "quarantine speech" at Chicago meant that America would carry through with its "responsibilities" in the Far Eastern crisis.

Stimson's call for action found enthusiastic support from various groups. Self-interest combined in some instances with a desire to aid China. Labor, for example, was glad to campaign against cheap foreign manufactures which undersold American products. Both the CIO and the AFL, in their 1937 conventions, passed resolutions favoring a boycott of Japanese-made goods. Business interests in competition with Japan also gave some support to Stimson's call for action. But when the *Nation* promoted a consumer's boycott on all purchases of silk stockings, American hosiery manufacturers who depended on Japanese silk imports denounced the boycott as a blow to American industry.

Arguments in behalf of an arms embargo and a consumer's boycott were also furnished by books like *Japan's Feet of Clay*. The author of this volume pleaded for the United States and Britain to call Japan's bluff and to cut off all trade with this imperialist nation. Japan was to collapse within a few weeks, her feet of clay crumbling under the strain of economic hardship, thus bringing the war in China to an end. Like other pleas for economic sanctions, this book claimed that such action would lead to peace. Any possibility of a conflict was denied, for the author believed that the Japanese were really mediocre fighting men whose characters were unfit for the strains of modern war.

These specious pleas were used by administration spokesmen in Congress in behalf of legislation which would give the President the power to curtail or suspend American economic relations with Japan. But congressmen were hesitant to act, reflecting on the uncertainty of public opinion. Despite the preference of the majority of Americans for a Chinese victory, a public-opinion poll in October, 1937, found that fewer than 40 percent of those questoned felt strongly enough about the Asiatic conflict to stop their purchases of Japanese goods.

The application of the so-called moral embargo by the Department of State in 1938 was the first official achievement of the supporters of economic sanctions. The decision, in 1939, to terminate the 1911 commercial treaty with Japan was an even greater victory. Within the Roosevelt Cabinet the movement for embargoes grew in strength. Secretary Morgenthau was the strongest advocate of ending American trade with Japan, and he gained a strong supporter in Henry Stimson when the latter entered the Cabinet in the summer of 1940. Six months earlier, Stimson had written another letter to the *New York Times,* again appealing for an end to the sale of war materials as the first step to a firmer policy. He assured his fellow Americans that Japan did not want war with the United States and that an embargo was the road to peace.

This simple program for winning a bloodless victory over Japan, with its "having one's cake and eating it" solution, began to win wider public support. Public-opinion polls were able to produce larger and larger percentages in favor of embargoes on trade with Japan. The administration kept pace with this movement of opinion and, by its licensing program, made successive inroads on the sale of strategic materials to Japan. By the end of 1940 the only item vital to Japan's effort being shipped by the United States was oil. The sanctionist groups therefore concentrated their efforts in 1941 on ending the trade in oil and in nonessential commodities.

In mid-June of 1941 oil supplies grew so short on the east coast of the United States that all shipments from east-coast ports were prohibited. Although the reason for this action was a genuine domestic problem, restricting purchases to West Coast ports produced a major cut in Japan's oil shipments.

The navy, and Admiral Stark in particular, argued strongly against cutting off Japanese oil purchases. Little hope was placed by the navy in this method of forcing a reversal in Japanese policy. The shortage of domestic oil supplies was expected to force Japan into war for the Dutch East Indies oil and into war with the United States as well. The navy, heavily burdened by its operations in the Atlantic in the convoying of arms to Britain, did not consider itself ready for war in the Pacific. Secretary Hull was also for months reluctant to give approval of the State Department to this drastic move.

Secretary Morgenthau, warmly supported by Stimson, continued his fight against the moderates in the Roosevelt Cabinet and called for the ending of Japanese trade by the freezing of Japanese assets. Outside the government he found many strong supporters. "Squeeze Japan Now!" was the title of one typical exhortation by a Far Eastern specialist. In a masterful oversimplification this writer promised that "terrorization of Japan by levying of penalties in advance as a token of what may come" was the only way to keep the European war from spreading to Asia.

President Roosevelt was finally moved to carry out the Morgenthau-Stimson program. On July 26, 1941, following the movement of Japanese troops into Indochina, he issued an order freezing Japanese assets and cutting off all Japanese trade. Britain and the Netherlands followed suit. Pressing the point home, American oil was then sent to the Soviet Union via Vladivostok by American tankers which passed not far from the shores of oil-hungry Japan.

Japan now had no alternative but to bow to American demands or fight for the resources by which her economic and military strength was to be maintained. Short of a miraculous revolution, overthrowing army leadership, no change of course could be expected from the Japanese government. The war with Japan, which Admiral Ingersoll said the navy had confidently expected for the last twenty years, was now at hand. The only question which remained to be answered was where and at what hour the attack would come. Pearl Harbor, the Philippines, and Guam were obvious Japanese objectives. But the vigor which had been applied to pressuring Japan in the previous months was not now applied in preparing to meet the results of that policy.

The Far Eastern policy of the Roosevelt Administration was born of an exaggerated conception of American political and economic interest in China. It was based on dream stuff rather than on the facts of Far Eastern history and statistics of American trade. It was based on the oft-disproved assumption that one major power can intimidate another by rapidly increasing its striking power without an arms race as the chief result. Yet this was the assumption stated most bluntly by Norman H. Davis, perennial American delegate to the naval disarmament conferences and one of Franklin Roosevelt's closest advisers in the realm of foreign affairs. In a memorandum which he prepared for the President in July, 1937, after the outbreak of war in China, Davis advocated the construction of two or three additional battleships "for the sake of peace and ultimate disarmament. I do not hold to the theory that the best way to preserve peace is to prepare for war, but I am convinced that the bigger our navy is the more influence we could bring to bear for disarmament." By these means American intervention in the Sino-Japanese conflict was to restore the pre-1937 or even the pre-1931 status quo of the Far East. When war appeared finally as an almost inescapable certainty, there was still faith in the validity of American policy since out of war were to come order and progress for China and more abundant economic opportunities for the United States.

These assumptions dominated the thinking of President Roosevelt and key figures in his Cabinet. When challenged by political opponents and others who were concerned with the maintenance of peace in the Pacific, the assumptions were dogmatically reaffirmed. On the basis of materials now available, there is no evidence that these assumptions were seriously reexamined at any time from 1933 down to Pearl Harbor. The warnings of Ambassador Grew and other students of the Far East, who managed to free themselves from the official frame of reference and the prevalent stereotypes, went unheeded. In 1935, for example, a former chief of the State Department's Division of Far Eastern Affairs warned his superiors that the defeat of Japan "would merely create a new set of stresses, and substitute for Japan the U.S.S.R.—as the successor of Imperial Russia—as a contestant (and at least an equally unscrupulous and dangerous one) for the mastery of the East. Nobody except perhaps Russia would gain from our victory in such a war. . . ."

This profound prophecy was ignored. The President and his policy-makers went ahead with a program of resistance to Japan which was logical and consistent, if their assumptions were accepted, but could only end in war.

Any study of the wisdom of American Far Eastern policy must note the unpleasant facts of its results. The end of all foreign policies is the protection and advancement of national interests. If American policy was sound, the results should testify to that soundness. But its results have only been negative. Into the vacuum created by the destruction of Japanese power moved the power of the Soviet Union. In place of Japan, the Soviet Union became the dominant force in the Far East and a China under Soviet influence has yielded far less for American interests than did China under Japan. A war with the "Open Door" as one of its objectives ended with the door closed more tightly than ever. Not only were American interests in China destroyed but in the war the more valuable trade with Japan was eliminated and Japan turned into a subject nation, dependent far into the foreseeable future on an American subsidy for its economic existence. Lastly, instead of bringing peace and order to Asia, World War II let loose in that vast area—as World War I did in Europe—all the passions of long-suppressed nationalism to create tumult and strife for decades to come.

"Wars begin in the minds of men," the framers of the UNESCO constitution concluded. So America's war with Japan began as much in the minds of Stimson, Roosevelt, and other architects of American policy, in the decade before Pearl Harbor, as in the minds of the leaders of Japan. It is unfair to ask that American leaders be endowed with superhuman powers of prediction and the ability to foresee all the results of their acts. But it is the responsibilty of statesmen and diplomats to avoid war and war-making policies unless there is a high degree of probability that unquestionably vital national interests can only be protected by war. A war policy must then be justified by the sanest of estimates of the outcome, evaluating the experience of the past and weighing the costs in blood and sweat against the benefits to present and future generations. By the standards of results—mankind's score sheet—the policies of Roosevelt and Stimson failed in their estimates of national interest and of the methods of achieving that interest. Their policy, paid for in American lives and resources, netted nought but ruin for Japan and assisted in the birth of an Asia more determined than ever to eject the Western interloper.

Akira Iriye

ONE WORLD WAR—THE REQUIREMENTS OF GLOBAL SECURITY

Akira Iriye, associate professor of history at the University of Rochester, views Japanese-American relations from the broad perspective of the world-wide collapse of a system of power politics based on the diplomacy of imperialism. In two books, After Imperialism: The Search for a New Order in the Far East, 1921–1931 *(1965) and* Across the Pacific: An Inner History of American–East Asian Relations *(1967), Iriye sees the crisis in East Asia as essentially a conflict between the status quo oriented policies of the satiated Western powers, and the old-style, acquisitive imperialism of Japan. Once this theoretical conflict degenerated into a military confrontation, the Western powers had little choice but to accept the challenge.*

The American-Japanese war was brought about by Japan's decision to extend its control over Southeast Asia and by America's determination to prevent it. Beginning in 1938, the Japanese military pushed their China campaign southward to offshore islands and eventually to French Indochina. Their undisguised aim was to achieve the control of the Dutch East Indies as well as Singapore. The inclusion of all these regions would enable Japan to form a gigantic Asian bloc, presumably an impregnable fortress and a source of most raw materials that were needed for national defense. It was such moves that ran counter to the American policy of defending the status quo in Southeast Asia. The survival of the British, Dutch, and French colonies in Asia necessitated America's involvement in that part of the world and led directly to war with Japan. It is obvious that Southeast Asia became a crucial factor in American-Japanese relations because of developments in Europe after 1938. Japanese penetration, actual and premeditated, of Southeast Asia was prompted by the German victories and expectation of further victories in Europe, while America's opposition to Japanese "southern advance" was designed to prevent the collapse of the British Empire, which was, Americans thought, essential to the survival of England itself. A Japanese victory over China would release resources for southern expansion, whereas a prolonged Sino-Japanese war would tie the Japanese military down on the continent of Asia and prevent them from penetrating the colonial empires to the south.

Thus, ultimately as a result of the European war, the Sino-Japanese war developed into a Pacific war via Southeast Asia. The United States became involved in the East Asian conflict because the survival of Britain in Europe and in Asia was considered vital to America's own security. Seen from such a perspective, it is clear that no single road led to Pearl Harbor. Without the German-British war there might have not been a Japanese-American war, and without the collapse of France in Europe there might not have developed a Southeast Asian crisis. The Sino-Japanese war did not automatically result in war between the United States and Japan. There had, after all, been no war between the latter before 1941, and no grave crisis before 1938. From new situations in Europe and in Southeast Asia grew distinct possibilities of armed conflict in the Pacific.

But if those were realities of prewar American–East Asian relations, what was perceived was very different. There still exists the myth, shared by many scholars in the three countries, that the United States and Japan went to war over China, and that, whether for moral, economic, or other motives, the United States was determined to prevent Japanese domination of China. Such a view of the recent past is convenient on many counts. For Americans it gives a psychologically satisfactory explanation for the origin of the Pacific war: America had gone to the rescue of the beleaguered Chinese. It is just a step from that to the corollary that the Chinese have betrayed American generosity, that they have bitten the hands that fed them. For the Chinese, also from the postwar perspective, the Pacific war appears as the beginning of America's unmistakable intervention in Asia, leading up to the postwar policy of interference in Chinese domestic politics. Many American, Chinese, and Japanese historians picture Japan as intent on establishing a predominant position in China ever since the Russo-Japanese War, and the United States as countering this intent with the policy of the Open Door. In fact, many still see in the Pacific war a culmination of the American-Japanese conflict in China that emerged after 1905.

Some contemporaries in the United States, China, and Japan, however, clearly saw the key issues in the late 1930s. In America, there is no doubt that, beginning in 1938, the conviction grew that the East Asian crisis was no longer an isolated phenomenon but was part of a developing world crisis. Italy and Germany had revealed their intention of altering the status quo by force even before 1936, but there was a time lag between these developments and the realization in the United States of the seriousness of the crisis. The crucial factor seems to have been the series of diplomatic crisis in Europe in 1938, culminating in the Munich fiasco. It was in this connection that Japanese action in China throughout 1938, conquering Hankow and Canton and enunciating the principle of a new order in East Asia, appeared particularly ominous. In the minds of American policy-makers, a clear link was established between the developments in Europe and in East Asia. There emerged the possibility, as they saw it, that the aggressive nations, in particular Germany and Japan, might band together and collectively menace the status quo and peace in the whole world. It seemed imperative to respond to the challenge if America's security and its concomitant, peace in the world, were to be maintained. Aggression in Asia must be resisted to discourage lawless action in Europe. Moral globalism was given official status by security considerations.

A few examples will illustrate the new language of global security. In July 1939 Secretary of State Hull told the Japanese ambassador,

> *We consider the preservation of peace so supremely important to the future of all nations that we draw the line between honest, law-abiding, peaceful countries and peoples, without reference to their form of Government, on the one hand, and those who are flouting law and order and officially threatening military conquest without limit as to time or extent; . . . we will work in a friendly spirit with every peaceful nation to promote and preserve peace, without serious thought as to who they are.*

In this unusually strong language Secretary Hull, the symbol of caution before 1938, put forth the philosophy of globalism in its simplest form. It is to be noted that he stressed the division of the world into peace-loving countries and aggressors "without serious thought as to who they are." It did not matter whether the aggressor or the victim of aggression was in Europe or in Asia, a democracy or a socialist state. What mattered was the distinction between the party of order and that standing for forceful alteration of the status quo.

From Hull's and his colleagues' point of view, Japan's self-styled new order in East Asia was the epitome of lawlessness. At the end of December 1938, the United States openly rejected the Japanese contention that a new situation had arisen in East Asia, necessitating changes in the principles of international conduct. The United States government did not admit, it declared, "that there is need or warrant for any one Power to take upon itself to prescribe what shall be the terms and conditions of a 'new order' in areas not under its sovereignty and to constitute itself the repository of authority and the agent of destiny in regard thereto." In a similar vein Ambassador Grew made his famous speech at an American-Japan Society meeting in Tokyo in October 1939. He reiterated the belief that international peace was dependent on law and order; this was particularly the case, he said, since nations were economically interdependent. Grew reminded the Japanese that "the present trend in the Far East, if continued, will be destructive of the hopes which [the American people] sincerely cherish of the development of an orderly world." The new order in East Asia ran counter to the American aspiration for "security, stability, and progress not only for themselves but for all other nations in every quarter of the world."

As often happens, military strategists perceived most clearly the trend toward global conflict. Before 1938 American naval and army planning vis-à-vis Japan had been conceived in terms of an "Orange war"—war in the Pacific against Japan. After 1938, however, strategic thinking was centered around a "Rainbow war," that is, war involving the Atlantic as well as the Pacific, Germany and Italy as well as Japan. Various possibilities were considered, depending on the timing of the war, capabilities of the belligerents, and geographical distribution of armed strengths. There was little doubt, after 1939, that the United States would cooperate with Britain to fight against an Axis alliance. Here the question of priority had to be raised; should the United States concentrate its resources first in the Atlantic or in the Pacific? Much depended on specific situations, and of the five Rainbow plans that were drafted in 1939, three envisaged a strategic defensive in the Pacific, while two specified an

offensive. In the end the strategy of defeating the enemy first in
Europe and then in Asia was adopted, but the tradition of global
strategy had been firmly established by the end of the 1930s.

Now that Japan was identified with Germany, the psychological
transition was made to identify China with the democracies in
Europe. As Hull's statement indicates, the United States was to assist the victims of aggression regardless of their form of government.
America would help China resist Japan just as it would encourage
British and French opposition to German militarism. Before 1938 the
United States had not been moved to come to the aid of China in
any substantial degree, and had rationalized its passivity in numerous
ways. Now a sudden turn to positive action was accompanied by the
image of the world divided between two camps. Without the awareness of the global crisis, one suspects, there would not have been
a shift of attitude toward China. One notices, for instance, that American business publications began denouncing Japan and expressing
support of China only after 1940. Some of them, in fact, maintained
an awkward silence on the East Asian situation throughout 1940 and
then began attacking Japan in 1941. It is obvious that the shift was
due to the awareness of the European war and its implications for
East Asia. Opinion polls, too, began to show signs that the American
public was now willing not only to express themselves unequivocally
in sympathy with China but to approve of certain measures short of
war to restrain Japan. The feeling was that the crisis in China was
closely related to America's own security problems, now that Germany and Japan were emerging as the twin threat to the peace of
the world. It is interesting to note, too, that such specialists on American East Asian policy as Paul W. Clyde and A. Whitney Griswold
were subly changing their attitude toward the East Asian question.
Earlier they had expressed the view that America's basic interest in
Asia was economic and that whatever Japan did in China was not
America's business. Griswold's classic *Far Eastern Policy of the
United States,* published in 1938, may be regarded as characteristic
of the era of isolationist writings on the subject. He eloquently pled
for America's noninvolvement in East Asia so long as its essential
economic interests were not injured. For him the whole adventure in
Asian politics, begun in the 1890s, had been misplaced politically
and confused morally. Clyde had written much in a similar vein. By
early 1941, however, they were talking of the relevance of the East

Asian crisis to America's security. In an extremely lucid analysis, Griswold pointed out that the East Asian crisis and the European crisis had been merged and that America's and Britain's security had become menaced. The best safeguard for Anglo-American security seemed to lie in an undeclared peace in East Asia and an undeclared war in Europe. The idea was that the United States should do all it could to assist the British effort at survival, and to this end it seemed best to take a cautious stand toward Japan. Clyde declared that Japan's new order rested upon "a system which, whatever its merits may be, is the antithesis of every ideal represented by a century of American policy in China." Although he had tended to be sympathetic toward Japan's aspirations in China and critical of America's unilateral adherence to the Open Door policy, he now came around to a solid denunciation of Japanese action.

Since they were predisposed to thinking in terms of global security, it was natural that Americans should find Japan's alliance with Germany, consummated in September 1940, final evidence that the two arch-aggressors had combined forces to challenge the democracies and conquer the world. In American thinking a point of no return seemed to have been reached when the Japanese recklessly, as it appeared, entered into a pact for universal aggression. The spectacle of Japan and Germany subjugating the weak nations and dominating the Atlantic and the Pacific was frightening. Should England and the British Empire fall, their rich resources and naval power would have been at the service of Germany and Japan. The United States would be surrounded by a formidable combination of hostile forces. The only safeguard, then, was to prevent the collapse of the British Empire. "The United States is isolated except for one great power and that's the British Commonwealth," Secretary of War Stimson wrote down in his diary, "and I already see signs of a realization of this among the thoughtless." He had long realized the need for cooperation with Britain, but even the "thoughtless" isolationists were slowly coming around to such a view. Perhaps the clearest exposition of the new state of American–East Asian relations was made by Ambassador Grew in his "green light message" of September 1940, a few days before the signing of the Axis alliance. In the telegram Grew, who had tried to understand the Japanese side of the East Asian question for nearly a decade, explicitly castigated Japan's as "one of the predatory powers." He went on,

American interests in the Pacific are definitely threatened by her policy of southward expansion, which is a thrust at the British Empire in the East. Admittedly America's security has depended in a measure upon the British Fleet, which has been in turn and could only have been supported by the British Empire. If the support of the British Empire in this her hour of travail is conceived to be in our interest, and most emphatically do I so conceive it, we must strive by every means to preserve the status quo in the Pacific, at least until the war in Europe has been won or lost.

Here was a clear rationale for new action to deter Japan in Southeast Asia. Stripped to essentials, Grew's message bespoke the fundamental truth, as he saw it, that American and British security were interdependent. That belief became the guiding principle of American policy and strategy, as well as of popular thinking from this time on.

The Japanese, too, perceived that Japan's new order was a threat to British and American security, although few at first were willing to accept the logical connection between the new order in Asia and the possibility of conflict with the United States. Even those who did accept it disagreed as to which stage of Japanese expansion in Southeast Asia would provoke forceful American intervention. This, however, was a question of military strategy, not of policy.

Southern advance was a basic Japanese policy after 1938. Partly this was a military move, an aspect of the new definition of national security. The military had explained their acts in Manchuria and China as an attempt to create an economically self-sufficient and militarily impregnable "defense state." The bloc embracing Japan, Manchukuo, and China was obviously far from being self-sufficient. From this point of view there was a logical necessity to include Southeast Asia, with its rich mineral and vegetable resources, in the Japanese Empire. Such a new order would help reduce Japan's dependence on American supplies of oil, iron, and other materials. Thus from a military standpoint the new order was often conceived of as an alternative to Japanese-American trade. The navy in particular, with its absolute need for fuel oil, came to view a southern advance as an inevitable choice forced upon Japan by America's policy. Since, in naval reasoning, unrestricted trade with America was being endangered by America's policy of opposing Japan in

Asia, the latter would have no choice but to strike southward. By 1940, when southern advance was made a national policy, top naval circles had also come to the conclusion that Japanese action in Southeast Asia would bring about conflict not only with Britain but also with the United States. This was because of the view, held by the navy, that Britain and America could not be separated; once Japan struck at British colonies, the United States would be bound to intervene. The question, therefore, was whether war with these two powers justified the policy of southern advance. By late 1940 section chiefs of the Navy Ministry and the Naval General Staff came to the belief that since war with America was sooner or later inevitable, Japan should take the initiative and advance into southern Indochina and the Dutch East Indies to secure naval bases and strategic raw materials. Circular reasoning here is notable. For naval strategists, the policy of southern advance would make conflict with the United States inevitable; since war was bound to occur, Japan should advance southward to prepare itself for the conflict.

The idea of a new order in Asia, however, was not totally a military notion. More and more civilian officials became believers in "pan-regions," several blocs into which the world was to be divided. Each bloc would be dominated by one or two superpowers, and all blocs would coexist harmoniously among themselves. World peace would be maintained on the basis of a balance of power among them. Japan was obviously to be the overlord of Asia, the term that came to include not only China but Southeast Asia. The "expulsion of Anglo-American influence" from Asia, to use an oft-employed phrase, was clearly a first step toward realizing this end. Already at the end of 1938 the Tokyo government had explicitly enunciated its new policy when Foreign Minister Arita Hachirō stated, in a note to the United States, that Japan was building a new order in East Asia and that the old ideas and principles of diplomacy would no longer serve to establish permanent peace there. At the same time, Japan's policy-makers believed that the pan-Asian order was compatible with peaceful relations between Japan and the United States, once the latter recognized the new order.

How it was felt that Japan could go on building a new order while avoiding open conflict with America, provides a clue to Japanese thinking. According to Matsuoka Yōsuke, who as foreign minister in 1940–1941 was the major ideologue behind Japanese policy, Japanese-American relations would form part of the global system in which Japan predominated in Asia, Germany and Italy in Europe, the Soviet Union would remain neutral, and the United States would keep its hegemony in the Western Hemisphere. As he wrote in January 1941, "The world is to be divided into the great East Asian zone, the European zone (including Africa), the American zone, and the Soviet zone (including India and Iran), though Australia and New Zealand may be left to England, to be treated in a similar manner as Holland." Matusoka seems to have been completely sincere in stating again and again that the Axis alliance and Japan's nonaggression pact with Russia, both part of the bloc policy, were designed to prevent war between Japan and the United States. America's influence in Asia and hostility to Japan were such, he thought, that only by presenting a determined stand would America be deterred from entering the war against Japan. Matsuoka's view of America is revealed in an informal statement he made in September 1940 at a government conference. He remarked that Japan was confronted with a choice between the United States and Germany. To choose understanding and cooperation with the former would entail a settlement of the China war in accordance with America's dictates, abandonment of the new order idea, and submission to Anglo-American influence for at least half a century. Amity with America and Britain would bring material benefits to Japan, he conceded, but the Japanese should remember what happened after the First World War, when Japan was their ally. Moreover, the Chiang Kai-shek regime would be emboldened and openly insult Japan. Thus Matsuoka justified the Axis alliance as essential to the completion of the new order. Japan would force American acquiescence in the new order by its very existence and splendor. From Matsuoka's and his supporters' point of view, the crisis with America had progressed to such an extent that only a bold new stroke of policy would work in maintaining Japanese-American peace. They were so captivated by their own logic that they did not note the primitive circularity of their reasoning. Nevertheless, their perception of America was realistic in that Americans, too, had come to view their relations with Japan in the light of the new order in East Asia.

Outside of the military and the government, there was in Japan a great deal of theorizing about what was called the Great East Asian Co-Prosperity Sphere. It is remarkable that the Japanese, who had developed few ideas of international relations, suddenly poured forth treatise after treatise about the meaning of East Asian conflict. A good example of Japanese thinking after 1938 is an article by Ozaki Hotsumi, a Marxist thinker, entitled "The Idea of the 'East Asian Co-operative System' and the Objective Bases of its Formation," which appeared in the January 1939 issue of *Chūōkōron*. Although he had China specifically in mind rather than the whole of Asia, the author wrote that nationalism was a basis of the new order. The cooperative state system in Asia would be a "regional, racial, cultural, economic, and defensive combination," which would shield itself against the West's imperialistic expansionism. There must be genuine cooperation among the member states, although it would be justifiable for Japan to assert its special status within the combination. The new order seemed economically inevitable, as an increase in productive power in Asia was destroying the equilibrium in the colonial societies. Their liberation and welfare would be promoted by economic cooperation within the East Asian bloc. This was also the best way for Japanese capitalism to survive in competition with Western capitalist nations. At the same time, Ozaki emphasized the need for Japan's internal economic and political transformation so as to enable it truly to play a central and leading role in the new order. Here an avowed Marxist was justifying Japanese policy while advocating internal reform, a response common to a vast number of Japanese liberals and leftists at this time. There was something appealing in the idea of a new Asian order, liberated from Western influence and truly integrated economically and politically. Such an image of Japan's mission was shared by a whole range of Japanese writers, from traditional ultranationalists to Marxist intellectuals. They had come to interpret the history of modern Asia as a story of Western capitalist exploitation. Japan was leading a crusade to free Asia. In the new dispensation the language of harmony would replace that of force, and the principle of co-prosperity would take the place of capitalism, materialism, and individualism. America was the symbol of the West, and the establishment of a new order necessarily meant rejection of America's role in Asia. It goes without saying that much ink was spent rationalizing the alliance with Germany and Italy while theoretically rejecting the West. Somehow these countries were seen as an antithesis of the United States and other democracies and therefore as more "Japanese." Such were the extremes to which the ideology of the new order led Japanese thinking. At any rate, the image of Western exploitation of Asia lay behind Japanese policy toward China, Southeast Asia, and the United States.

*   *   *

American action in the Pacific prior to December 1941 reveals a view of Japan that was a product of wishful thinking. There was the idea that strong determination on the part of the United States would keep Japan in check, that force was the only language the Japanese understood and that concessions would encourage further aggression. Since Japan was pictured as inferior militarily and economically to the United States, it was not expected to risk American retaliation by precipitous action. At the same time, delaying diplomatic action would serve to gain time for the United States and keep Japan from becoming desperate. In other words, the Japanese would behave as Americans would if placed in a similar situation. America's show of determination, backed up by superior economic resources and military potential, would moderate Japan and prevent it from challenging the United States. There is no question that here was an element of self-complacency. American military leaders as well as American policy-makers wanted to believe that the measures they were taking would suffice to hold Japan in check. Some, notably Ambassador Grew, tried to warn that the Japanese could be extremely erratic and irrational, that out of desperation they might resort to extreme measures. President Roosevelt and his senior advisers, however, held to the view that war could be avoided or at least postponed through military preparedness coupled with diplomatic talks.

It was such a view of Japan that was put to a severe test as months went by in the year 1941. As seen already, some in Japan, particularly naval officers, had come to believe in the inevitability of war with the United States. The point of no return had been reached in Japanese-American relations, they argued; therefore Japan should worry only about how to wage war against the United States most effectively. Advocated most forcefully by the navy's section chiefs, such a view came to be accepted by their superiors as well as by army strategists. After the spring of 1941 both the armed services were in virtual agreement on the inevitable logic of coming events; Japan would strike southward, the United States would retaliate by imposing a total embargo on exports to Japan, and Japan would finally decide on war with America. The Japanese military became so captivated by their own logic, which, it must be admitted, was not far wrong, that it became more and more difficult for them to transcend it and think of alternatives. The only logical alternative they could accept would have been restoration of normal trade with the United States, which would ensure the navy of continued oil supply and render unnecessary the forceful seizure of Southeast Asia. It was this alternative that the civilian government in Tokyo sought to pursue in the peace talks in Washington. Put simply, Japan's leaders embraced a clear formula of choosing between American oil and Southeast Asian oil. Believing that the United States would welcome a deal, they carried on their last-minute nego-tiations with Secretary of State Hull and sought to hold a leaders' conference in Honolulu. The burden of the Japanese offer was that Japan would give up its southern advance if the United States would consent to the resumption of trade. The Japanese, too, were guided by military considerations. Even the navy advocates of war admitted that it was doubtful if Japan could win an American war; war, however, was considered preferable to the continuation of the stalemate, with the stock of oil running out. If war had to be faced, the decision must be made quickly. It would be impossible to wait past the end of November, 1941.

The Japanese attitude throughout 1941, like the American, re-veals an image of its potential antagonist. That the Japanese pre-pared for war against the United States as they advanced southward indicated that they could not separate America from Britain and the Dutch East Indies. The United States, they realized, was to enter the scene as soon as Japan attacked British and Dutch possessions in Southeast Asia. At the same time, they recognized that America desired peace in the Pacific in order to concentrate on the Atlantic. Furthermore, in the Japanese view, the United States would be ready to buy peace with oil and iron; it would be willing to resume trade if Japan refrained from attacking Southeast Asia. Such a view of America persuaded the Japanese government that it was worthwhile pursuing a modus vivendi with Washington. The idea that the United States really did not want war with Japan encouraged some opti-mism. Thus the Japanese tended to read into America's policy state-ments what they wanted to find there, as revealed for instance when

Ambassador Nomura Kichisaburō misrepresented Hull's remarks to Tokyo. Though the secretary's tone was always uncompromising if not belligerent, the ambassador desperately sought in it some indication of a conciliatory spirit. The conviction that United States in the end would compromise explains why the Japanese regarded Hull's November 26 note as an ultimatum and decided on war.

The "Hull note" visualized the return to the status quo, not of 1940, 1939, or even of 1937, but virtually of 1931, by demanding that Japanese troops be withdrawn from Indochina and China in return for resumption of trade with the United States. The presentation of the note signaled the end not only of negotiations in Washington but also of the fiction of peace between the two countries. This was well recognized by leaders in Tokyo as well as in Washington. What is crucial, however, is the intrusion of the China question at the very last moment. American and Japanese military planning, as well as Japan's civilian diplomacy, had visualized the alternative of war or peace in terms of Southeast Asia, not of China. The Japanese had hoped for a compromise on the issue of oil, and the American military had sought to prevent Japan's southern advance. In the fall of 1941, as the sense of crisis heightened on both sides of the Pacific, serious thought was given to averting war on the basis of the resumption of limited trade in return for Japan's abstention from a southern thrust. In Washington the military planners felt such a bargain was worthwhile, in order to gain time and wait for the outcome of the European conflict. It was considered imperative to prevent Japan's advance into Malaya and elsewhere and this could be done, it was felt, only by agreeing to the resumption of trade. It was at this point that the question of China assumed decisive proportions. Partially it was a military question. Japan might refrain from advancing into Southeast Asia and even withdraw forces from Indochina, but it would still be predominant in China. There was no assurance that Japanese troops might not again attempt to thrust southward. Moreover, the British were adamant on the question of China. Winston Churchill believed that the collapse of China would menace the British position in Southeast Asia. Thus he would have the United States insist on total evacuation of Japanese troops from Indochina, and he also opposed concessions in China. The United States, committed to joint defense with Britain and the Dutch, had to consider such views.

More fundamentally, however, there was American revulsion at the idea of sacrificing China in order to arrive at a deal with Japan merely to gain time. Here was, as Americans saw it, a moral question. It seemed morally wrong to compromise with Japan without considering China's destiny. Harry Dexter White, assistant secretary of the Treasury, was expressing a commonly held opinion when he wrote, in August 1941, "To sell China to her enemies . . . will not only weaken our national policy in Europe as well as in the Far East, but will dim the bright luster of America's world leadership in the great democratic fight against Fascism." The dualism in American thinking, dividing the world into fascist aggressors and peace-loving peoples, dictated the conclusion that the destinies of America and China were bound closely together, as two free, democratic nations fighting against totalitarianism. When the State Department considered accepting a temporary modus vivendi with Japan in November, Treasury Secretary Henry Morgenthau wrote a note, drafted by White, opposing such moves. "No matter what explanation is offered the public of a 'truce' with Japan," the note asserted, "the American people, the Chinese people, and the oppressed peoples of Europe, as well as those forces in Britain and Russia who are with us in this fight, will regard it as a confession of American weakness and vacillation." From Chungking, Owen Lattimore, adviser to Chiang Kai-shek, telegraphed, "A relaxation of American pressure while Japan has its forces in China would dismay the Chinese. Any modus vivendi now arrived at with [Japan] would be disastrous to Chinese belief in America and analogous to the closing of the Burma Road, which permanently destroyed British prestige."

Similar statements can be multiplied. Here was normal concern with the destiny of China, or rather with an image of Chinese-American relations. America was pictured as having built up good will in China; Free China, a phrase that began to be used in official documents, looked to the United States for support and cooperation. Any compromise with Japan would do irreparable damage to the state of Sino-American relations. It was simply unthinkable to betray the Chinese trust in America. In the light of what we now know about Chinese Communist thinking at the time, the American image of China appears hollow, a product of the liberal American imagination. There is no question that America's view of China was part of its global picture, a picture in which the democracies of the world were seen as fighting against dictatorships.

Robert A. Divine

ONE WORLD WAR—JAPANESE AGGRESSION

The traditional view of Roosevelt's diplomacy has a persuasive and pro-lific proponent in Robert A. Divine, professor of history at the University of Texas in Austin. He has written about every phase of American Foreign policy between 1933 and 1945, including The Illusion of Neutrality *(1962),* Second Chance: The Triumph of Internationalism in America *during* World War II *(1967),* Roosevelt and World War II *(1969), and numerous articles. He edited* Causes and Consequences of World War II *(1969) and surveyed American prewar diplomacy in* The Reluctant Belligerent: American Entry into World War II *(1965), from which the following selection is chosen. Divine sees Roosevelt as initially an isolationist whose movement toward intervention and internationalism came about largely because of German and Japanese actions. Though he criticizes certain aspects of American policy toward Japan, Divine writes largely in the tradition of Herbert Feis, William Langer, and S. Everett Gleason, all of whom emphasized Japan's aggressiveness and refusal to compromise. To all these writers the crisis in Asia is integrally connected to the one in Europe; not only because their coincidence in time strained Allied resources and in particular threatened British survival, but more importantly because there was an ideological unity between the facism of Europe and the militarism of Japan. In short, it was all one war.*

Just before midnight on July 7, 1937, a volley of shots rang out between Chinese and Japanese troops stationed near the Marco Polo Bridge on the main railroad line connecting Peking and Central China. Thus the Pacific phase of World War II began only ten weeks after the passage of permanent neutrality legislation. Although a truce was arranged two days later, it lasted but a few hours. The fighting again stopped on July 11, but when Japan used this respite to rush reinforcements into China, any hope of heading off a major clash disappeared. By the end of the month heavy fighting was under way, which quickly led to the defeat of the Chinese forces and Japa-nese occupation of Peking. When the fighting spread to Shanghai in mid-August, the China Incident, as the Japanese referred to it, had become a full-scale war.

The Sino-Japanese war was the logical result of Japan's determination to dominate Asia. The seizure of Manchuria had marked the beginning, not the climax, of Japanese expansion in the Far East. Confronted with a population growing at the rate of 1 million a year and a basic scarcity of raw materials for an industrial economy, Japanese leaders were bent on exploiting the wealth of China. Civilian statesmen in Japan had planned traditional methods of trade and diplomacy to achieve this end, but in the 1930s the army leaders began to destroy the party system and take over the government. The militarists, fearful of both the expanding power of the Soviet Union in Siberia and the weak but ambitious Chinese government at Nanking under Chiang Kai-shek, were determined to dominate as much of China as possible. In 1935 and 1936 Japanese army leaders were undermining Chinese sovereignty in the five northern provinces bordering on Manchuria. They met with stubborn resistance from the Chinese Nationalists, who decided to challenge the Japanese to an all-out conflict rather than surrender their territory piecemeal.

The outbreak of war in the Far East came as a surprise to most Americans. Many observers had expressed concern in December, 1934, when the Japanese had announced their intention of withdrawing from the Five Power Treaty signed at the Washington Conference in 1922 to limit battleships and aircraft carriers. A year later at the London Naval Conference the United States and Great Britain rejected Japanese demands for naval equality. The Japanese responded by walking out of the conference and announcing a program of large-scale naval construction. Rebuffed by the western democracies, Japan aligned herself with Germany in November, 1936, by signing an Anti-Comintern Pact. Although the open clauses of this treaty merely provided for cooperation between the two nations in resisting Communist propaganda and subversion, there were secret sections that virtually amounted to a defensive alliance against the Soviet Union.

Yet despite these signs of Japan's increasing restiveness, the United States was completely caught off-guard by the war in China. The initial response of the American government was very mild. Rejecting Chinese pleas for American mediation and British overtures for joint protests to Tokyo, Hull released a statement of moral principles on July 16, 1937, to which he asked other nations, including Japan, to subscribe. His answer came two weeks later when the Japanese army launched its offensive in North China. When the Japanese assault shifted to Shanghai, the major port of China and a center of American commercial interests, Hull announced that the government was dispatching 1200 marines to guard American lives and property in China. Clearly, while the United States would attempt to defend the interests of its citizens, it did not intend to uphold the Nine Power Treaty of 1922, to which Japan was a signatory, preserving the territorial integrity and political independence of China.

The immediate problem confronting the Roosevelt Administration was whether or not to invoke the Neutrality Act in the Far Eastern war. Since no formal declaration of war had been issued by either side, the President could exercise discretion in regard to imposing the arms, travel, and loan bans, as well as the cash-and-carry provisions for general trade. The Neutrality Act would favor Japan, who produced her own munitions and who could put her control of the sea to maximum advantage if trade were placed on a cash-and-carry basis. China, on the other hand, needed to import arms from abroad and lacked both the ready cash and the ships to buy supplies on a come-and-get-it basis. After a long conference with his aides, Roosevelt announced at a press conference on August 7, 1937, that he was keeping the question of invoking the Neutrality Act on a "24-hour basis." Despite a great outcry from isolationists in Congress, Roosevelt continued to withhold the Neutrality Act. On September 14, after the Japanese announcement of an extensive blockade of the Chinese coastline, the President did halt trade with China in government-owned ships and warned American exporters that they engaged in commerce with China at their own risk. This order had little effect on American shipping, which was largely privately owned, and the American people, sympathetic to China, generally approved of Roosevelt's refusal to invoke the Neutrality Act for the Far Eastern war.

In mid-September China appealed to the League of Nations. On October 6 the League Assembly found that Japan had violated the Nine Power Treaty and the Kellogg-Briand Pact and recommended that the signatories of the Nine Power Treaty call a conference to consider this violation. The Chinese were greatly encouraged, for only the day before President Roosevelt had delivered his Quarantine address in which he condemned "the epidemic of world lawlessness" then raging and called for "positive endeavors to preserve peace."

When Hull announced that the United States concurred in the League judgment of Japan and would attend a conference at Brussels of all nations with interests in East Asia, it seemed as if American policy was undergoing a major reversal.

President Roosevelt dispelled any such thoughts in his Columbus Day address on October 12; the sole purpose of American policy at the Brussels conference would be to cooperate with China and Japan to seek an end to the fighting. The conference convened on November 3, and it quickly proved a fiasco. Neither Britain nor the United States was willing to take the lead against the Japanese, who refused even to attend the session. Only the Soviet Union recommended strong action, but Russian sincerity was never put to the test. When the conference adjourned on November 24, it had failed to take a single concrete step to aid China or restrain Japan. Indeed, the conference had probably thwarted the one real opportunity to end the fighting. In October, the Japanese leaders had made a set of moderate proposals to Chiang Kai-shek to halt the conflict. Chiang, believing that the United States and England were behind him, turned down the offers to await the outcome at Brussels. During the conference the military situation in China changed drastically— Japanese forces completed the conquest of Shanghai and routed the Chinese armies before Nanking. By early December Chiang was ready to negotiate with Japan, but the Japanese leaders now increased their demands until the Chinese preferred a losing war to submission.

The collective appeasement of the Brussels conference marked another step in the American retreat from the Open Door policy. The United States had deep economic, religious, and emotional faith in the future of China, but when confronted with Japanese aggression, the American people preferred to withdraw from the Far East rather than risk war. When Japanese naval aviators bombed the American gunboat *Panay* on the Yangtze in December, there was a brief flurry of public indignation, but most people were relieved when Japan quickly apologized and paid an indemnity for this unprovoked attack. In 1938, following Japanese bombings of Chinese civilians, Secretary Hull inaugurated an unofficial but quite effective embargo on the export of aircraft to Japan. Americans, however, continued to supply Japan with very large quantities of petroleum and scrap iron which were essential to the Japanese war effort in China. Thus the

United States tacitly assented to the Japanese sweep into China and gave Japan the dangerously misleading idea that the American government and people would acquiesce in future Japanese aggression in the Far East.

*   *   *

In 1939 American public opinion became increasingly hostile to Japan. The American Committee for Non-Participation in Japanese Aggression, headed by Henry L. Stimson, mounted a very effective campaign against the export of oil and scrap iron to Japan; a poll taken in the summer indicated that 82 percent of those surveyed favored the prohibition of the sale of war supplies to the Japanese. The idea caught on in Congress, and in June and July of 1939 a series of resolutions were introduced to restrict trade with Japan. Secretary of State Cordell Hull, fearful that embargoes would lead to war, opposed these resolutions. To offset this movement he finally decided to accept an idea advanced by Senator Arthur H. Vandenberg, Republican isolationist from Michigan, to give Japan the required six months notice that the United States was terminating the commercial treaty of 1911 between the two countries. When the six months were up, the United States would be legally free to institute restrictions on commerce with Japan. Hull hoped that this maneuver would quiet the public discontent without leading to a showdown.

The outbreak of war in Europe resolved Hull's dilemma. The hostilities across the Atlantic captured the attention of the American people and thus eased the pressure for embargoes in the Far East. Japan also became preoccupied with the European conflict and its implications. Japanese leaders, who had been angling for an alliance with Germany against Russia, were stunned by the Nazi-Soviet Pact; and in the months of confusion and indecision that followed, they were not prepared to challenge American abrogation of the commercial treaty of 1911.

Throughout the fall of 1939, the State Department wrestled with the problem of American Far Eastern policy. Ambassador Joseph Grew, who had been in Japan since 1932, was in Washington on a furlough, and he pressed repeatedly for a policy of accommodation, urging that the United States ease its opposition to Japan's ambitions in the Far East and negotiate a new commercial treaty as part of an overall settlement with Japan. Hull, outraged by the aggression in

China and fully aware of public antagonism to Japan, rejected Grew's advice. Unwilling either to appease or challenge Japan, Hull finally persuaded Roosevelt that the United States should continue a modest policy, upholding American rights in China without risking war with Japan.

On January 26, 1940, when the commercial treaty of 1911 expired, the State Department informed Japan that trade would continue on a day-to-day basis. Henry Stimson protested vigorously in a letter to the *New York Times,* and his committee renewed its efforts to curb trade with Japan. But the administration held firmly to its new policy. Hull was not ready to force a crisis with Japan, but he hoped that the ever-present threat of trade embargoes would serve as a brake on Japanese expansion. "I was careful to give them no enlightenment," he later wrote. "I felt that our best tactic was to keep them guessing. . . ."

The cautious policy of the United States toward both Japan and the Soviet Union in the early months of the European war indicated the Roosevelt Administration's belief that Germany posed the major threat to American security. Despite the public indignation expressed over the plight of Finland and China, Roosevelt and Hull refused to take action that might restrict their freedom to move against Hitler in the future. The American people were not ready to go beyond the mild cash-and-carry aid to Britain and France, but their leaders were already looking forward to more active measures in Europe. Passive acceptance of the "dreadful rape of Finland," as the President termed it privately, and a diplomatic holding action against Japanese aggression, were the price that Roosevelt was willing to pay to insure that the United States would contribute to the destruction of Nazi Germany.

*   *   *

The sweeping German victories which ended American neutrality toward the European war also had a profound impact on American interests and policies in the Far East. The Japanese, entering into the fourth year of a seemingly endless campaign to conquer China, were astonished by the speed and completeness of the German success in Europe. Japanese militarists quickly perceived that the defeat of the Netherlands, France, and Britain gave them a perfect opportunity to expand southward to Indo-China, Malaya, and the Dutch

East Indies. Southeast Asia, with its vast reservoir of oil, rice, rubber, and tin, now lay exposed. The Japanese army could turn from the stalemate in China to win new glory by achieving the Greater East Asia Co-Prosperity Sphere so long heralded by Japanese propagandists. Only the United States stood between Japan and dominance of all Asia.

*   *   *

The advent of the Konoye cabinet and fear that Japan was embarking on a more aggressive policy brought reconsideration of the embargo issue toward the end of July. Stimson and Morgenthau stressed the importance of petroleum to the Japanese economy, and argued that an oil embargo would force the Japanese to moderate their policies. Hull disagreed, but during his absence from the capital, Morgenthau and Stimson persuaded the President to include all petroleum products and all scrap iron and steel in the list of materials essential for national security and hence barred from export. When Under Secretary of State Sumner Welles learned of this plan, he immediately protested, warning that it would mean war with Japan. The White House announced an embargo on these items on July 25, but the next day, after a heated discussion in the Cabinet, Welles succeeded in limiting the embargo to aviation gasoline, rather than all petroleum products, and only the highest grade of scrap iron and steel. Despite this modification by the State Department, the July 26 order was a major departure in American foreign policy. Since the outbreak of the Manchurian incident in 1931, American officials had often discussed and rejected the idea of economic sanctions against Japan. Now the United States had finally embarked on the policy of economic pressure, and though the beginning was cautious and limited, it was a clear warning that the United States would no longer acquiesce in the creation of Japan's new order in Asia.

. . . On September 23 Henry Morgenthau wrote in his diary, "My own opinion is that the time to put pressure on Japan was before she went into Indo-China and not after and I think it's too late and I think the Japanese and the rest of the dictators are just going to laugh at us." It was too late. On September 27 the Japanese Ambassador to Germany signed a treaty of alliance with Germany and Italy in Berlin. In this Tripartite Pact the three powers agreed to respect each other's spheres of influence in Europe and Asia and undertook "to assist one another with all political, economic and military means when one of the three contracting Parties is attacked by a power at present not involved in the European War or in the Sino-Japanese Conflict." To make it absolutely clear that the alliance was directed against the United States, a further clause specifically exempted the Soviet Union. In effect, Japan had joined with Germany in an effort to frighten the United States by raising the specter of a two-ocean war. The chief architect of the treaty, Japanese Foreign Minister Matsuoka, clearly stated the purpose of the alliance. "Germany wants to prevent American entry into the war," he told an Imperial Conference on September 26, "and Japan wants to avoid a war with the United States."

The scrap iron embargo and the Tripartite Pact, both coming in late September 1940, revealed that Japanese-American relations had reached an impasse. Each nation had adopted a new and bold policy in hope of influencing and restraining the other. The Japanese had thrown in their lot with Germany to compel the United States to withdraw its opposition to Japanese expansion. This policy backfired. News of the Axis alliance stiffened the determination of American leaders to resist Japanese encroachments. What had once seemed to be a local thrust in Asia now had become part of a worldwide danger to American security. The American people also reacted strongly, viewing Japan as the Asiatic branch of a conspiracy by the dictators to control the world. The American embargo policy was equally ineffective. The stoppage of scrap exports inconvenienced the Japanese but failed to cripple their war potential. It confirmed their decision to join with Nazi Germany and made them more sensitive than ever to their continued dependence on the United States for petroleum products. Even if the United States had embargoed oil, as Morgenthau wanted, it is doubtful if Japan would have been restrained. The oil which Japan needed was available in the Dutch East Indies, and the scrap embargo compelled the Japanese to begin laying plans to seize this vital area. An embargo on oil would simply have forced the Japanese to launch their assault on Southeast Asia in 1940, at a time when America was completely unprepared to defend the region.

The policies adopted by the United States and Japan in September 1940 made war between the two nations nearly inevitable. Each antagonist threatened the vital national interests of the other to the

point where compromise was impossible. Japan could not accept any
accommodation which denied her the opportunity to create a new
order in Asia; the United States could not agree to Japanese domination of Asia in cooperation with Nazi Germany at the expense of the
British Empire.

II WARTIME DIPLOMACY, 1941-1945

The Contemporary View

Walter Lippmann
THE CONTINUATION OF SPHERES OF INFLUENCE

Although Americans are often reputed to abhor power politics, one of the nation's most respected commentators on international affairs, Walter Lippmann, advocated a clear balance of power settlement with the Soviet Union even before the war had really been decided. In U.S. War Aims, excerpted below, Lippmann warned that Russia would demand concessions in both Eastern Europe and Asia, and that American leaders should recognize the fact that the vital interests of the United States lay in the Western Hemisphere and Western Europe—a position he has been reiterating for the entire period of the cold war.

Other regional combinations are forming in the world, the most important being that of which the Soviet Union is the nucleus. The relations of the Atlantic Community with this system, which I shall call the Russian Orbit, will decide the outcome of the war both in Europe and in Asia, and the settlement for as much of the future as we can now foresee. The boundaries of the Russian Orbit are not clearly defined. But it certainly extends from Prague to Vladivostok, from Eastern Europe to the shores of Eastern Asia, and its heart is the Soviet Union.

The Russian Orbit

During this century Russia has fought two wars against Germany. These wars have convinced the Russians, and that is what counts in this matter, that the Western nations are unable to enforce peace east of the Rhine and to prevent a German invasion of Eastern Europe and of Russia. Therefore, the Russians are bound to consider the region eastward from Germany as a separate strategic system of security.

From Walter Lippmann, *U.S. War Aims* (Boston: Little, Brown & Company, 1944). Reprinted by permission of the author. Footnotes omitted.

In 1914–1917 all of Central and Eastern Europe and the Balkans was overrun by Germany; Russia was defeated, invaded, and dismembered. Again in 1938, beginning with Austria and Czechoslovakia, Germany proved that the Western powers cannot protect this Eastern region. In 1941, for the second time in twenty-five years, Russia was invaded by Germany. Now no matter how high we rate the help that Britain and America have given Russia, the plain fact is that the expulsion of the German armies from Russian soil, and from Polish, Czechoslovak, Romanian, Finnish, and Bulgarian soil as well, depends preponderantly upon the Red Army and the exertions of the Russian people. It is, therefore, clear that Russia exists in, and depends upon, a region of strategic security separate from the Atlantic powers.

This does not mean that the Atlantic and the Russian regions are not interdependent. They are. It is evident that Russia alone could not have defeated Germany, and certainly not Japan as well. It is equally evident that if the Western nations had not been allied with Russia, they could not hope for a decision against both Germany and Japan. Upon these conditions rests the Western alliance with the Soviet Union. We all have the same enemies and without mutual aid none of us could defeat these enemies.

Our primary war aims are, therefore, the same. The conclusive defeat of Germany and Japan will make Russia invulnerable for as long a time as can be foreseen. The primary Russian war aim must be, in its simplest terms, not to lose the security which victory will have given her. This also is our first war aim. The conclusive defeat of Japan will make the United States and the whole Atlantic Community invulnerably secure in the Pacific; the conclusive defeat of Germany will make Western Europe and the Americas secure.

Quite evidently, the crucial question of how long and how confident can be the peace after this war will be determined by the maintenance of the substance of the alliance between the Russian Orbit and the Atlantic Community. Whether there is to be a third World War in the twentieth century depends upon whether the Russians come to rest within their orbit, the Atlantic States in theirs, and whether they then concert their policies towards Germany and Japan. We shall, therefore, return to the crucial question of our relations with the Soviet Union when we have discussed the settlements with Germany and Japan.

I do not say that such a concert of power with the Russian Orbit is a world order of peace. But I do contend that such a concert must be achieved in order to found a world order. The concert, as we shall see, is absolutely indispensable to any lasting settlement with Germany and with Japan.

It is also necessary if there is to be any prospect of order and good relations with the emergent peoples of Asia and Africa.

The Chinese Orbit

China has two great neighbors. They are Japan and Russia. When we put away the maps of the age of sailing vessels and use a globe for our geography, we realize that to the heart of China the direct routes from the United States by air are over Russian territory, and that even by sea they pass through Russian and Japanese waters. Russia, and also Japan, are between America and China.

The course of this war has indicated how this bears upon China's position in the world. Japan was able to cut China's sea connection with the United States. Yet with little help from us the deep interior of China has long resisted Japanese conquest. If Owen Lattimore, who is a tried and true friend of China, is right in thinking that the center of the China of the future will be not along the coast and the Yangtze River but in the deep western hinterland, that the industrialization of China "will be firmly built in the heart of the country," and that "from there it will expand back to the coast," then when China is freed of the Japanese menace, she will also be strategically independent of us.

When Japan has been defeated, China will necessarily look for her primary peace and security not across the Pacific to us, but backwards, so to speak, across the Eurasian land mass. China and Soviet Russia have an immense land frontier which runs for four thousand miles from the Pacific to the Pamirs in the very heart of Asia. Surely, Lattimore is right when he says that "the things that will happen along that land frontier, far beyond the reach of any American gunboat or battleship, or airplane carrier or air base . . . are of greater significance than anything that will happen in the Pacific Ocean."

Another regional system will form around China. That it will in time encompass not only the Chinese dependencies in the north but also the whole or the greater part of the mainland of Southeast Asia is probable. We cannot know how soon this will take place because we cannot know how soon China, freed of the menace of Japan and of the tutelage of the Western powers, will achieve her internal political unity and her industrial development. When she does achieve them, China will be a great power capable of organizing her own regional security among the smaller states of Indo-China, Burma, Thailand, and Malaya. China and the Soviet Union will have to come to terms along their great Asiatic frontier. The rise of China will also precipitate great questions for the British Commonwealth and Empire, and indeed also for the other Atlantic powers, including the United States. But these questions are not yet clearly posed, and though they can be foreseen dimly, they cannot yet be answered and settled.

Emergent Asia

It is equally evident that the future will bring momentous developments among the peoples of India and in the Moslem societies. We cannot see that future at all clearly. We might wish we could. But in truth we cannot in our own time settle everything for all time. All we can hope to do is to stabilize and organize as much of the world as is ready for it, and thereby make it easier for our children and our grandchildren to deal with their problems.

We must take it as decided that the tutelage of the Western empires in Asia is coming to its predestined end. We cannot doubt that the thousand million people of China, India, and of Islam will achieve an importance and a power they have not hitherto, had in the modern world. But as the Western empires recede and before the newly independent states are well established, the peoples of Asia will almost certainly pass through a long interregnum. It will be a time of troubles. Only by a miracle can effective civil authority be established throughout Eastern and Southern Asia without prolonged and complicated civil and international strife.

The history of the Western world as a whole, and of each nation which has formed within it, teaches us what to expect. Possibly, but not probably, the peoples of Asia may learn so much from our long and hard history that their own will be easier. The Western nations have had to win, earn, and pay for independence, unity, self-government, and position in the world, by labor and hard experience, and with blood.

But of one thing we may be certain. It is that since the tutelage of the Western powers is ending, their influence even in guiding, much less in controlling, the evolution of Asia will become increasingly remote and indirect. Yet they must take what measures they can to prevent the emergence of Asia from disrupting the peace of the world. It will disrupt the peace of the world if the Soviet Union and the Atlantic nations become rivals and potential enemies in respect to China, India, and the Middle East. The emergence of Asia can also disrupt the peace of the world if the members of the Atlantic Community act separately. What France, or Great Britain, or the Netherlands, or Australia does in respect to China, the Middle East, India, Burma, Malaya, and the East Indies can lead to consequences among the great masses of Asia that none of them, acting individually, might finally be able to deal with. Therefore, they cannot afford to adopt policies which will not surely command the support of the nations whose interests may also be involved. This means that colonial policy can no longer be the sole prerogative of the imperial state, and will have to be set by consultation and agreement. . . .

SETTLEMENT WITH JAPAN

If a reader asks why a book on war aims has had so much to say about the Allied world, and nothing as yet about the settlement with our present enemies, my answer is that nothing can in fact be decided about Germany and Japan until we have made up our minds about what we can and should do with the alliance of the United Nations in the postwar period.

I am assuming that no responsible person wishes to dissolve it. Yet it is evident that when the fighting comes to an end the improvised war alliance will have to be transformed if it is to be stabilized. So I have suggested that the next phase in the development of what I have called elsewhere the nuclear alliance of Britain, Russia, China, and the United States, is the formation of regional systems: the Atlantic Community, the Russian Orbit, the Chinese Orbit, and later, in a form which I am unable to foresee, Indian and Moslem Communities. In these transformations the wartime alliance of the big powers would be broadened and, I believe, stabilized.

Unless the alliance is victorious, we can, of course, impose no terms on our present enemies. Nor can we settle with them permanently until we know whether the Atlantic Community will hold together and what will be its relations with the Russian Orbit and with the Chinese. The settlement with the vanquished will depend upon the organization of the victors; the conditions they can impose must be determined by the test of how long they can enforce them. What kind of place can be made for Japan and for Germany and offered to their people is a question that can be answered only if there is a prior agreement on how the postwar world is to be organized.

The Cairo Terms

The Cairo Declaration commits the United States, China, and Great Britain to definite terms which fix new boundaries for Japan. . . .

Taken as a whole these terms mean that Japan is to be expelled from the Asiatic mainland and is to lose her sea power in the Pacific. Japan becomes once more an island nation. She is to be an island nation near a continent where she has no foothold, and in an ocean which others command.

There would be no point in imposing these terms now if we did not incorporate them in a settlement which would last. It must begin as a settlement which Japan cannot undo; it must become a settlement which the Japanese nation will in the end accept.

This is the general aim of any lasting settlement of a war of aggression: to extinguish the war party and to protect the peace party by making the defeat irrevocable and the peace acceptable.

For Japan the defeat is irrevocable if she cannot return to the mainland of Asia from which she is to be expelled, if she cannot recover command of any part of the Pacific Ocean. Within her own islands, having no military control over, but only commercial access to, the resources and manpower of Asia or of the Pacific, Japan cannot restore her military power. Her three nearest great neighbors —the Soviet Union, America supported by Great Britain, and China as she achieves her development—will be indubitably stronger.

Once Japan is ousted from the mainland, she cannot return without the consent of Russia and China. Once she is ousted from the islands of the Pacific, she cannot return to them if the United States is determined to prevent her. . . .

In the end, it seems to me, a disarmed Germany can come safely and properly to rest within the international exchange economy of the Atlantic Community. But Germany can be so placed only with the sincere consent of the Soviet Union. Therefore, there must be no question of Germany's being included in the military system of the Atlantic powers. By making a demilitarized Germany dependent on sea-borne commerce, the best guaranty will be provided that the age-long German expansion to the east, the *Drang nach Osten,* is ended.

To end it conclusively and forever, the strategic security of the Russian Orbit will then have to be reinsured by firm alliances between Russia and the other eastern neighbors of Germany. If the borderland between Germany and Russia is a diplomatic no man's land, the small states within it cannot hope to be independent and secure, and no settlement can be made with Germany that Russia as well as the Western nations will agree on.

The organization of this Eastern regional system is the guaranty Russia is bound to take against a third German invasion in this century, and against any sort of anti-Russian combination by the Western states. It is, moreover, a real guaranty. For it places Russia, which will now surpass Germany as a military power, in a position to prevent the revival of Germany's military power. It is the one sure guaranty that can be given to Russia that no Western country will seek to revive German power for use against Russia. For the Soviet Union will be there to prevent it.

We have to look at these things as the most pessimistic and suspicious Russian might see them if we are to reach conclusions that are solid and sound. Now if Germany is by these means rendered innocuous to Russia, she will also be innocuous to the Atlantic Community. On that foundation of reciprocal security, it will then be clear to Russia why it is her interest as well as ours, and also Germany's, that for a German democracy, neutralized as a military power, a place should be reserved within the Atlantic Community.

There is no other place for a peaceable Germany. For Germany must have a place somewhere. The German people cannot live a self-contained economic life within their frontiers. They will either expand overland in Europe, or they must be allowed to live by trading overseas, by being accepted into the oceanic international exchange economy.

German economic expansion in Europe means German militarism

and pan-German domination; this war is being waged to exterminate both. It will be safer for all of Europe, and also for Russia, if Germany becomes dependent upon maritime commerce. The less self-sufficient Germany is, the better for her neighbors whom she has sought to dominate, and for the Atlantic nations which will emerge from this war with the command of the seas.

This does not mean that the Germans can or should be given a free run in the markets of the world. Not until the period of probation is over, and there have been radical changes in their way of doing business, can German trade pass unregulated. But it does mean that a trade, which the Allies regulate and supervise as to its amount, its origins, its destination, and its terms, should be developed between Germany and parts of the extra-European world. It might well be that for the probation period German nationals should not be permitted to have business agencies abroad because they are known to be the foci of political conspiracy and propaganda. It might even be that Germans should do their international trading only at German ports, and beyond them through Allied agencies. These are, relatively speaking, details. The main point at the moment is that within Germany an important part of the working population should manufacture for non-European markets in payment for imports from overseas.

This conclusion will at first be unpalatable to the Western countries which would have to receive Germany into their trading community; it may well be highly suspect to the Russians on the ground that it extends the political influence of the Western states to the very frontiers of their strategic neighborhood. Yet these first reactions must be weighed against the alternatives.

The permanent isolation of Germany is not a solution of the German problem. The attempt to isolate Germany will surely fail if it is extended beyond the time when her victims, and the Germans who now oppress them, are still in active life. The peoples of the world simply will not spend many long years supervising Germany in a reform school. Eventually Germany must have a recognized place of her own in the scheme of things. The real alternatives are a place in the Atlantic Community or in the Russian Orbit.

But in the Russian Orbit there is no place for Germany which is safe and tolerable for the Eastern states or for the Western. A Germany integrated with Russia would be a dangerous and menacing internal enemy of the Soviet Union. The very essence of pan-Germanism, which is German infiltration and domination to the east, would remain in the form of a subversive movement within the Russian Orbit. Moreover, a Germany facing east would be a crushing weight upon the political and economic life of the border nations from Poland to the Danubian countries and the Balkans. And as the inclusion of Germany within the Russian Orbit would bring it to the shores of the Atlantic, this solution would be intolerable for the Western world.

But as a demilitarized trading nation within the Atlantic Community, Germany would be made as safe as it is possible to make her for Europe and for the world.

Sumner Welles

POLITICAL COOPERATION DURING THE WAR—A LOST OPPORTUNITY

Walter Lippmann was not the only influential American who advocated settling postwar questions before the end of the war. Sumner Welles, assistant secretary of state and a personal adviser and troubleshooter for President Roosevelt, also believed the United States should have negotiated arrangements with the Soviet Union early in the war—but his rationale differed from that of Lippmann. Welles, reflecting traditional American rhetoric, blamed power politics for the outbreak of war and advocated just settlements along the lines of the principles of the Atlantic Charter. Welles himself sounded like an old style power politician however, when he bemoaned Roosevelt's failure to force the Russians to accept such a set of agreements early in the war when America could bargain from a position of strength. In Seven Decisions That Shaped History, *from which the following selection is chosen, Welles wrote in 1951 that a world structured along American ideals could have been established had Roosevelt made political settlements before the Red Army went on the offensive.*

Experience had shown during the Paris Conference of 1919—even though we were dealing primarily with Great Britain, France and Italy, all Western nations—how appallingly difficult it was to overcome the exaggerated forms of selfish nationalism to which a victorious war gives rise. This time we would be dealing with the Soviet Union. The Kremlin's course following the Stalin-Hitler deal in August, 1939, hardly gave ground for confidence in the inherent altruism of the Politburo's foreign policy. There was little reason to think that after the defeat of Germany and Italy a triumphant Russia would be disposed to give the just claims of humanity priority over her own demands for what Stalin would term "security." If the great peace conferences of Vienna in 1815 and of Paris in 1919 had taught any one lesson clearly, it was surely this: that victorious allies invariably quarrel among themselves over the division of the spoils.

In this case, all the "spoils" that the United States wanted for herself was a peace founded on justice and practical common sense so that future wars might be avoided. But we would hardly be likely to attain this single end if we postponed action until the quarrels of the victors had again broken out around the peace table.

Yet the possibility of such action seemed to be precluded at the outset. Early in December, 1941, Anthony Eden, then Britain's foreign secretary, was about to go to Moscow. Though the United States was not yet at war, he had let us know that the future status of the Baltic republics would undoubtedly come up in his talks with Stalin and Molotov. I myself expressed the strong hope in talking with the President and Secretary Hull that we would urge the British government not to make any final agreement that would commit Great Britain to support the permanent obliteration of Lithuania, Latvia, and Estonia. A message in that sense was sent to Mr. Eden through Ambassador Winant in London.

But the message sent by Secretary Hull went much farther indeed than a mere note of caution on this specific issue. The position he took was that, since the Soviet, British, and United States governments had bound themselves to be guided by the Atlantic Charter in all postwar settlements, no specific terms of settlement should be agreed upon before the final peace conference. The secretary of state very properly concluded by also urging that in any event no secret commitments should be made.

At the moment when the message was sent (only two days before Pearl Harbor) the terms in which it was couched seemed innocuous enough. The principles for postwar policy laid down by the Atlantic Charter provided an altogether desirable pattern. Yet they constituted a pattern, and nothing more. They gave no slightest indication, for example, of the justice or injustice of a given settlement covering eastern Poland. The Soviet Union might claim quite plausibly that her retention of eastern Poland would not be territorial aggrandizement of the sort prohibited by the first article of the Atlantic Charter, but, on the contrary, a "territorial change" that fully accorded "with the freely expressed wishes of the peoples concerned," as authorized by the second article. Yet the Polish government-in-exile would inevitably maintain that such a "territorial change" was aggrandizement at its worst, and that the wishes of "the peoples concerned" could not be "freely expressed." Agreement upon the broad principles of the Atlantic Charter would never in itself prevent future bitter controversies over frontiers and zones of influence.

In any event, the message of December 5, 1941, to Anthony Eden created a precedent upon which a policy was soon erected.

When Mr. Eden left for Moscow he took with him instructions from his Cabinet that were similar in intent to the request made by the United States government. In Moscow, however, he was met with an insistent demand that Great Britain without further ado formally commit herself to the recognition of Russia's 1941 frontiers as established by Stalin's 1939 deal with Hitler. . . .

In accordance with his instructions, Mr. Eden limited himself to the promise that the Russian claims would at some future time be considered by the British Commonwealth as well as by the United States. But upon his return to London he was further pressed by Mr. Molotov for a categorical acceptance of the Russian demands. It appeared from Mr. Eden's messages that he was impressed with the need to comply, unless the English-speaking powers were willing to risk an early break with their Soviet ally and a separate peace treaty between the Soviet Union and the Nazi government.

The issue was, of course, clear-cut. It was evident that even at the climax of the furious German assault upon the Soviet armies Stalin wished to be sure that he would retain the fruits of his earlier collusion with Hitler. The Soviet government had just subscribed to the United Nations Declaration and, consequently, to the provisions of the Atlantic Charter. Yet it was now pressing for a commitment that certainly in the case of the Baltic states, would violate the spirit as well as the letter of the charter.

From our standpoint in Washington such an agreement was unthinkable. Our acquiescence in it would have been interpreted in every quarter of the globe as meaning that the Atlantic Charter was, in fact, no more than a hollow sham, a collection of high-sounding phrases designed merely to impress the ingenuous. It would have lost the United States that invaluable measure of moral support which she was given in every country where people were still able to think and speak freely, and which eventually proved to be of such great avail in winning the war.

We found that Mr. Churchill stood four-square with us on this issue. He stated flatly then, during his first visit to Washington as Prime Minister, what he has since frequently reiterated, "The Baltic

States should be sovereign independent peoples." In a message to Mr. Eden of January 8, 1942, he said:[1]

> *The transfer of the peoples of the Baltic States to Soviet Russia against their will would be contrary to all the principles for which we are fighting this war and would dishonor our cause. This also applies to Bessarabia and to Northern Bukhovina and in a lesser degree to Finland, which I gather it is not intended wholly to subjugate and absorb. . . . In any case there can be no question of settling frontiers until the peace conference. I know President Roosevelt holds this view as strongly as I do, and he has several times expressed his pleasure to me at the firm line we took at Moscow. . . . There must be no mistake about the opinion of any British Government of which ·ᵢam the head, namely, that it adheres to those principles of freedom and democracy set forth in the Atlantic Charter, and that these principles must become especially active whenever any question of transferring territory is raised.*

Thus, barely a month after the United States entered the war, the American and British governments reached a firm agreement that no commitments upon postwar political and territorial settlements should be made until the peace conference. For the time being the Soviet government acquiesced. When Molotov visited Washington six months later in June, 1942, he made no demand that the American and British reconsider their refusal to recognize Russia's frontiers prior to June, 1941.

Yet it was, of course, inconceivable that some of our smaller allies who had territorial or political problems should not try during the war to get by direct negotiations a settlement that would be confirmed after the victory. If any demonstration of this had been needed, it was soon afforded, first, by the several visits to Washington of General Sikorski, the Prime Minister of the Polish government-in-exile, and, later, by the visits of President Beneš of Czechoslovakia.

Sikorski I found one of the most stalwart and attractive statesmen of the war years, and I conferred with him at great length during his weeks in Washington. He recognized, of course, as he told me repeatedly, that no final commitments on the future status of Poland or the future extension of Polish territory could be made by any Polish government-in-exile, but must await the freely expressed decision of the Polish people themselves. Nevertheless, he felt he would

---

[1] Winston Churchill, *The Grand Alliance* (Boston: Houghton-Mifflin Co., 1950), p. 629.

be criminally short-sighted not to try during the war to reach an agreement with the Soviet Union and with Czechoslovakia on political and territorial issues, so that the entire problem could be successfully clarified before any peace conference was held.

He foresaw, and correctly I think, no difficulty in finding an agreement with Czechoslovakia, notwithstanding the previous Polish government's dastardly seizure of Czechoslovakian territory when Hitler occupied that country. Whether he was equally justified in speaking so confidently, on the basis of his conversations with Stalin in Moscow in 1941, of his ability to negotiate a fair settlement with the Soviet Union is another matter. I remember he told me that Stalin had, with apparent approval, quoted to him Lenin's remark that the Soviet government must realize that the Poles had reason to hate Russia, and that consequently the Bolshevik Revolution must treat the Poles in a friendly way, and give Polish nationalism full recognition.

In any event, Sikorski succeeded, with British help, in restoring diplomatic relations between his own government-in-exile and Moscow, and arranged for the formation of a Polish Army to fight against Germany on Russian soil. He felt then that he had concrete evidence that he was not unduly optimistic in believing that fair political and territorial adjustments might be negotiated with Stalin.

President Beneš, because of his greater experience in the international arena, was far less sanguine. He recognized, as he told me, that the future independence and security of Czechoslovakia lay solely in her ability to walk the tightrope over the abyss between the East and the West. For that reason he made his wartime visits to Moscow, believing that only through an understanding with Stalin could his country hope to be saved from Russian hegemony in the years to come.

While I have cited only the two cases of Poland and Czechoslovakia, almost all our smaller allies spoke to me of this, that or the other territorial rectification or reparation which they hoped to consolidate by agreement before the end of the war.

As I have said, the question whether the United States was not losing an unparalleled opportunity to ensure the kind of peace that the American people wanted was much in my own mind during the two years after Pearl Harbor. By the spring of 1942 we have already commenced within the State Department our intensive study of the kind of world organization and of the kind of political and territorial settlements that we wanted to see made. But necessarily our decisions represented merely what we Americans believed to be wise, right, and just. We could assume that our views coincided largely with those of the British Commonwealth, of our neighbors of the Western Hemisphere and of the lesser powers of Western Europe. But in the light of our past experience with the Soviet Union, what possible assurance could we have that at the peace conference Moscow would accept even a small percentage of our recommendations? Would it not be wise, as soon as our own views were formed and we learned what the views of our American neighbors and of some of the smaller European countries were, to try to do exactly what Mrs. Roosevelt had suggested three years before, namely, set up officially an international group "continuously to plan for future peace"?

Should we not create a body, similar in composition to what later became the Security Council of the United Nations, and representing all the United Nations, to begin without delay to study the future structure of the world, to iron out as far as possible difficulties among its member nations, and to be prepared at the end of the war to present for the final approval of the peace conference a series of settlements and of postwar policies already agreed upon in principle?

I naturally discussed this possibility with the other members of the Advisory Committee on Post-War Foreign Policy in the Department of State. There the suggestion met with general approval, enthusiastic on the part of some and tepid on the part of others. Yet at the highest level it was summarily turned down.

I think it is wholly accurate to say that, while the President decided to reject the proposal, the intrinsic idea commended itself to him. In judging his decision we must remember the influences that were being brought to bear upon him, and the considerations by which as commander-in-chief he must be guided. Winning the war was and must remain the foremost objective. No step could be taken politically, however beneficial it might promise to be later on, if it jeopardized or threatened to postpone the victory.

The first ten months of 1942 were for us the darkest period of the war. We had to face not only the succession of disasters that had struck us in the Pacific, but the series of calamities—such as the setbacks in Libya, the occupation of Greece, the fall of Crete, and the growing threat to the security of Egypt—that had attended the British war effort since Pearl Harbor. The Russian armies were magnificently resisting the German onslaught, but how long could they hold?

It was altogether natural that the Joint Chiefs of Staff should constantly warn the President that, whatever the theoretical future advantages of trying to settle political and territorial problems during the war, they were offset by the immediate dangers of the controversies with Russia that might be aroused. In any such attempt, we would run headlong, probably immediately, into a renewed demand that we recognize Russia's 1941 frontiers. How could we comply, in view of the position we had already taken? Russia might later demand control of the outlet from the Black Sea to the Mediterranean, a predominant position in Iran, and strategic and territorial concessions in the Far East. Would we not find it impossible to concede these claims without endangering our own security in the postwar world, and without incurring the legitimate resentment of the peoples of Turkey, the Middle East and China?

On the other hand, would not the firm rejection of Russia's claims cause a breakdown in Russian cooperation in the war against Germany or, even worse (and this possibility was uppermost in the minds of the Joint Chiefs of Staff throughout the war), encourage the Kremlin to negotiate a separate peace with Hitler. The Joint Chiefs frequently emphasized the significance of the British Cabinet's belief that a message received from Moscow as early as September 5, 1941, implied that Stalin was already thinking of separate peace terms with Germany. Such arguments as these would at any time have been persuasive. During the dark year of 1942, they proved to be decisive.

There were other considerations as well. The secretary of state was temperamentally disposed to put off dealing with controversial issues as long as possible. He preferred not to cross the proverbial bridge until he came to it. A remedial policy was to him preferable to a preventive policy, even though, as events so often showed, a preventive policy adopted at the psychological moment and carried out with decision and dispatch might later save a world of remedy. If the discussion of such exceedingly thorny problems as the Baltic states or Poland's eastern frontiers could be postponed until a peace conference, that was infinitely better than grasping the nettle firmly now. And this was a moment, it is to be remembered, when as a result of the extreme friction that had arisen between President Roosevelt and Mr. Hull in January, 1942, the President was making every effort to avoid decisions that ran counter to Mr. Hull's recommendations.

Nor must we lose sight of the President's preoccupation with his role as wartime leader of the American people. He was determined to preserve national unity. If it became known that the government was discussing with other nations the future status of Poland, the future status of the Baltic states, and other East European settlements, there was little doubt that large racial minorities in this country, hearing wholly unfounded versions of the government's decisions, would at once be greatly exercised and split into quarreling and antagonistic groups.

Last, but by no means least, was the fact that while the President clearly saw the advantages in going to the peace conference with prior agreements on political and territorial problems, he by no means felt that to postpone discussion of these issues need seriously prejudice our hope of securing a good peace. For he had, and justly, great confidence in his own ability as a negotiator.

It is perhaps only fair to add that Roosevelt was occasionally apt to rely too greatly upon a few favorite panaceas for problems that were actually too basic and far-reaching in their origins and nature to admit of any easy solutions. For example, he had faith in the efficacy of plebiscites for most of Europe's territorial controversies. He was even more wedded to the idea that plebiscites are a universal remedy than Woodrow Wilson had been. It was at about this time that he talked to me for well over an hour one evening about the desirability of using plebiscites to settle once and for all the friction between the Serbs, the Croats and the Slovenes which had so beclouded the history of Yugosalvia as an independent state. He did not apparently attribute much importance to the harm that would be done to the national economies of all three peoples should they decide to become independent entities; nor did he have much in mind the impoverishment and general misery that had spread over most of the Danube basin after the Treaty of Versailles had dissolved the Austro-Hungarian Empire and the economic federation that the empire represented. His strong sense of justice responded instinctively to a freely held plebiscite as a means of preventing the subjugation of national minorities. But he failed fully to take into account the very practical consideration that the further fractionization he proposed would merely increase the economic maladjustments that had been one of the chief causes for Europe's woes during the years between the two World Wars.

He also intended to recommend the plebiscite principle if and when the time came to discuss the future of the Baltic states with Stalin. He said he was certain he could get Stalin to agree to a freely conducted plebiscite, under international auspices, in all three of the republics. As is now well known, the President found out at Yalta how vain this illusion had been. Stalin told him that the subject was one that he refused to discuss, since the Baltic peoples had already voted to join the Soviet Union.

Yet as the months passed, it became plain that while it might be much easier, and in some ways perhaps more expedient, to postpone such problems as these until the peace conference, the morale of certain countries, like China, would be seriously impaired if their government could be given no firm assurances about their future status. It was also becoming more and more apparent that the appetite of a victorious Soviet Union might well become inordinate if no effort to check it was made before the end of the war.

The recognition of these imperious necessities resulted in a number of purely political declarations. A declaration covering the restoration of Austrian independence and the future status of Italy was issued when the foreign ministers of the four major allies met in Moscow in October, 1943, and another covering Korean independence, and the restoration to China of Manchuria, Formosa, and the Pescadores was made when the President met with Chiang Kai-shek and Churchill at Cairo in December of the same year.

Necessity also paved the way for the agreement to establish a European Advisory Commission to consider the treatment to be accorded the European enemy states. Because a number of highly qualified advisers were appointed to the commission, useful documentation on Europe's political and territorial problems was compiled, but the commission itself failed during the year and a half of its existence to negotiate any political agreements of importance whatever.

At Tehran and at Yalta, new and significant political agreements were reached. It was at Tehran that the President first brought up the suggestion that Russia should have access to the Manchurian port of Dairen. It was at Tehran that Stalin temporarily reversed the position he had taken in his conferences with Eden the year before, stating that there was no need for him at that moment to speak of Russia's future territorial interests, but adding, not without grim significance, that "When the time comes we will speak." It was at Yalta that Roosevelt and Churchill conceded Stalin's Far Eastern demands covering the return of southern Sakhalin and the Kurile Islands to Russia, and a position in Manchuria that was tantamount to full control of that ancient province. At Yalta, also, the precise limits of Poland's future territory were taken up, together with the political composition of her future government.

What this brief record shows is that the position so confidently and firmly taken by the British and American governments in January, 1942, was wholly at variance with the course that they later actually pursued. This change of policy on a matter of vital significance was apparently due to no conscious decision by either of them; rather they seemed to have drifted into it without any real apprehension of all its implications.

It must be ruefully admitted also that many of our discussions of postwar territorial and political problems with the Soviet Union were undertaken in a singularly haphazard fashion, and without full consideration or preparation. The United States had two clear-cut alternatives in January, 1942. One was to create the official international planning commission that Mrs. Roosevelt had suggested, in the hope that the major allies would at that crucial moment in the war be able to work out political and territorial solutions that would be found acceptable at the end of the war. The other alternative was to refuse resolutely to discuss any political or territorial question until a peace conference assembled.

Each course has its advantages and its disadvantages. My own judgment now, as it was then, is that the advantages of the former far outweighed its disadvantages. By sticking neither to one course nor the other we fell, as so often happens in such cases, between two stools. The immense influence that we possessed immediately after Pearl Harbor was not exercised. When we did attempt to negotiate political settlements, our influence was no longer decisive.

And it would be hard to deny that our influence before 1943

would probably have been conclusive if we had used it to secure postwar settlements that, while insuring legitimate security to the Russian people, would have seemed just and wise to a majority of the remaining peoples of the world. At that stage the moral influence of this country was incomparably greater than that of either of its major allies. It is true that Mr. Churchill had roused the hearts and souls of the English-speaking world by his resplendent war leadership. But the part his predecessors had played in European affairs during the decades between the two World Wars, his own more recent quarrel with the French, and Britain's role as a colonial power in Asia, Africa, and the Near East, deprived the British government of the measure of popular confidence that the United States then enjoyed in every part of the world.

As for the Soviet government, the suspicion and mistrust aroused by its policy after 1917, and the long war waged by the Kremlin upon organized religion, had lost for the Soviet Union the moral support of a large part of the world outside the Communist Party membership. Her struggle against Hitlerism had regained for her a measure of the popular backing she had forfeited. Nevertheless, it was to the United States and, in particular, to Roosevelt himself, that countless millions in every part of the globe were turning, in the hope that American leadership would win them freedom and security. Even within the Soviet Union there were no few signs that the people were beginning to realize that Roosevelt was not the pawn of Wall Street, nor a "capitalist reactionary," but rather the spokesman for a free and generous nation joined with them in the struggle to defeat the invaders of "Mother Russia."

The political influence of the United States was then at its peak. Our military strength was already far greater, in proportion to the strength of our allies, than it had ever been during the First World War. The success of the North African operation was to most observers convincing evidence of the reserve power that the United States possessed and soon would bring into play. It is true that two years later the ground forces and the air force were to be immeasurably greater in striking power. But by then the Soviet armies had demonstrably defeated the Nazi invaders.

The Historical Debate

Lloyd C. Gardner

FDR AND COOPERATION WITH THE SOVIET UNION—A POLICY OF PROCRASTINATION

Professor Lloyd Gardner of Rutgers University claims that Roosevelt's essential mistake was that he wanted to achieve the goals that Welles thought the President had abandoned; that is, the ideals set forth in the Atlantic Charter. Unfortunately, to Gardner's way of thinking, those goals conflicted with Russian security and interests, both political and economic. Like Lippmann, though for somewhat different philosophical reasons, Gardner believes Roosevelt should have accepted the spheres of influence he seemed initially to accept during the early stages of the war. Gardner, who proceeds from a moderate left-revisionist viewpoint regarding the origins of the cold war, infers that Roosevelt came very close to breaking out of the traditional mold of American foreign policy when he placed cooperation with the Soviets above all other postwar goals, but that break never came as Second Front diplomacy degenerated into sleight-of-hand and procrastination designed merely to keep the Soviets in the war. In the end, Roosevelt could not hold on to the aims of the Atlantic Charter and keep the Soviets friendly because the Atlantic Charter reflected the Open Door style expanding political economy of the United States. Professor Gardner has written widely in the field of American foreign policy, most notably Economic Aspects of New Diplomacy (1964), as co-author of The Origins of the Cold War (1970), and Architects of Illusion: Men and Ideas in American Foreign Policy, 1941–1949 (1970) from which the excerpt below is taken.

" 'Dear Mr. President:' John Sherman said in 1877, 'The only way to resume specie payments is to resume.' Similarly, the only way to get the initiative in this war is to take it." Distrustful of British objections to a large cross-channel invasion of Western Europe in 1942, Secretary of War Stimson urged Roosevelt in this letter to "lean" on those charged with production of "landing gear for the ultimate invasion." He hoped thus to put an end to Churchill's obstructionist claims that such an invasion was logistically impractical for the next twelve months and more. "The rate of construction of a number of landing barges," Stimson counseled, "should not be allowed to lose the crisis of the World War." The "crisis" Stimson wrote about, of course, transcended the war and referred to the shape of the postwar world.

Stimson's letter came at a time when several of the President's advisers were reassessing their decision to postpone territorial and political questions to the end of the war. Cables from London in recent weeks had further revealed England's deep fear that unless Stalin received a countersigned deed from his Allies to much of the Baltic and large parts of Poland he would negotiate a separate peace in the East. The issue before American policy-makers was whether or not it was already necessary to compromise their war aims.

"The Government is widely split," noted a State Department officer, "one group, headed by the State Department, Bill Bullitt, and others, maintaining that if we make a single commitment regarding the peace we have lost the chance of being free agents; that the acid test of our good faith in Russia is whether we deliver the supplies we promise. . . . There is intense bitterness, and meanwhile Stalin in his recent speech tried to hurry matters by throwing out the possibility of a treaty with Germany."

Bullitt had indeed renewed his warning that if Roosevelt should assure an Anglo-Russian victory over Germany without previously obtaining definite written pledges in regard to the political shape of the postwar world, "he would find himself in a far worse situation at the end of the Second World War than that in which Woodrow Wilson found himself at the close of the first." A Russian victory might well mean "one vast dictatorship extending from the Pacific to Western Europe," imperiling American interests now "covered by our Atlantic Doctrine and our Open Door doctrine."

"Bill, I don't dispute your facts," the President had replied (according to Bullitt), "they are accurate. I don't dispute the logic of your reasoning. I just have a hunch that Stalin is not that kind of man. Harry [Hopkins] says he's not and that he doesn't want anything but security for his country, and I think that if I give him everything I possibly can and ask nothing from him in return, *noblesse oblige,* he won't try to annex anything and will work with me for a world of democracy and peace."

Bullitt first made this exchange public in a 1948 *Life* article. By that time he had already joined Roosevelt's critics who were denouncing the late President's foreign policies and looking especially for his footprints on the path to Pearl Harbor. Bullitt was suggesting that the real clue to the mystery was Roosevelt's naiveté. Some of his readers remained convinced that something more sinister had occurred; meanwhile, the President's defenders explained his wartime policies as a strategy of postponement.

Roosevelt's policy toward his Allies during the war *was* indecisive, but the responsibility for the strategy of postponement cannot be placed upon the President's shoulders alone, nor confined to his personal direction of Big Three conferences during the war. His ambiguity had broad consequences for the future, as did his reduction of complex issues to matters of personality where he functioned best. But Bullitt's characterization of presidential actions neglects the setting of the war and the problems of alliance warfare. Indeed, it was Roosevelt's effort to get all that Bullitt and other universalists wanted, albeit by a different means, which left crucial issues unsettled at his death.

As Stimson's letter implied, most American policy-makers believed that logistical strength and productive capacity would be America's principal weapons in the diplomatic end game. The war secretary's own feeling (most of the time) was that the United States should concede parts of Eastern Europe to the Soviets, then strengthen its position in the Far East, where, he felt, Russian-American interests ran along more parallel lines.

Bullitt and Secretary of State Cordell Hull also viewed a second front as a counter to British political aims, but they were more universalist in their approach to the peace. They agreed that America's economic power would not be at its height until the end of the war, but, they argued, that power could never be effective (either abroad or at home) without the opportunity to function in a completely open world—including Eastern Europe. Regionalism, spheres of influence, and bilateral pacts would choke off American potential and plunge the nation back into depression. The main task for wartime diplomacy, therefore, was to prevent such divisions before American economic power could influence England and Russia.

It was up to Roosevelt to find the proper means to accomplish this feat. The President's efforts to please both groups and yet secure the postwar peace among the Big Three was an impossible undertaking from the outset. But what sounded naive to Bullitt—"if I give him everything I possibly can and ask nothing from him in return"— was actually Roosevelt's analysis of what he could offer Stalin to accomplish this end that Churchill could not. A little more than two weeks after Stimson's plea that he seize the initiative, Roosevelt wrote Stalin: "I have in mind a very important military proposal involving the utilization of our armed forces in a manner to relieve your critical Western Front. This objective carries great weight with me. Therefore, I wish you would consider sending Mr. Molotov and a General upon whom you rely to Washington in the immediate future. Time is of the essence if we are to help in an important way."

What Roosevelt thought he alone could offer was a military second front, large-scale economic aid for Russian reconstruction, and, finally, security guarantees against a rearmed Germany. Churchill's perception of imperial interests also integrated Russian desires into a postwar system, but one which cut against Roosevelt's policy from the very beginning. Churchill offered Stalin good fences in the Balkans; Roosevelt wanted them both to help him build the town meeting hall.

Within a few days of the German attack on Russia, on June 22, 1941, Roosevelt's second ambassador to the Soviet Union, Joseph E. Davies, had come to the White House to plead the case for all-out aid to Russia. Aid to Russia, Davies submitted, would preclude a second Nazi-Soviet pact—a separate peace between the two totalitarian powers that would divide Europe once again. After talking with Stalin about Russia's ability to resist the German onslaught, Special Ambassador Averell Harriman reported much the same thing to Roosevelt: "I left feeling that he had been frank with us and if if we came through as had been promised and if personal relations were retained with Stalin, the suspicion that had existed between the Soviet Government and our two governments might well be eradicated." From Harriman and others, then, Roosevelt received positive assurances that economic aid and personal diplomacy could bring the two nations together. But trust in such assurances was not the basis of second-front diplomacy. American leaders were determined to redeem their past mistakes. Even if there had been no such suggestion from Stalin, the means they planned to use would not have been altered at all.

That was why Churchill's overtures to Stalin in the summer of 1941 so disturbed the State Department. If the British preempted American policy by coming to terms with the Soviets on a detailed political settlement, economic aid to the Soviets would not produce anything: German hegemony would be replaced by Anglo-Russian dominance. Unhappy rumors about such a settlement were spreading, Roosevelt wrote the Prime Minister. "I am inclined to think that an overall statement on your part would be useful at this time, making it clear that no postwar commitments as to territories, populations or economies have been given." The White House would back up such a statement with one of its own.

This exchange led to an agreement between the two English-speaking powers to discuss this problem off the coast of Newfoundland around the 1st of August. Their meeting ended with an eight-point "Joint Declaration," known thereafter as the Atlantic Charter. . . .

The first three points dealt specifically with the old "secret treaty" problem, though much of the literature on the Atlantic Charter at the time and in later years placed greater stress upon its relevance to colonial questions. At the time London was deeply engaged in Asia with the Congress party's demands for Indian independence. Soon after the Prime Minister returned to England, he found widespread speculation that he had committed the whole empire to the charter. The Joint Declaration, he reassured the House of Commons, in no way applied to internal imperial questions.

This caveat was matched two weeks later when the Russian ambassador to Great Britain, Ivan Maisky, added his signature to the Atlantic Charter, and appended verbally a statement about the "historic peculiarities of particular countries" in Eastern Europe. The whole episode was reminiscent of the way European rulers had replied to John Hay's "Open Door Note" concerning China in 1899. What George F. Kennan wrote of Hay's note was certainly as true of the Atlantic Charter: it amounted to asking everyone in the room who was not a thief to stand up. In each instance American reactions were also remarkably similar. Washington gave these nominal acceptances the widest possible circulation, presuming that a combination of "pitiless publicity" and growing economic power would make good most of the promises in the two documents. At the time of the Atlantic Charter, however, the Open Door policy in China had already led to an increasingly frustrating effort to block Japan's forward movement through such means.

Anglo-Russian negotiations in the summer of 1941 did not produce anything like agreement between the two powers actively engaged in fighting Hitler. This was something of a pleasant surprise to Washington, which accounted for it by the timely issuance of the Atlantic Charter. Churchill still had not yielded to Stalin's demands for Russia's 1941 frontiers even by November, when the Kremlin sent a sharp message to His Majesty's government through Ambassador Maisky. Stalin began with a complaint that Great Britain had not declared war on Finland, Hungary, and Rumania, implying that the British had political reasons for not doing so. Then he asserted bluntly that there could be "no mutual trust" until this problem had been resolved and "plans for the post-war organization of the peace" agreed upon. Stalin's diplomatic problems were seriously complicated by the exile governments in London (especially the Polish exiles), whose disposition toward the Soviet Union was less than friendly. Though neither the "Battle of Britain" nor the "Battle of Russia" had been won, or even assured, Stalin was determined to settle postwar matters at once.

Maisky was deeply troubled by Stalin's approach. He regarded all diplomatic and political issues as secondary matters when compared with the urgent need for agreement on a second front in the West. After long thought about how to minimize the impact of the message, he finally took it to the Prime Minister, and said quietly as he handed it over: "I very much ask you, Mr. Churchill, to treat this with the greatest possible calm." As the Prime Minister began reading, his face "immediately went red, and then his left hand began agitatedly closing and opening." When he rose and began pacing the room, Maisky grew fearful that nothing could save the situation. But after his anger subsided, Churchill was persuaded to send Foreign Minister Anthony Eden back to Moscow.

The State Department's warning of December 5—"Above all there must be no secret accords"—went with Eden to Moscow. Maisky went too, to keep Stalin on the matter of a second front; but his apprehensions turned to utter dismay when Stalin demanded that recognition of the 1941 frontier could be put off no longer. Eden replied evasively that Britain had agreed to postpone politcal decisions, and to seek a peace in conformity with the Atlantic Charter. "As regards your repeated references to the necessity for His Majesty's Government to consult the United States Government," Stalin said angrily, "I must confess that I had overlooked this fact and believed your Government to have more freedom of action in these matters. That is perhaps why it is difficult now to reach an agreement." Then he added: "I thought the Atlantic Charter was directed against those people who were trying to establish world domination. It now looks as if the Charter was directed against the U.S.S.R." Stalin was only half-right: it was also aimed at British imperialism. Germany's defeat was simply assumed in the charter.

There was no way around this impasse in December 1941. Eden did promise to present the Russian case to the War Cabinet when he returned to London, but the Prime Minister was in serious trouble: if Stalin should make a separate peace with Hitler sometime in 1942, wouldn't everyone be worse off than if the Soviets kept their spoils? At Christmastime Churchill arrived in Washington for the "Arcadia" conference with Roosevelt with these problems very much on his mind. The President was waiting for him with an enlarged version of the Atlantic Charter, a proposed Declaration of the United Nations against the Axis. Once again press coverage and later historical accounts concentrated on American public concern with British colonialism in India. The State Department wanted the Dominion government to sign the document separately so as to demonstrate London's good faith toward colonial peoples. At the time the public did not perceive the relationship of the document to Anglo-Russian negotiations.

"Several times," Churchill confided to Eden, the President "expressed his pleasure to me at the firm line we took at Moscow." The reasoning behind American policy in this matter, he told the Foreign Minister, was as follows:

> No one can foresee how the balance will lie or where the winning armies will stand at the end of the war. It seems probable however that the United States and the British Empire, far from being exhausted, will be

*the most powerful economic bloc the world has ever seen, and that the
Soviet Union will need our aid for reconstruction far more than we shall
need theirs.*

Plans were laid at the Arcadia meeting for a combined British-
American expedition to North Africa. But the two months following
the conference brought chilling disasters for British arms in the
Middle East and Asia. In Europe, meanwhile, the Russians were
fighting desperately against the main force of Hitler's armies. In
London the exile governments were demanding of the British government that their nationhood be preserved against Russian in-
truders. "In a deadly struggle," an exasperated Churchill confessed
to his personal physician, "it is not right to assume more burdens
than those who are fighting for a great cause can bear."

Not long after, Churchill sent a cable to Washington: "The Atlantic
Charter ought not be construed so as to deny to Russia the frontiers
which she occupied when Germany attacked." When Roosevelt read
it to his cabinet he explained that he had emphatically advised the
British not to accede to Stalin's demands—not even to his claims to
the Baltic states. Such a concession would lead to ever more demands, FDR thought, eventually including the eastern half of Poland.

At a London diplomatic reception several evenings later, the
American ambassador, John G. Winant, called his Russian colleague
aside and confided: "I can give you a pleasant piece of news: President Roosevelt and General Marshall, the Chief of our General Staff,
consider Germany, not Japan, enemy No. 1, and think the immediate
action by the USA and Britain should be an invasion of Northern
France." On April 3, 1942, Roosevelt officially informed Churchill
that he was sending Harry Hopkins and General Marshall to London
to explain to the British government a proposal that "has my heart
and *mind* in it. . . . Your people and mine demand the establishment
of a front to draw off pressure on the Russians, and these peoples
are wise enough to see that the Russians are today killing more Germans and destroying more equipment than you and I put together.
Even if full success is not attained, the *big* objective will be."

Though he had not secured Churchill's final agreement to his plan
for a 1942 invasion of northern France, Roosevelt urged Stalin to
send Foreign Minister Molotov and some reliable general to Washing-

DOES HE NEED A CONSULTATION OR A CHANGE OF MEDICINE?

FIGURE 4. The image of American ideals versus European imperialism (1944). *(Chicago Tribune)*

ton. Molotov talked once more with British leaders in London in an effort to solve the political issue in Eastern Europe. The American ambassador kept close to the talks—to make sure they followed the prescribed adherence to the Atlantic Charter. Molotov arrived in Washington in late May 1942, after he had concluded a short treaty in London which contained no secret protocols about Eastern Europe. The Russian foreign minister made it plain to Roosevelt that his government felt it had given up near-vital security arrangements in his talks with Churchill. Roosevelt expressed his understanding of the Russian position and began speaking about the "formation" of a second front in 1942. Military aid, however, was only the preface to an entirely new book on Soviet-American relations, the President suggested. The first chapter of this new book, he continued, had been tentatively titled "The Big Four"—in which the Soviet Union is taken into full partnership with the Anglo-American trust to manage the postwar world. Declaring the League of Nations defunct, Roosevelt then outlined his conception in greater detail, explaining that each member of the big-power trust would be responsible for general obligations in connection with the treatment of the defeated Axis nations, and each would have specific regional obligations as well. One of these last concerned the problem of strategic areas to be put under some kind of international trusteeship. "The President hoped Mr. Molotov would discuss this suggestion with Mr. Stalin."

No Western statesman had ever spoken to a Bolshevik in such fashion. Without doubt it was one of the President's most remarkable performances: a dramatic attempt to strike through Molotov's mask-like countenance to the man who sat impatiently in the Kremlin waiting for his emissary's reports. It was also a one-time performance; it is not unfair to say that America reached the height of its wartime diplomatic efforts at this moment. No action at Casablanca, Teheran, or Yalta went so far toward genuine diplomatic adjustment with the Russians. In part this was because Roosevelt was soon put on the defensive by British unwillingness to go ahead with the American plan; in part it resulted from pressures by Roosevelt's advisers against reducing the Big Four to concrete terms. But it was also because FDR had no real faith in the concept, other than as a way of establishing rapport with his Allies. It was the same "pragmatic" style he applied to domestic problems.

Ever since the Roosevelt-Churchill meeting of August, 1941, the State Department had been trying to persuade the President to commit himself to an effective international organization to keep the peace after the war. Roosevelt had refused to do it. The last paragraph of the Atlantic Charter, Churchill observed after the war, "was a plain and bold intimation that . . . the United States would join with us in policing the world until the establishment of a better order." Cordell Hull and his aides did not regard the Big Four as a better order at all; in fact, they asserted, it would probably be even worse, and at best hardly more satisfactory than an outright concession of Eastern Europe to Russia.

Stalin considered all this talk about a Big Four no more than algebra; he preferred solid mathematics. Roosevelt's proposal for a Big Four directorate was in fact, as Stalin said, an abstract formula. China, whom Roosevelt proposed as the fourth member, could not be called a big power under any circumstances. Post-war "planning" that depended upon Chiang Kai-shek's government for any kind of international responsibility was speculative beyond all likelihood. In fact, FDR's continuing insistence upon this Big Four rhetoric, even as he undertook to act as China's guardian during Big Three conferences, left his allies puzzled and disturbed. One conclusion they drew was that Roosevelt sought China's "faggot" vote either in support of American anti-colonialism or to increase his influence against Britain and Russia on European questions.

Of more immediate concern to American policy planning and the Allies, however, was Churchill's ultimate refusal to risk an invasion of the European continent in 1942. The only offensive action against German land forces that the British would countenance at all was a modified African campaign, which the American chiefs of staff had never liked from the beginning. Roosevelt's political advisers were equally upset by this development, which meant that Churchill would gain a double measure of diplomatic success at America's expense: (1) he would obtain American power in support of his overall strategy for winning the war through the Mediterranean, at least for the time being; and (2) he would retake the immediate diplomatic initiative among the Big Three for his own purposes. He even "volunteered" to carry the news to Moscow. Roosevelt had been trying to achieve a personal meeting with Stalin for several months; now it was to be Churchill who spoke for the West on this crucial question. At Moscow the Prime Minister played the role to the hilt. "Stalin will make a great mistake," Churchill, at his imperial best, warned Molotov, "to treat us roughly when we have come so far." "Stalin," replied the Foreign Minister, "is a very wise man. You may be sure, however he argues, he understands all."

In all of his explanations of the North African campaign, the Prime Minister insisted that the British and the Americans were "preparing for a very great operation in 1943." Stalin's military advisers could not have been any more skeptical about that claim than the American chiefs of staff, who were insisting even as Churchill left for Moscow that the Germany-first strategy be reexamined if the British persisted in their resistance to a cross-channel attack.

Critics later charged that Roosevelt had felt the United States "owed" the Soviet Union a second front, and that he had over-compensated with numerous "concessions" to the Kremlin on a whole series of questions. This is a shortsighted criticism: FDR's central purpose was to realize a second front—when it still mattered to the Russians. The North African campaign not only failed to serve that end, it raised unexpected issues in the so-called deal with Vichy French authorities in North Africa which facilitated the Anglo-American landings.

But while American liberals attacked the compromise with Germany's semifascist allies as a "separate peace in the West," Stalin's people were more concerned that the West planned a series of holding actions until the tide had turned in Europe, then a rush for Berlin. Roosevelt fully understood this and renewed his efforts to persuade Stalin to come to a Big Three meeting when the North African campaign ended. The site selected was Casablanca, but neither the geographical nor the political climate suited the Russian leader, who decided to stay home to make the most of his role as the injured party. FDR went ahead with the meeting with Churchill alone. To the Prime Minister's complete surprise, Roosevelt then issued his "Unconditional Surrender" ultimatum. The gesture was aimed at convincing the Kremlin that the United States would fight until Germany was crushed—that there would be no separate peace in the West.

Roosevelt's advisers had come to Casablanca in an angry mood. They were irked by Allied political maneuvering and their inability to do very much about it. Determined not to be a fluttering tail on the Britsh kite any longer, they found it difficult to counter British arguments for a full-scale Mediterranean strategy. Had Stalin come to Casablanca, ironically, he would have found Americans grateful for his aid in this matter. The Prime Minister's advisers had brought literally boatloads of documents to bolster their position. Though the British finally "compromised," wrote American Ambassador Robert K. Murphy, their so-called concession still kept Americans "fighting for more than two years in this traditional sphere of British influence. . . . Instead of the quick campaign which Eisenhower had expected to fight in Africa, he had to plan and direct several additional campaigns in Mediterranean islands and in southern Europe. More than a year passed before he could even get back to England to prepare at last for the kind of invasion of Europe which he and other Americans had wanted in the first place. . . ."

Russia's victory at Stalingrad in January and February 1943 was a turning point not only in the military history of World War II but in world history as well. Any assumption that the German Eastern front would hold the Russians until Britain and America were ready to fight in the West had to be abandoned. The question now was where the Allies would meet, and what they would find when they got there, particularly in Italy, France, and Germany.

Roosevelt had already discussed this problem with British Foreign Minister Anthony Eden and Harry Hopkins. The President's close adviser kept a record of what he had contributed to the discussion: "I said I thought there was no understanding between Great Britain, Russia and ourselves as to which armies would be where and what kind of administration should be developed. I said that unless we acted promptly and surely I believed one of two things would happen— either Germany will go Communist or an out and out anarchic state would set in; that, indeed, the same kind of thing might happen in any of the countries in Europe and Italy as well."

In the light of this post-Stalingrad awakening, the "Unconditional Surrender" statement seemed completely outdated, even foolish. Germany could be expected to fight hard against the Russians, but, as many postwar critics pointed out, the unconditional surrender statement weakened the West's bargaining posture. Now that Russia was on the offensive, hard decisions had to be reached quickly. In talks with Eden and Averell Harriman, his newly appointed ambassador to the Soviet Union, Roosevelt took the position that Churchill had held in 1942: Russia could no longer be denied the Baltic states, a readjustment of the Soviet-Polish frontier up to the so-called Curzon line, and East Prussia as well. But he still counted on Russia's economic dependence on the United States to ameliorate East-West relations on terms favorable to the West. He instructed Bernard M. Baruch to inform Churchill of his continuing belief in the efficacy of economic diplomacy with the Russians. The Prime Minister "was impressed by the argument," reported Baruch, "and even said it was a brilliant idea."

But Roosevelt moved neither to activate this plan nor to prepare the public for diplomatic adjustments. The public face of American wartime diplomacy, the Atlantic Charter, remained unchanged despite the deep lines in Roosevelt's private worries. His indecision about postwar treatment of Germany, for example, may well have been the by-product of the Russian dilemma—or perhaps vice versa. Baruch and Henry Morgenthau, Jr., argued that the "more of Germany that is destroyed, the more the United States becomes the source of rehabilitation in peace as she was the source of materiel, munitions, ships, planes and food in the war." Hull and Stimson countered that this was a shortsighted and foolish position. Roosevelt could not choose between them. . . .

In the months leading up to the Teheran Conference in November, 1943, where Roosevelt would finally confront Stalin face to face, talk of second-front diplomacy shifted to new ground. Now it became a defensive tactic to guarantee the United States enough time to complete its postwar plans before Britain and Russia settled everything between them. Roosevelt in fact told his military advisers at Teheran that he foresaw a race to Berlin, and quite probably the need to put several army divisions into Germany at once to prevent disorder should the surrender take place before American troops managed to fight their way to the German capital. On the other hand, Herbert Feis comments, Roosevelt planned to appeal more positively at Teheran to the "presumed" Soviet desire for collective security and an "equal" place at the peace conference. "He was also going to try to satisfy Stalin's wish for more direct security by agreeing to join in the sponsorship of such protective measures as the dismemberment of Germany. He hoped that his views could be made more persuasive by offers of American help in repairing war damage in the Soviet Union."

Aside from suggesting that the Big Three consider German dismemberment, and sending Stalin a brief post-Teheran message saying he was sorry he had not been able to take up the matter of economic aid to the Soviet Union personally during their discussions, Roosevelt failed to appeal to the "good side" of Stalin's nature or, as Feis put it, to "presumed" Soviet desires.

Negotiations over a postwar credit to the Soviets did take place in 1944 on Roosevelt's instructions, but as Harriman advised the State Department:

If aid for Russian reconstruction is to be of real value in our overall relations with the Soviet Government, as a benefit which they can obtain from us if they play the international game with us in accordance with our standards, we must have a well-forged instrument to offer them. Vague promises excite Soviet suspicions, whereas a precise program offered now to them but kept always within our control to suspend will be of extreme value. Stalin must offer his people quick reconstruction to retain supreme leadership. We on the other hand want Russian business quickly during our period of conversion from war production.

But, as in the 1930s, Roosevelt did not intervene when these negotiations became entangled in legalisms and secondary matters.

Searching for an answer to this phase of the strategy of postponement is a frustrating task. Clearly, as Allied momentum toward final victory increased, events foreclosed the President's options; the strategy of postponement strengthened the hand of those advisers who generally shared Bullitt's outlook, if not his ideas on strategic warfare.

British-American attempts to organize a provisional Italian government without close consultation with the Russians, moreover, brought out several facts neither East nor West was exactly happy to acknowledge. Churchill wanted to promote the most conservative promonarchy government possible. To most Americans, it looked like North Africa all over again. The Russians at first demanded an equal voice in the Allied Control Commission for Italy, but were granted only a nonparticipatory "advisory" role. Western diplomats realized they were setting a precedent, but a new factor had entered the situation which they simply could not gauge adequately. Until they could do so they were unwilling to test Russian intentions. The swelling power of Italian communism left few doubts that the Russians, if they so chose, could invoke all the dreadful force of revolutionary Marxism against any provisional government. In March, 1944, the Russians dropped a bombshell by negotiating an exchange of diplomatic representatives with the Royal Government. When the British raised objections to this independent action, the Russian Foreign Office informed the ambassador, Sir Archibald Clark Kerr, that its action was intended to strengthen the antifascist forces fighting the Germans by unifying the dissidents under the Royal Government's directives. In other words, the bomb had been aimed at Italian Communists.

This impression was confirmed by further conversations in Rome with the Russian "advisory" representatives to the Allied Control Commission. There was no doubt, concluded a British aide, that the "Russians intend to take a strong line with the Parties of the Left in Italy and that they intend to ensure that these Parties do nothing to upset the war effort by actions which might dislocate the administration." At the same time, this reporter cautioned London, the Russian diplomat gave him "the impression of a Penitent Cobra being matey."

Despite Stalin's dissolution of the Comintern in 1943, Russian intervention in Italy demonstrated that the political power of the Soviet Union would be far greater after the war than it had ever been before, and that Great Britain and the United States would either have to tolerate such intervention or face the likelihood of Moscow-inspired disruptions. No matter what the Russians said, their power to do all sorts of unpleasant things in Western Europe after the war was all the more disturbing because it could not be calculated. As the Russian representative in Rome explained to Sir Noel Mason-MacFarlane, if Moscow had wanted to do any "abnormal" business in Italy, it would not have been "so stupid as to exchange representatives. They had quite different and much more effective ways of doing that sort of thing."

On April 1, 1944, the Soviet ambassador in Washington frankly informed Secretary Hull that Russian penetration into Rumania "was the beginning of a full re-establishment of the border delineated in 1940," but he gave assurances that no further extensions were planned. Stalin's behavior since the Anglo-Russian talks in 1941 had been consistent in this regard, and calculated to discourage those in the West who warned that Russia had not given up its revolutionary aims. But the louder he talked of Soviet honor, the faster the State Department counted its spoons. This paradox arose (as in Italy) from a situation that neither Russia nor the West could control.

*   *   *

During the war political polarization in Europe had actually intensified. The most dynamic resistance groups were communist or militant left-partisan forces in northern Italy, France, Yugoslavia, and Greece. Barbara Ward suggested what larger ramifications this would have in a 1946 *Foreign Affairs* article: the Russian Revolution had been followed by the rise of Italian fascism and then German National

Socialism. This had created a Left-Right division throughout Europe long before the war itself, "with the issue of nationalization at the center of the resulting tension." Political leaders in the postwar period, even those on the moderate right, would espouse some form of socialism (at least temporarily) to contain the growing demands of militant socialists and communists. Fascism might well be replaced in many countries by communism.

Realizing the possibility of such developments, Churchill and Stalin tried to settle their affairs before postwar politics overwhelmed them both. The Prime Minister wanted to secure British interests in Greece and the Eastern Mediterranean; Stalin wanted security in the Balkans. FDR reluctantly agreed that Churchill might try to reach a temporary modus operandi with Stalin, but he warned the latter that in a global war there was "literally no question, military or political, in which the United States is not interested." Any decision they might reach on Eastern Europe must be regarded as only preliminary to a second Big Three meeting some time after the American elections in 1944. And to Ambassador Harriman he wrote that the United States must retain complete freedom of action when the conference ended.

Despite Stalin's "surprise" at this message—he had assumed Churchill was coming as the result of an Anglo-American under-standing—the two settled their business in no more time than it took for Churchill to scrawl some figures across a half-sheet of paper and pass it to Stalin, who took a blue pencil, made a large tick upon the paper, and passed it back. After this brief exchange there was a long silence broken finally by Churchill's suggestion that they burn the paper, lest they be thought "rather cynical" for having disposed of these issues, "so fateful to millions of people, in such an offhand manner." "No, you keep it," said Stalin.

Churchill's figures called for 90 percent Russian "predominance" in Rumania and 90 percent British-American interest in Greece. Yugoslavia and Hungary were to be divided equally, and Russia was to have 75 percent influence in Bulgaria. In the wake of the retreating German army, Churchill directed British forces to restore order—and the monarchy—in Greece. American reactions to British policy pointed up Roosevelt's dilemma and the pressures upon him to do something to head off the division of Europe in spheres of influence. The dreaded "secret treaty" had in fact been signed; now Roosevelt was left with Wilson's predicament in full.

Even worse, though Russian military observers had joined the British and their Greek clients in the effort to persuade partisan leaders to lay down their arms, the solution did not stick. The partisans had been led to believe that all other groups contending for power in Athens and the countryside would also be required to put aside their weapons. When this renuniciation did not occur, the partisans called for a protest march in Athens on December 3, 1944. British authorities first granted permission for the parade, then grew fearful and revoked the permit at three in the morning; but by that time—even if they had been willing to do so—it was too late for the partisan leaders to call it off. As the crowd neared the Grande Bretagne Hotel, the royalists opened fire on the unarmed marchers, killing or wounding nearly two hundred people. From the point of view of local communists, this panicky act successfully completed the polarization of Greek politics. As in Italy and France, communists occupied key positions in the movement, but its popular support stretched across nearly the whole Greek political spectrum, except for an inch or so at the end controlled by British-supported royalists and conservatives. "Do not . . . hesitate to act as if you were in a conquered city where a local rebellion is in progress," Churchill instructed the British commander. "We have to hold and dominate Athens."

Not since the Indian question in 1942 had the American press reacted so violently as it did to this blatant display of British imperial policy. It was a perfect editorial subject to illustrate—and condemn—American acquiescence in Russian and British "spheres of influence." Only the Soviet Union, busy with its own share of the Balkans, kept silent—a stance gratefully acknowledged by Churchill during parliamentary debates on Greece. "Naturally I felt the sudden way in which very large sections of the American press which has hitherto appreciated my ceaseless efforts to keep our two countries in harmony turned upon me over the Greek affair," the Prime Minister wrote an American friend at the height of the controversy. "How stultified they must feel today when, after infinite toils and many hazards, every ideal in the Atlantic Charter is being secured for Greece, and when the gratitude of her people for their deliverance from a dictatorship of a Communist gang is expressed on every side."

As reports of daily events in Greece and Eastern Europe came in to the American press during December, 1944 and January, 1945, the new Secretary of State, Edward R. Stettinius, put a worried notation in his priviate memoranda: "United States military people were going so far as to say that we ought to withdraw from Europe and 'go to the Pacific now and win the war there.'" A political columnist flatly told Stettinius that "we are letting the British and Russians ride roughshod over us." The secretary asked him to be patient yet a while.

Business Week, usually well informed on such questions, suggested (and probably hoped) that the President would finally use his economic leverage to secure reasonable terms from Stalin not only on Poland but on other questions as well. Though no more than a surmise, it was still a logical one; during those weeks the press was filled with suggestions for dealing with the imperialists and social revolutionaries. The problem they all perceived so well was how to convert economic power into political advantage, how to save the United Nations from the spheres of influence agreements—the secret treaties of World War II.

As Ambassador Harriman explained it to Stimson, it would be practically impossible for the United States to convince the Russians to eliminate the secret police from the areas where the Red Army penetrated. Therefore the administration had to find a way to keep the Russians from introducing the OGPU and communism into Hungary and other Eastern European countries. Harriman was still convinced that the answer was economic diplomacy. On January 3, 1945, Foreign Minister Molotov made a formal request for a $6 billion credit for postwar purchases in the United States. The way he made the request irritated Harriman—a gratuitous offer to save capitalism from serious surplus crises in the transition period—but the ambassador remained convinced that the Russians really needed American aid and would make political concessions to get it.

Almost at the same time, Henry Morgenthau proposed a different use of American economic power: he argued that the United States should extend an even bigger credit, $10 billion, without such obvious strings as Harriman's crude "Dollar Diplomacy" plan, though with other less visible ties and obligations to the American postwar economic system then being formulated. "If we were to come forward now and present to the Russians a concrete plan to aid them in the reconstruction period [as had already been promised the British]," contended Roosevelt's old friend and adviser, "it would contribute a great deal towards ironing out many of the difficulties we have been having with respect to their problems and policies."

*   *   *

Harriman and the State Department succeeded in forestalling serious consideration of Morgenthau's proposal, and in convincing Roosevelt that he must keep foremost in mind the "tactical point of view." It would be "harmful for us to offer such a large credit at this time and thus lose what appears to be the only concrete bargaining lever" America had. FDR told Harriman he had a "keen interest" in taking up the subject at Yalta; consequently, it should "not be pressed" until he had a chance to talk with Stalin personally. But once again, as at Teheran, Roosevelt did not broach the subject at Yalta.

The State Department had also been urging Roosevelt to confront his Allies in another way, through the creation of a European High Commission to enforce the Atlantic Charter throughout liberated Europe. The department wanted the President to introduce a Declaration on Liberated Europe at Yalta, and insist upon the creation of a commission to see that it was in fact carried out. Quite obviously something had to be done—and soon. On January 1, 1945, the Soviet Union had extended formal diplomatic recognition to the so-called Lublin government in Warsaw, its own creation. As these pressures mounted, Roosevelt's temper flared up at Ambassador-designate to Poland Arthur Bliss Lane, who told him to get tough with the Russians. "Do you want me to go to war with Russia?" FDR snapped.

The Polish question brought a loud protest from Senator Arthur Vandenberg of Michigan, the most important convert to "internationalism" the war had made. But wrapped inside the Senator's denunciation of Anglo-Russian secret diplomacy on the floor of Congress was a concrete plan for testing Allied intentions—if only the President could find some way to use it. After demanding a peace with justice for all the small nations, Vandenberg suddenly shifted to a consideration of the legitimate "security" problem posed by postwar Germany: "I know of no reason why a hard-and-fast treaty between the major allies should not be signed today to achieve this dependable end. We need not await the determination of our other postwar relationships. This problem—this menace—stands apart by itself."

The American response to Vandenberg's speech was tremendous. "I wish somebody would psychonanalyze that speech," the senator confided to his wife. "I can't understand why it has been such an appalling sensation." Walter Lippmann called it one of the few speeches ever to affect the course of events: "The immense importance of Senator Vandenberg's proposal is that it would end the policy of postponement and thus restore American influence in the settlement of Europe."

Another of Vandenberg's listeners was equally struck: Secretary of War Henry L. Stimson wrote Stettinius that the speech had caused him to reconsider what had happened at the end of the last war. He now recalled that President Wilson had tried to create a League of Nations without a strong security foundation first. Wilson had belatedly recognized this failure in his offer of a security treaty to France "as the pillar of western Europe" against a new German menace, but it had been too late. Stimson urged Stettinius to present this point of view to the President before he reached any Big Three decisions at Yalta.

Life devoted an editorial to the senator's speech and press reaction to it, observing that while incorrigibly isolationist papers and journals like the *New York Daily News* and the *Chicago Tribune* considered the speech a mortal blow to the Republican Party and their cause, sound thinkers like John Foster Dulles had praised it: "Having made such a treaty—and only after having made it—America would then have the 'duty and right' to demand that political and boundary questions in Europe be kept open and subject to postwar review. Thus we might stop the present series of unilateral acts. If we do not stop it we are heading for trouble."

Vandenberg noted in his personal diary that Roosevelt had in fact asked for several copies of the speech to take with him to the Crimea. But as far as one can tell from the published records of the Yalta Conference, FDR made no use of them. Deeply concerned about the coming "isolationist" reaction to the United Nations, Roosevelt may well have decided that Wilson's greatest mistake had been to divide his supporters by demanding *two* kinds of internationalism at once—a League of Nations *and* a security treaty with France. At any rate,

Stimson heard indirectly that the President was not much interested in his suggestion for settling the German question by an Allied treaty before tackling other problems at Yalta.

Since 1941 Roosevelt's prinicipal advisers had been steering him away from Big Four trusteeship and toward a new League of Nations. By the time of the Teheran Conference he was moving rapidly in that direction. How that affected his consideration of a proposal for a Big Four treaty over Germany is problematical, but this much is clear: Roosevelt had allowed his alarm at Anglo-Russian secret diplomacy (and the politics of American reaction to it) to inhibit his genuine desire for good postwar relations with the Soviet Union. His concern about spreading communism also inhibited necessary decision-making. Responsibility for the public face of American diplomacy was not his alone, but when opportunities arose for direct use of economic diplomacy or political initiative, the President retreated into a protective ambivalence, waiting for something to turn up.

Plans were well advanced for the new United Nations when the Allies sat down at the first plenary session of the Yalta Conference. Despite all his efforts to prevent history from repeating itself, FDP found himself where Wilson had sat before him. Churchill and Stalin had seen to their security and their ambitions outside the framework of the new collective-security organization, and Roosevelt was left with the task of reversing an accelerating course of events. A few days before leaving Washington, Roosevelt had himself outlined the situation in his 1945 State of the Union message:

> *During the interim period we and our Allies have a duty, which we cannot ignore, to use our influence to the end that no temporary or provisional authorities in the liberated countries block the eventual exercise of the peoples' right freely to choose the government and institutions under which, as free men, they are to live.*

But at Yalta Roosevelt demurred when the State Department offered him the Declaration of Liberated Europe to accomplish this end, extracting from it the mechanism which Secretary Stettinius and his aides had put behind the rhetoric to see that something would come of it. Why the President acted in this fashion has never been satisfactorily explained, but Churchill's behavior at Yalta was perhaps as much responsible for the lack of effective action on Eastern Europe as Roosevelt's, and it illustrated how complex the President's problems were. After exploding at one session that he would never allow fifty or more nations to put their interfering fingers into imperial affairs, the Prime Minister made a bad slip when the American secretary of state read the proposed Declaration on Liberated Europe. Obviously worried about American postwar policy toward the Empire, Churchill remarked, to the dismay of American policy-makers, that he did not dissent from the President's declaration "so long as it was clearly understood that the reference to the Atlantic Charter did not apply to the British Empire." He added that he had long ago informed Wendell Willkie, then on his famous "One World" tour, that the Empire was excepted from all that kind of talk. Roosevelt inquired in mock seriousness if that was what had killed Mr. Willkie.

Stalin, however, kept his silence. He had seen that the Prime Minister had overlooked the fact that the American proposal referred only to the former German satellites in Eastern Europe. While FDR did insist at this plenary session that there be free elections as soon as possible in Poland, the final protocol of the Yalta Conference stated only that the new Polish provisional government should be a "reorganization" of the Lublin government. This was to be accomplished by consultations with "other Polish democratic leaders from within Poland and from abroad." Admiral William D. Leahy, Roosevelt's military aide, saw the document and threw up his hands. "Mr. President," he said, "this is so elastic that the Russians can stretch it all the way from Yalta to Washington without ever technically breaking it." "I know, Bill—I know it," FDR replied. "But it's the best I can do for Poland at this time."

On board ship during the return voyage from Yalta, reporters asked the President if Churchill's subborn attitude on colonial issues did not negate the Atlantic Charter. Roosevelt answered simply: "The Atlantic Charter is a beautiful idea." Although he explained a bit, the report of this interview set off another public discussion of Russian and British imperialism. Against these charges, Roosevelt's appeal for the United Nations sounded like an unhappy echo from an earlier day. His report to Congress on the Big Three conference ended with a dangerously overoptimistic assessment of the future. Yalta, he declared, spelled the end "of the system of unilateral action and exclusive alliances and spheres of influence and balances of power and all the other expedients which have been tried for centuries—and have failed."

Roosevelt put all his failing strength into the fight for an international organization; unlike Wilson, he had the votes in the Senate to complete the task. Yet the only way to make this new League work was to have reached prior agreement on issues left by the war itself, and hope that postwar questions could be handled as they arose. But the President had not been able to make decisions on any of the really crucial problems, issues that were fundamental to the peace. The United Nations was designed to be a peacekeeping device; but it could not be made into a peacemaking device without dividing the Big Three. Stalin's demand for three votes in the United Nations was primarily his way of calling attention to this fact. America could build up numerical majorities with its allies and the Latin American nations, but the Russians would regard the result as meaningless because it was based upon the assumption that there was a genuine consensus in the world when such a thing did not exist. Roosevelt did not tell the American people this—or even the Vice-President.

John L. Gaddis

FDR AND COOPERATION WITH THE SOVIET UNION—A REALISTIC APPROACH

The traditional interpretations of Roosevelt's wartime policies, particularly those that related to Soviet-American relations, have often reflected critiques of the President rather than offering positive theses. Initially those historians who agreed with the basic thrust of American foreign policy during the war years wrote largely in defense of Roosevelt against charges from the Right that he had sold out to the Soviets on such issues as the Polish boundary, aid to the Chinese Nationalist government, and self-determination for the countries of Eastern Europe. Vigorous justifications of Roosevelt's actions on those issues provided ample ammunition for a left-revisionist critique since the President's scholarly defenders tended to emphasize his anti-Soviet policies when arguing against accusations of naiveté or Communist sympathies. With the publication of John L. Gaddis' The United States and the Origins of the Cold War, 1941–1947, *excerpted below, the pendulum has clearly swung in the other direction. Gaddis incorporates much of the recent left-revisionist critique in his book, admitting that American economic plans and support for self-determination in Eastern Europe proved incompatible with Soviet demands and policies. Gaddis ultimately agrees with what he sees as Roosevelt's decision to realistically live with the spheres of influence which ultimately developed, but faults the President for misleading the public by emphasizing the idealistic rhetoric of such items as the Declaration of Liberated Europe. Gaddis, who was a student of Robert A. Divine, is currently associate professor of history at Ohio University.*

If Russian resistance to Hitler could help Britain, it followed logically that the United States should do what it could to keep the Red Army fighting. Diplomatic and military advisers gave the Russians little chance to withstand the German onslaught, but Roosevelt, impressed by Harry Hopkins' optimistic reports of his talks with Stalin late in July, chose to disregard these warnings. On August 2, while Hopkins was still in Moscow, the President admonished his special assistant for defense matters to speed up aid to Russia: "Please, with my full authority, use a heavy hand—act as a burr under the saddle and get things moving!" Three months later Roosevelt proclaimed the survival of the Soviet Union vital to the defense of the United States,

From John L. Gaddis, *The United States and the Origins of the Cold War, 1941–1947* (New York, 1972). Reprinted by permission of Columbia University Press. Footnotes omitted.

159

and ordered that Lend-Lease aid be made immediately available to the Russians.

Hitler's declaration of war four days after Pearl Harbor made the United States and the Soviet Union formal allies. From now on victory over Germany would depend upon cooperation with Russia, whatever past differences had been. Roosevelt appraised the value of this coalition realistically: "Put it in terms of dead Germans and smashed tanks," he told a press conference early in 1942. To General Douglas MacArthur he wrote in May that "the Russian armies are killing more Axis personnel and destroying more Axis materiel than all other twenty-five United Nations put together. Even after the collapse of Mussolini in July, 1943, the President could still tell the American people that "the heaviest and most decisive fighting today is going on in Russia," and that Britain and the United States had been fortunate to have been able to contribute "somewhat" to the Russian war effort.

But Roosevelt's "grand design" encompassed far more than simple military collaboration with the Soviet Union to defeat Germany—cooperation with Russia would also be vital to ensure postwar peace. Keenly aware of the realities of power, Roosevelt knew that the United States and the Soviet Union would emerge from the war as the world's two strongest nations. If they could stay together, no third power could prevail against them. If they could not, the world would be divided into two armed camps, a prospect too horrible to contemplate. "We either work with the other great Nations," FDR told the Foreign Policy Association in 1944, "or we might some day have to fight them. And I am against that."

The President knew that vast differences in culture, language, and ideology separated the Soviet Union from the United States. He had no illusions about the nature of Stalin's regime, which he regarded as no less rigid a dictatorship than Hitler's. But he believed the Russian form of totalitarianism to be less dangerous than that of Germany because the Kremlin had not sought world conquest through military aggression. Moscow had tried to use the Comintern to overthrow foreign governments, Roosevelt admitted, but these sporadic efforts seemed far less of a threat than Hitler's more direct methods. Much of Russia's hostility toward the West, he believed, stemmed simply from lack of knowledge: "I think the Russians are perfectly friendly; they aren't trying to gobble up all the rest of Europe or the world. They didn't know us, that's the really fundamental difference. . . . They haven't got any crazy ideas of conquest, . . . and now that they have got to know us, they are much more willing to accept us." Proud of his decision to recognize the USSR in 1933, Roosevelt sought to bring Russia into the postwar community of peace-loving states. The post-World War I policy of treating the Soviet Union as an international pariah had been silly—after World War II it would be suicidal.

The President believed that he could obtain Stalin's postwar cooperation by meeting legitimate Russian security needs, provided the Soviet Union had given up its attempts to force communism on the rest of the world. Convinced that World War I diplomats had erred in not agreeing on war aims before the fighting had stopped, Roosevelt attached great importance to reaching an early settlement with Stalin. Personal diplomacy, he felt, would demonstrate America's good intentions, thereby creating the basis for peaceful coexistence after the war. "I 'got along fine' with Marshal Stalin," FDR told a nationwide radio audience after the Teheran Conference; "I believe that we are going to get along very well with him and the Russian people—very well indeed."

But the President's "grand design" for cooperation with Russia was only part of a larger American scheme for preventing future wars. This vision of the future, based primarily upon the lessons of the past and shared, to a remarkable extent, by most Washington officials and by a large portion of the informed public, imposed limits on how far Roosevelt could go in accepting Stalin's postwar objectives. The President could never move too far from the American peace program without calling into question the reasons for fighting the war. The extent to which Russian postwar aims conflicted with those of the United States would thus determine, in large measure, the possibilities for keeping the alliance intact after victory.

*   *   *

To its credit, the Roosevelt Administration generally avoided attempts to picture the Soviet Union as a budding democracy or to defend past actions of Stalin's regime, preferring instead to justify collaboration with Russia in terms of military necessity. The one significant exception to this pattern occurred before American entry into the war, when President Roosevelt became worried that powerful religious organizations might oppose Lend-Lease shipments to Russia because of that country's restrictions on freedom of worship. In August, 1941, the White House arranged on two days' notice to fly Dr. Daniel A. Poling, president of the International Christian Endeavor, to London in a bomber to defend aid to the Soviet Union before a meeting of his organization. On September 3, FDR pointedly advised Pope Pius XII that "leaders of all churches in the United States . . . should not . . . by their present attitude on this question directly assist Germany in her present objectives." Since the Pope presumably had little influence over American Protestant denominations, it may be assumed that Roosevelt had potential Catholic opposition chiefly in mind.

"If Moscow could get some publicity back to this country regarding the freedom of religion [in Russia]," Roosevelt told Soviet Ambassador Constantine Oumansky on September 11, "it might have a very fine educational effect before the next lease-lend bill comes up in Congress." As if to jog the Russians' memory, the President some days later read to a press conference Article 124 of the largely unimplemented 1936 Soviet Constitution, which contained guarantees of religious freedom. Roosevelt regarded this question as one of "outstanding importance . . . from the standpoint of public opinion in the United States," Secretary of State Hull cabled Ambassador Laurence A. Steinhardt in Moscow. "It is desired that you make every endeavor to see that some statement of this kind is made by the Soviet authorities at the earliest possible moment." The Russians dutifully complied on October 4, 1941, publicly proclaiming that freedom of worship was allowed in the Soviet Union so long as it did not challenge the authority of the state.

Like Davies and Wallace, Roosevelt saw some possibility that the Soviet and American systems of government might, through evolution, become similar. The President once explained to Sumner Welles that since 1917 the USSR had advanced "from the original form of Soviet Communism . . . toward a modified form of state socialism," while at the same time the United States had progressed "toward the ideal of true political and social justice":

> He believed that American democracy and Soviet Communism could never meet. But he told me that he did believe that if one took the figure 100 as representing the difference between American democracy and Soviet Communism in 1917, with the United States at 100 and the Soviet Union

at 0, American democracy might eventually reach the figure 60 and the Soviet system might reach the figure of 40.

As long as this trend toward convergence continued, Roosevelt saw no reason to regard conflict between the communist and capitalist worlds as inevitable. Unlike many prominent figures during the war, however, the President refrained from publicly encouraging the belief that time would erase ideological differences between the two nations.

After Pearl Harbor, the Roosevelt Administration felt little need to polish the Soviet Union's image in the United States. For most Americans, the simple fact that the Russians were fighting Hitler was reason enough to accept them as allies without worrying too much about ideological conflicts. As one Georgia newspaper editor put it: "I'd be willing to fight alongside the Devil himself to win this war." The uncritical descriptions of Russia which became so prevalent in the mass media during World War II reflected the desire of those Americans sophisticated enough to concern themselves with contradictions in international affairs to find complete ideological consistency in the war aims of the anti-Axis coalition. This well-intentioned but misguided effort generated a false sense of euphoria which led to disillusionment and recrimination later on, when it became apparent that, aside from common interest in defeating their enemies, the Soviet Union and the United States had radically different concepts of what the postwar world should be like.

. . . In August, 1943, William C. Bullitt submitted a lengthy memorandum to his old friend Franklin Roosevelt warning of an imminent "political catastrophe" in Europe. The United States and Great Britain had rightly judged Hitler's conquest of Europe to be "an intolerable menace to . . . their free institutions," Bullitt asserted, but "domination of Europe by Stalin's Communist dictatorship would be as great a threat." Unfortunately, the British and Americans needed Russia's help in the war against Germany if they were to keep their casualties within tolerable limits. The problem, therefore, was to find some way to prevent "the domination of Europe by the Moscow dictatorship without losing the participation of the Red Army in the war against the Nazi dictatorship."

Bullitt's argument reflected a central dilemma of American military strategy during World War II: victory over the Axis depended upon cooperation with the Soviet Union, yet defeat of Germany and Japan would mean a vast increase in Russian power in Europe and the Far East, a development which might well preclude realization of such vital postwar objectives as self-determination and the revival of multilateral trade, Bullitt's solution to this problem was to devise operations against Germany which would place Allied forces in a position to counteract Russian influence in Eastern Europe—an Anglo-American invasion of the Balkans would accomplish this, he believed —while at the same time making further aid to the Soviet Union, both for wartime and for postwar purposes, contingent upon Moscow's acceptance of Washington's war aims. "War is an attempt to achieve political objectives by fighting," he reminded Roosevelt, "and political objectives must be kept in mind in planning operations."

FDR did not have to be warned of risks of collaborating with Moscow. "I don't dispute your facts," he told Bullitt. "They are accurate. I don't dispute the logic of your reasoning." But the President made it clear that he did not intend to follow Bullitt's advice:

> *I just have a hunch that Stalin is not that kind of man. Harry [Hopkins] says he's not and that he doesn't want anything but security for his country, and I think that if I give him everything I possibly can and ask nothing from him in return,* noblesse oblige, *he won't try to annex anything and will work with me for a world of democracy and peace.*

Bullitt retorted that Stalin was "a Caucasian bandit whose only thought when he got something for nothng was that the other fellow was an ass," but Roosevelt cut him off: "It's my responsibility and not yours; and I'm going to play my hunch."

As was often the case with Roosevelt, his "hunch" was based on sound reasoning. No one could yet exclude the possibility that Stalin, if pressed too hard, might make a separate peace with Hitler. Even if the Russian dictator did agree to support American war aims, there could be no assurance that he would keep his promise. Furthermore, Roosevelt was extremely conscious of the limits of American power. United States troops could not counteract Russian moves in Eastern Europe without imposing unacceptable demands on the nation's manpower pool and productive facilities—already stretched to the limit by simultaneous operations against Germany and Japan. Such a maneuver would also endanger prospects for Soviet assistance in the Far East, which American military leaders badly wanted.

Finally, the President felt certain that public opinion would not tolerate keeping United States forces overseas after the war, a clear necessity if Soviet influence was to be contained. Roosevelt therefore rejected Bullitt's suggestion that he reorient military strategy in accordance with postwar poltical objectives. Instead he concentrated on achieving total victory over the Axis, trusting that a mutual desire to avoid further conflict would compel Russians and Americans to coexist peacefully after the war.

Roosevelt failed to see, however, how his strategy for winning the war might undermine his effort to build trust between Washington and Moscow. FDR sought to defeat the Axis through the maximum possible use of American industrial power, but with the minimum possible expenditure of American lives. Such a policy precluded launching military operations when chances for success were not high. Yet to the Russians, who did not enjoy the luxury of deciding where and how they would fight Germany, a "blood sacrifice" in the form of an early second front seemed the acid test of Anglo-American intentions. Roosevelt led the Russians to expect such a front in Europe in 1942, but then endorsed a British proposal to invade North Africa, thereby delaying the full cross-channel attack until 1944. At the time, each decision appeared to be in the best interests of the anti-Axis coalition, but the two-year gap between promise and performance convinced the Russians that their capitalist comrades had decided to let them carry the main burden of the war. The resulting atmosphere of suspicion was hardly conducive to Roosevelt's "grand design" for placing postwar Soviet-American relations on a firm basis of mutual understanding. . . .

Roosevelt's second-front diplomacy, in both Europe and the Far East, reflected his overall strategy of seeking victory over the Axis as quickly as possible with the minimum possible loss of American lives. Despite the Soviet Union's minor role in the war against Japan, this strategy paid off handsomely in Europe. For three years, from June of 1941 to June of 1944, the Soviet Union carried the main burden of the fight against Hitler. On the day Anglo-American forces established the long-awaited second front in Normandy, the Red Army was still confronting more than 250 German and satellite divisions along the thousand-mile eastern front. British and American troops, in France and Italy, faced less than 90 divisions. Partly because of Russian military successes, the United States Army got through the war with less than half the number of divisions prewar plans had indicated would be necessary for victory. Casualty figures reflect with particular vividness the disproportionate amount of fighting which went on in the east. A conservative estimate places Soviet war deaths—civilian and military—at approximately 16 million. Total Anglo-American losses in all theaters came to less than a million.

But Roosevelt's reluctance to incur heavy American casualties could not help but undermine his plans for postwar cooperation with the USSR. The long delay in establishing the second front confirmed Soviet fears that their capitalist allies had deliberately let communist Russia bear the brunt of the fighting. As a result, the suspicion with which Stalin had always viewed his Anglo-American associates intensified considerably. Convinced that they had won the war, the Russians showed little inclination to compromise on major postwar objectives which the West found unacceptable. Roosevelt probably felt that he had no other choice—the American people would not have supported sacrificial operations to meet the Russian timetable for a second front. Given ideological differences, it seems likely that the Russians would still have distrusted their allies, even if the Anglo-Americans had hurled their forces against Hitler's Europe in 1942. But by promising such a maneuver in 1942, and then delaying it until 1944, Roosevelt needlessly aggravated Soviet hostility toward the West, thereby imperiling his own hopes for the postwar world.

. . . The President had sought to make Stalin trust him, feeling that only in this way could postwar Soviet-American cooperation be assured. To this end, he had furnished the Russians with lend-lease supplies on an unconditional basis, had twice traveled halfway around the world to meet with the Soviet leader, and had incurred considerable political risk at home in order to satisfy Moscow's postwar territorial demands. Yet Roosevelt refused to pay the one price which might, but only might, have convinced Stalin of his sincerity—the massive American casualties which would have been necessary to establish an early second front. There were limits to how far even Roosevelt could go in trying to overcome Soviet suspicion. While the bankruptcy of his policy of openhandedness was not fully apparent at the time of his death, events such as Berne made it seem unlikely that Roosevelt, had he lived, would have continued it much longer.

In contrast to their confusion over Germany, Washington officials knew what they wanted in Eastern Europe: maximum possible self-determination for the people of that region without impairing the unity of the Grand Alliance. Unfortunately these two goals—both fundamental elements in the American program for preventing future wars—conflicted with each other. Stalin had made it clear since the summer of 1941 that he would not tolerate hostile states along his western border, yet in most of Eastern Europe free elections, if held, would produce governments unfriendly to Moscow. The existence of two clear objectives thus did not simplify the task of Roosevelt and his advisers, because both could not be attained. A choice would have to be made, in the light of American interests, between self-determination for Eastern Europe and cooperation with the Soviet Union.

With characteristic optimism, Roosevelt hoped he could avoid making this decision. Throughout the war he worked to convince the East Europeans that they had nothing to fear from Russia and that they could afford to choose governments acceptable to Moscow. Simultaneously he sought to persuade Stalin that the defeat and disarmament of Germany, together with maintenance of big-power unity into the postwar period, would do more to guarantee Soviet security than would territorial gains and spheres of influence in Eastern Europe. If a choice became inevitable, however, Roosevelt knew in which direction he would move. Self-determination he had always regarded as an ideal to be striven for, but not practically attainable in all situations. Cooperation with the Soviet Union, though, was essential both to win the war and to keep the peace after victory. By the end of 1943, the President had cautiously indicated to the Russians that they could count on a free hand in Eastern Europe.

At the same time, however, the President hoped that Stalin would be discreet, for any appearance of abandoning self-determination would cause FDR serious political problems inside the United States. Several million Polish-Americans might defect from the Democratic Party in 1944, endangering Roosevelt's chances for reelection. Even more important, any flagrant violations of the Atlantic Charter might give critics of international organization sufficient ammunition to kill American participation in the United Nations, just as Wilson's departures from the Fourteen Points a quarter-century earlier had con-

FIGURE 5. The ultimate realism: the Big Three shape the postwar world.
(© *Punch* 1943).

tributed to the Senate's rejection of the League of Nations. For these
reasons, Roosevelt felt that he could not publicly back away from his
promises of a peace settlement which would allow the people of
Europe to determine their own future, even though he knew that
the likelihood of this happening in countries bordering Russia was
small

But by failing to prepare the American people for Stalin's demands in Eastern Europe, Roosevelt inadvertently undermined the domestic consensus necessary for his postwar policy of cooperation with the Soviet Union. Having been led by the President's own rhetoric to expect self-determination everywhere, Americans reacted angrily when the Soviet Union proceeded to extract territorial concessions from its neighbors, and to impose spheres of influence on them. Interpreting these actions as first steps in a renewed bid for world revolution, Americans, lessons of the past firmly in mind, gradually came to regard Stalin as an aggressor with unlimited ambitions who, like Hitler, would have to be resisted and contained.

*   *   *

Roosevelt may well have expected the Russians to allow free elections in Poland and the rest of Eastern Europe. The habit of wartime collaboration was still alive, and the readiness of the Russians at Yalta to promise these elections had been encouraging. When it began to look as though Moscow was stalling, the President became concerned. He never wavered, however, in his insistence that governments installed in power along Russia's borders be "friendly" to the Soviet Union. FDR's superficial knowledge of Eastern Europe kept him from fully realizing the contradiction between freely elected and pro-Russian governments in that turbulent part of the world. It was like a labor-management conflict in the United States, he once told Polish Prime Minister Mikolajczyk: all that was necessary was an impartial mediator to prod the negotiations along. But whatever his expectations, the President by his actions had led the American people to expect free elections in Eastern Europe, while at the same time leading the Russians to expect a free hand. The peculiar mixture of naiveté and realism which characterized Roosevelt's East European policy had created a painful dilemma, which it would now be up to Harry S Truman to resolve.

American diplomats had never really divorced political considerations from the question of financing postwar reconstruction in the Soviet Union. Ambassador Harriman consistently regarded aid to Russia as "one of our principal levers for influencing political action compatible with our principles." But during 1943 and 1944, most discussions of this subject had taken place within a primarily economic framework.

The main benefit which Washington expected to receive from the proposed loan to Russia—full peacetime employment—was economic in nature, as were the principal factors impeding the extension of credits—the difficulty of ensuring repayment and the existence of legal restrictions on foreign lending. But by January of 1945, when the Russians again raised the question of a postwar loan, the atmosphere had changed. As the approach of victory exposed conflicts of interest with the Soviet Union, particularly in Eastern Europe and Germany, Washington officials came to feel that the political advantages of withholding the loan might well surpass the profits to be gained from extending it.

On January 3, 1945, Russian Foreign Minister Molotov told Harriman that if the United States would extend to the Soviet Union a $6 billion loan at an interest rate of 2.25 percent, the Soviet government would place large orders for capital equipment in the United States. Molotov pointedly reminded Harriman of "the repeated statements of American public figures" that such large orders would ease the American economy's transition from war to peace. Coming with no previous warning, the Russian "offer" surprised the American ambassador, who considered it "extraordinary both in form and substance."

Nevertheless, Harriman advised the Department of State to disregard the unconventional form and unreasonable terms of Molotov's proposal, ascribing them to "ignorance of normal business procedures and the strange ideas of the Russians on how to get the best trade." The United States, he felt, should do everything it could through the extension of credits to help the Russians develop a sound economy. Friendly postwar relations would depend to some extent on American assistance in solving Russian reconstruction problems. Moreover, the sooner the Soviet government could provide a decent life for its people, the more tractable it would become. At the same time, the United States should make it quite clear to the Russians "that our willingness to cooperate with them . . . will depend upon their behavior in international matters." Washington should retain full control of any credits granted to Moscow in order to derive from them the maximum political advantages.

Meanwhile, and apparently coincidentally, Treasury Secretary Morgenthau was reviving his department's plan for extending credits to Russia. In a letter to Roosevelt early in January, he proposed giving the Russians a loan of $10 billion at 2 percent interest for the purchase of American products. The Russians would repay the loan mainly by exporting strategic raw materials, with amortization to extend over a period of thirty-five years.

But Morgenthau encountered unsympathetic responses from both President Roosevelt and Secretary of State Stettinius when he talked this matter over with them on January 10, 1945. Roosevelt did not want to discuss credits with the Russians until after the forthcoming Yalta Conference, and seemed to favor using them as a device to extract concessions on other issues: "I think it's very important that we hold this back and don't give them any promises of finance until we get what we want." Later that day Morgenthau remarked to Stettinius that in dealing with the Russians one should offer the carrot and not the stick. Stettinius replied: "Henry, I don't think you'd feel that way if you knew all . . . if you had all the chips before you." On the following day Roosevelt told a group of senators that the loan might be a strong bargaining point to use in dealings with the Soviet Union, and that he had decided to take no action on the Russian request until he had talked to Stalin.

The State Department now began to formulate a response to the suggestions of both the Russians and Morgenthau. Emilio G. Collado, chief of the Division of Financial and Monetary Affairs, did much to establish the department's position. Collado did not attempt to evaluate the wisdom of extending the loan itself, but emphasized the domestic political and economic difficulties it would entail. Congressmen would almost certainly balk at legislating credits for either the Soviet Union or Great Britain. Morgenthau's plan to use the Russian loan to obtain stockpiles of strategic raw materials would not arouse enthusiasm on Capitol Hill, but would antagonize petroleum and mining interests. Consequently credits, if granted, would have to be extended through the Export-Import Bank, where special legislation would not be required. But this approach too would create problems, for Congress would have to extend the bank's lending authority before it could make a substantial loan. The lowest rate of interest which the bank could charge without discriminating against other borrowers was 4 percent, a rate almost twice what the Russians had proposed to pay. Collado admitted that a loan could benefit Soviet-American political relations, but thought that the economic boost it would give to American industry had been exaggerated. . . .

The administration therefore postponed action for the second time on a Soviet loan request, evidently with the intention of extracting political concessions. Ironically, Treasury Secretary Morgenthau's simultaneous proposal probably stiffened State Department opposition to the idea. Top State Department officials still strongly resented Morgenthau's recent attempts to influence policy on Germany, and doubtless bristled automatically at this new Treasury incursion into diplomacy. When James F. Byrnes became secretary of state in July, 1945, he expressed the general departmental attitude by placing Morgenthau's proposal in the "Forgotten File," taking time only to muse that "our Treasury officials were not always the cold-hearted, glassy-eyed individuals all bankers are supposed to be."

Meanwhile, the administration's efforts to arrange for the orderly termination of Lend-Lease had collapsed, owing to the obstinacy of the Russians. During the spring of 1944, the United States government had proposed that the Soviet Union comply with congressional requirements by providing reimbursement for Lend-Lease materials used in postwar reconstruction. The Roosevelt Administration offered to lend the Russians whatever amount of money was necessary to pay for these goods, at an interest rate of 2⅜ percent for thirty years. Moscow accepted the basic outline of this arrangement, but balked at the interest rate. Negotiations bogged down, and the Russians refused to sign the Fourth Lend-Lease Protocol, covering shipments of supplies from July of 1944 through June of 1945. This in no way impeded the flow of Lend-Lease goods to Russia, but it did delay agreement on how to distinguish between items of purely military value and those potentially useful for reconstruction.

Both Roosevelt's advisers and congressional leaders were demanding with increasing regularity that such a distinction be made. Ambassador Harriman and General Deane repeatedly warned from Moscow that the Russians were taking advantage of American generosity by ordering more material under Lend-Lease than they needed to fight the war. *Newsweek* reported in August, 1944, that senators who had never criticized the use of Lend-Lease in wartime were now planning to oppose its use for reconstruction. Secretary of War Stimson pleaded with Roosevelt in October not to try to employ Lend-Lease supplies for postwar rehabilitation without securing new congressional authorization. Lauchlin Currie, one of Roosevelt's administrative assistants, warned him early in 1945 that "should the Russo-German war end and Russia *not* be at war with Japan, there will be great pressure from Congress and the press to cease lend-lease unless Russia goes to war with Japan."

When the annual lend-lease extension bill came before the House of Representatives in March of 1945, Representative John Vorys, Republican of Ohio, introduced an amendment categorically prohibiting the use of Lend-Lease for postwar relief, rehabilitation, or reconstruction. Worried over congressional suspicions regarding the use of Lend-Lease after the war, the Roosevelt Administration decided not to oppose the Vorys Amendment, which had attracted considerable support from Republicans and some Democrats. Foreign Economic Administrator Crowley instead suggested a compromise which would forbid use of Lend-Lease for reconstruction but would allow recipient nations to obtain all goods contracted for provided they paid for what arrived after the end of the war. The Foreign Affairs Committee unanimously approved this arrangement, advising the full House of Representatives that such a clear expression of congressional intent would prevent future misunderstandings. Representative Karl Mundt told the House that "with this amendment added, there can be no post-war economic activities by Lend-Lease except through the most flagrant violation of the intent of Congress." The amended version of the Lend-Lease Extension Bill passed the House on March 13, 1945.

The Foreign Economic Administration now recommended withdrawing the American proposal to let the Russians order reconstruction materials through the still unsigned Fourth Protocol. Instead the government should adopt a new policy, in line with the wishes of Congress, which would see to it that the Soviet Union did not receive significant amounts of heavy industrial equipment under Lend-Lease after the war. Ambassador Harriman approved this idea, pointing out that many of the arguments which a year earlier had caused him to recommend making American goods available for Russian rehabilitation were no longer present. On March 23, 1945, President Roosevelt officially approved the FEA's suggestion.

When the Senate took up Lend-Lease extension early in April, it showed that it felt even more strongly than the House about the postwar uses of Lend-Lease. One group of senators regarded the Crowley-Vorys compromise as a clever loophole designed precisely to conceal the employment of Lend-Lease for reconstruction. Their attempt to remove this provision from the bill, thereby cutting off all Lend-Lease upon the termination of hostilities, failed on a 39-39 tie vote. On April 17, 1945, President Truman signed the amended Lend-Lease bill into law. The mood of Congress impressed itself vividly on the new chief executive. Truman regarded European reconstruction as a cause worthy of American assistance, but felt that this assistance should come through the Export-Import Bank. "If we undertook to use any Lend-Lease money for rehabilitation purposes we would open ourselves to Congressional criticism."

Roosevelt's decision not to allow the Russians to obtain reconstruction materials through Lend-Lease, and his reluctance to discuss a postwar loan "until we get what we want," do not indicate that the President was about to give up his long-standing policy of cooperation with the Soviet Union at the time of his death. They do suggest, however, that recent developments—the Berne incident, the quarrel over German reparations, the Polish and Rumanian crises—had convinced him that appeals to "world opinion" or "high morality" alone would not move Stalin. In order to get the Russians to go along with the American postwar peace program, firm but friendly pressure would have to be applied, in much the same way that the United States had dealt with its British ally since 1941. Holding back aid to Russian reconstruction was one of the few means which Washington had of applying such pressure. Roosevelt's successor in the White House went on to implement this policy, but in a manner far less tactful than the smooth and sophisticated squire of Hyde Park would have employed.

Gaddis Smith

FDR AND COOPERATION WITH THE SOVIET UNION—FOOLISH OPTIMISM

Gaddis Smith, professor of history at Yale University and author of Britain's Clandestine Submarines, 1914–1915 *(1964), and* Dean Acheson *(1972), one of the volumes in the series* American Secretaries of State, *wrote a survey,* American Diplomacy during the Second World War, 1941–1945, *which typifies the approach taken by most traditional studies written since the end of the war. Although Smith criticizes certain of Roosevelt's decisions and points to the gap between stated ideals and actual practice, he clearly believes that the American attempt to create a cooperative relationship with the Soviet Union was based upon a foolishly optimistic belief that the Russians would be reasonable and cooperative. In short, the origins of the cold war lay primarily with Soviet actions and policies.*

A factor that influenced the style and results of American wartime diplomacy as well as the nation's optimistic interpretation of the past was the personality of President Roosevelt. He took crucial diplomatic negotiations more completely into his own hands than any president before or since. One way to examine Roosevelt's qualities as a diplomat is to compare him with Woodrow Wilson. There was nothing cheerful about Wilson's solemn crusade of Christian good against the forces of evil. Roosevelt, in contrast, always gave the appearance of a happy man, sometimes to the point of an unbecoming and inappropriate frivolity. Wilson found it hard to like the individuals with whom he was forced to deal; Roosevelt's first instinct was to like everybody. Wilson was solitary; Roosevelt loved the crowd, huge parties, the feeling of presiding over a numerous family.

Associates found both Wilson and Roosevelt difficult to work with, but for different reasons. Wilson enjoyed admitting that he had a "one track mind." For long periods he would concentrate on a single issue and ignore others of equal importance. Roosevelt's mind, in contrast, was trackless. He would dabble in a dozen questions simultaneously and acquire a superficial acquaintance with thousands of details in which Wilson would have had no interest. Subordinates found it difficult to keep Roosevelt's mind focused for long on any one problem. He loved to ramble and he seldom studied deeply.

Wilson was stubborn and opinionated; his dislike for advice that did not conform with his own conclusions often became dislike for the adviser. Roosevelt, on the other hand, had a compulsion to be liked. In dealing with others he would feign agreement with an opinion rather than produce disappointment. In domestic politics this habit of trying to please everyone caused confusion but no lasting harm. When Roosevelt's final views on an issue emerged, the man who had been misled could resign. Many did.

But this Rooseveltian technique had doleful results when applied to international affairs, where all the favorable conditions that Roosevelt enjoyed at home were missing. Disagreements in domestic affairs were over means, not basic objectives. All Americans desired a healthy economy, an end to unemployment, and a broadening of security among the whole population. There were no disagreements that could not be faced and thrashed out by reasonable men of good will. But how different the conduct of international affairs, especially in the emergency conditions of a world war. The nations in uneasy coalition against the Axis disagreed not only on the means of winning the war, but also on fundamental objectives for the future. Differences were too profound to be dissolved by geniality, and disgruntled allies, unlike subordinates, could not be ignored. Roosevelt either forgot these truths, or else believed that his power to make friends was so irresistible that all opposition could be charmed out of existence. He was wrong.

There was another unfortunate connection between domestic politics and Roosevelt's diplomacy. As the most successful American politician of the century, Roosevelt had a superb sense of how much support he could command for his domestic programs. But in his understanding of what the people would accept in foreign affairs he was timid and unsure. Often he shied away from problems that needed to be confronted—Russian treatment of Poland, for example —because he feared that publicity might lose votes. He overestimated the strength of isolationism and underestimated the ability of the American people to absorb bad news and undertake new responsibility. As a result Roosevelt sometimes gave the public a falsely optimistic picture of our diplomacy, especially in regard to Russia and China. He also gave the Russians the impression that the United

States would probably withdraw into partial isolation after victory and that Russia, therefore, need not worry about American opposition to her postwar ambitions in Europe.

Two further traits of Roosevelt's character should be noted. The President had a small boy's delight in military and naval problems. Under the Constitution he was commander in chief of the armed forces and he set out to give practical as well as theoretical meaning to the title. Much of his time was spent in close consultation with military and naval authorities. Usually, he took the advice of the chiefs of staff, but on occasion he made important military decisions independently. Roosevelt's fascination with strategy and tactics intensified the American emphasis on military objectives to the neglect of those long-range political conditions to which military operations should always be subordinate. For example, in 1944 and 1945 Roosevelt concentrated so hard on the military objective of bringing Russia into the war against Japan that he seriously weakened American bargaining power in the settlement of permanent political objectives in Europe and Asia.

Finally, Roosevelt, unlike Wilson, was a pragmatist who lived in a world in which good and bad were somewhat mixed. He had no qualms about further blending the two, and for settling by way of compromise for the best that seemed available. Roosevelt was no metaphysician losing sleep by wondering if evil means could contaminate a worthy end. He was more inclined to act and let the historians worry about the philosophical problems involved in his behavior. The historian must conclude, however, that much of Roosevelt's diplomacy fails of justification even on its own terms. Too often the means were questionable and the results worse.

Roosevelt's character produced the worst results in his diplomacy with Stalin; with Churchill the best. Churchill and Roosevelt enjoyed the closest personal and official relationship that has ever existed between an American president and the head of another government. It was not, however, a relationship of equality. Roosevelt had the power and Churchill the ideas. Churchill, acutely aware of the British Empire's dependence on the United States, kept Roosevelt informed and entertained with an almost daily stream of incomparably lucid and persuasive letters and telegrams. Frequently, he traveled to meet Roosevelt in Washington, at Hyde Park, or in Canada. Roosevelt never went to Churchill in Great Britain, although both Roosevelt and

Churchill did meet Stalin on or near his home ground. Churchill's sincere liking for Roosevelt, his understanding of the President's character, and above all the range and penetration of his intellect served the British Empire and the Anglo-American cause well. No other man could have won Roosevelt's approval to such a large measure of British policy. But sometimes Roosevelt and his advisers did refuse Churchill's requests. On those occasions Churchill gave way with a grace that was as uncharacteristic of his past political behavior as it was serviceable for the preservation of the even tenor of Anglo-American relations.

Roosevelt's personal relations with Stalin were the least effective aspect of his diplomacy. The President met Stalin's displays of temper, suspicion, and churlish obstructionism with redoubled efforts at conciliation. Early in the war he tried to please Stalin by an implied promise of an immediate second front, and later he remained silent in the face of barbarous Soviet conduct in Poland. Sometimes he tried to win Stalin's confidence by ridiculing Churchill and hinting at a Soviet-American alignment against British colonialism. In personal relations and in diplomacy it is unwise and dangerous to pretend to denounce a proven friend in order to ingratiate oneself with a third party. Churchill bore the humiliation manfully; Stalin was not fooled. He listened to Roosevelt's chatter, said little himself, and coolly pushed the Soviet advantage in Europe and Asia without regard to the idealistic principles of political liberty to which Russia, as one of the United Nations, had subscribed. Stalin acted on the assumption, which Roosevelt's words and behavior amply confirmed, that the United States would raise no effective opposition to hostile Russian expansion. By the time Roosevelt's policy was reversed after the war, the Russian position had been consolidated, and the lines of the cold war drawn.

The results of Roosevelt's personal diplomatic contact with the proud and haughty leaders who ranked just below the triumvirate, Chiang Kai-shek of China and Charles de Gaulle of France, were poor. Chiang and de Gaulle were similar in many ways. Each claimed to represent a great power suffering from temporary adversity; each was quick to resent the slightest reflection on his personal prestige or the sovereign prerogatives of his nation. Roosevelt, however, treated the two leaders in opposite fashion, acting more in terms of his preconceived notions about France and China than the actual situation. The President was an infatuated captive of the myth that China under Chiang Kai-shek was one of the world's great powers and deserved to be treated as such. He even toyed with the idea of giving Chiang a voice in the settlement of European affairs. No amount of evidence concerning Chiang's maladministration, the disunity of the country, the strength of the opposition, or the inefficiency of the Kuomintang armies appeared capable of shaking Roosevelt's illusion, at least until the closing months of the war.

For modern France, in contrast, Roosevelt had acquired an attitude of contempt as extreme as his admiration for China. He considered France a source of decay in the world, a politically and socially sick nation which by lying down before Hitler and giving way to the Japanese in Indochina had forfeited the right to be respected. Roosevelt saw de Gaulle as a pompous adventurer who represented only a clique of followers and who secretly intended to assume the dictatorship of his country after the liberation. Ultimately, Roosevelt's attitudes led to severe friction with France and to bitter misunderstandings on the part of the American people when Chiang Kai-shek collapsed so ignominiously in his civil war with the Communists.

Although wartime diplomacy, pervasively influenced by the personality of President Roosevelt, dealt principally with military operations, one overriding question was always present: what kind of world did each of the three major allies desire after the war? Each power sought, first of all, a victory that would prevent recurrence of a war as catastrophic as the one in which the world was then involved. American leaders gradually developed among themselves some broad ideas on how this might be done, but they believed that their objectives could be best achieved if specific discussions concerning the future were postponed until the fighting was over. Assuming that no postwar problem could be as important or difficult as the defeat of the Axis and that there would be time enough after victory to make detailed arrangements, they were insensitive to the way in which the conduct of war can prejudice the results.

From the American point of view, there were several ways that the goal of postwar security might be sought. Isolation had failed and was now discredited, more thoroughly than Roosevelt realized. A unilateral armed *Pax Americana* in which every threat to security was instantaneously smashed by the exercise of the superior force of the United States was technically worth considering, but was not politically or morally tolerable. A *Pax Anglo-Americana* in which the United States and Great Britain together ran the world had appeal for some Americans, and briefly for President Roosevelt, but it, too, was not feasible. Roosevelt until 1944 favored a peace secured by the armed cooperation of "the Four Policemen": the United States, Russia, China, and Great Britain—in that order of importance. Little countries would be required to keep quiet and take orders. This concept had numerous flaws. A power vacuum would be left in Western Europe where, according to Roosevelt, neither Germany nor France would again be factors in world politics. This would be especially dangerous if Roosevelt's assumption of an identity of interest between Russia and the West proved unfounded. In Asia there was considerable doubt whether the Chiang Kai-shek regime in China could survive, much less serve as a policeman for others. In addition, the outcry of small nations at being herded about by the great powers would be too loud to ignore in the United States and Great Britain, countries which prided themselves on respecting the rights of others.

Churchill felt that Roosevelt intended to relegate Great Britain to a position of undeserved and unrealistic inferiority while encouraging the disintegration of the British Empire, a development which Churchill resisted with skill and energy. The Prime Minister's own program for securing the peace was equally objectionable to most Americans. Churchill, a strong believer in the traditional British reliance on the balance of power, assumed that the fate of Europe still determined the fate of the world; that there was a basic conflict of interest between Russia and the West; that these differences should be faced openly and realistically; that Western Europe had to be rehabilitated as quickly as possible with France and eventually Germany rejoining the continent's power structure; that the United States ought to cooperate with Britain in rebuilding Europe and be prepared, if necessary, to oppose Russian ambitions. Churchill believed that colonial peoples should receive increased self-government, but that the imperial powers should continue to exercise responsibility for their colonies in the interests of world stability.

Roosevelt abandoned the concept of "the Four Policemen" in favor not of Churchill's balance of power program but in response to the rising enthusiasm in the United States for the formation of a universal collective security organization, the United Nations. Secretary of State Cordell Hull, for example, argued that postwar antagonism between Russia and the West was unthinkable and that a third world war was the only conceivable alternative to full cooperation. Great power cooperation must be embedded in a world organization, a resurrection of the Wilsonian League of Nations. From 1944 onward Roosevelt and his advisers were fully committed to the early establishment of the United Nations as the only way to lasting peace. They became increasingly suspicious of Churchill's ideas. Ironically, many Americans came to believe that British imperialism and continued adherence to the idea of the balance of power were greater threats to security than anything Soviet Russia might do.

This does not mean that American leaders were hostile to Great Britain; rather they looked upon Britain as a misguided friend unfortunately wedded to dangerous and outmoded patterns of behavior. It was the duty of the United States to set this friend right for her own good and the good of the world. Russia, in contrast, was seen as the unfairly maligned giant, a bear too long harassed by an unsympathetic world. Russia had been so badly treated in the past that it was now necessary for the United States and Great Britain to make an extra effort to be warm and understanding. Roosevelt and many of his advisers believed that inwardly the Soviets yearned to be friends with the West, but were too scarred with unhappy memories to take the initiative. Russia's enormous loss of life in the war, approximately ten times Anglo-American losses, strongly reinforced the sympathetic American attitude. How callous it seemed to think ill of a nation that was suffering so horribly in what Americans thought of as the common cause of humanity against the barbaric Axis. In the face of this suffering, to treat Russia as a potential adversary, as the British were inclined to do, would perpetuate the atmosphere of suspicion.

While Roosevelt, Churchill, and their advisers privately wrestled with different theories for the maintenance of peace, the official public declaration of Anglo-American war aims remained the Atlantic Charter, a generalized statement drafted by the two leaders in August 1941, and subsequently accepted by all countries joining the war against the Axis. The Atlantic Charter denied that its adherents sought self-aggrandizement; it condemned territorial changes against the will of the peoples concerned, and favored self-government, liberal international trading arrangements, freedom from fear and want, and permanent security against aggression. Soviet Russia adhered to the charter with the capacious qualification that "the practical application of these principles will necessarily adapt itself to the circumstances, needs, and historic peculiarities of particular countries." In other words, Russia would not be deflected in the slightest by the charter from the pursuit of her own aims in her own way.

Roosevelt thought that Russia wanted nothing but security from attack and that this could easily be granted. Personally uninterested in theory and president of a country where ideological passion was out of style, Roosevelt tended to assume that national security meant approximately the same thing in Moscow as it did in Washington. Unfortunately, even the Russians could not say where the line lay between the normal requirements of national security and the imperatives of Communist ideology. Russia's minimum territorial objectives in Europe were clearly stated. They included restoration of the June 1941 boundary, which meant that Russia would enjoy the full fruits of the 1939 Nazi-Soviet Pact, specifically the annexation of the three Baltic states, nearly half of prewar Poland, and pieces of Finland and Rumania. Germany was to be dismembered into a cluster of weak separate states and hunks of territory were to be given to Poland and Russia. Politically, Russia insisted on "friendly" governments along her central European borders. In practice this came to mean Communist regimes imposed by totalitarian means. In Asia the Soviets sought the expulsion of Japan from the mainland and the restoration of Russia's position as it existed at the height of Tsarist imperial power in 1904. This would entail serious limitations on Chinese sovereignty in Manchuria.

The United States shared these aims as far as they applied directly to Germany and Japan, but everything beyond that was in actual or potential conflict with the Atlantic Charter. By postponing decisions on these conflicts, Roosevelt convinced himself that he was preventing discord with Russia without making concessions that violated the charter. But inwardly the President was quite prepared to concede these Russian aims on the assumption that once they were attained Russia would feel secure and would cooperate without reservations in the new world organization.

In retrospect it seems clear that Roosevelt's basic assumption was false. The evidence indicates that Soviet leaders believed that their state and ideology could never be secure as long as the world contained any large concentration of non-Communist power. Defensively they could assign no limits to the requirements of security; offensively they were under a compulsion rooted in Russian history as well as Communist ideology to expand the area of their domination wherever practical. Russian security and expansion were two sides of the same coin. A collective security organization was for the Russians an instrument to be joined or abandoned solely in terms of its usefulness in advancing Russian power in a world of irreconcilable conflict between capitalism and communism; it was not the beneficent organization of universal cooperation envisioned by the more idealistic Americans. . . .

That, in brief, was the optimistic background to the year's political discussions. The British, convinced of the necessity of making political plans, took the initiative by sending Foreign Secretary Eden to Washington in March 1943. The significant portion of the Eden conversations took place in the White House with Roosevelt and Harry Hopkins, who filled the role of secretary of state while unhappy Hull, the real secretary, was pushed farther into obscurity. The President's habit of excluding Hull from all important conversations meant that the professional officers of the State Department were isolated from the conduct of foreign policy. They worked hard, wrote detailed and often discerning memoranda, and made recommendations, but the President seldom acknowledged their existence.

Russia was the first topic in the White House talks with the British Foreign Secretary. Roosevelt asked Eden for an opinion on the thesis "that the Soviet Government was determined to dominate all of Europe by force of arms or by force of communist propaganda." Eden replied with an optimistic analysis which the British later abandoned. Stalin, he said, hoped for cooperation with the United States and Britain but "in any event a wise and expedient thing was to cultivate to the utmost . . . the friendship and confidence of the Soviet Government." Roosevelt agreed wholeheartedly. The conversation turned to Russia's territorial objectives. Eden said Stalin would insist on permanent annexation of the three Baltic states. Roosevelt answered that this was lamentable but also unpreventable. He hoped for the sake of appearances that Russia would conduct new plebiscites to show that the Baltic people wanted to be incorporated into the USSR. Next came some discussion of the friction between Russia and the Polish government-in-exile. It was agreed that the London Poles were troublemakers whose complaints and unreasonable demands were endangering relations with Russia. Roosevelt said that a Polish settlement would have to be dictated; "as far as Poland is concerned, the important thing is to set it up in a way that will maintain the peace of the world." This readiness to dictate to a small power reflected Roosevelt's conviction that the "Four Policemen" would run the world. He said there might be a world organization with general membership, "but . . . the real decisions should be made by the United States, Great Britain, Russia and China, who would . . . have to police the world." The President laid particular emphasis on the importance of strengthening China as the leading power in Asia. Eden disagreed and said he "did not much like the idea of the Chinese running up and down the Pacific." Positions were reversed in regard to France. Roosevelt said France should be disarmed and Eden said she should be restored as a European power. Germany, they both agreed, "must be divided into several states, one of which must, over all circumstances, be Prussia."

The conversations were rambling and inconclusive, but of great importance as a revelation of Roosevelt's attitudes. Many of his passing remarks to Eden were soon to broaden into basic themes of policy for the remainder of the war. Later decisions would be based on his easy faith in the possibilities of cooperation with Russia, his annoyance with the claims of small countries and especially Poland, his preference for a postwar world ruled by great powers, his exalting of China's potential and his antipathy to France, and his belief in the need to create a power vacuum in the heart of Europe in the place of Germany.

Roosevelt, who avoided bringing discordant topics into a conversation, did not mention to Eden one of the most significant aspects of his thinking: the idea, encouraged by several of his advisers, that Britain, rather than Russia, might be the principal disruptive force of the postwar world. The President had two vague anti-British apprehensions. First, he feared that the British might return to an old-fashioned scramble for political spheres of influence in Europe, thus frightening the Russians who were naturally sensitive about their security, and ultimately provoke a third world war. Roosevelt also believed that British imperialism, especially in India, would produce explosive unrest unless the colonial peoples were granted independence or placed under trusteeship in preparation for independence.

Notwithstanding Eden's insistence on the importance of cultivating Russian friendship, Roosevelt had many reasons for believing that a serious Anglo-Soviet rivalry for power in postwar Europe was a possibility. There was British procrastination over establishing the second front and reluctance to make sacrifices to maintain the flow of convoys to north Russia. There was also Churchill's obsession with Mediterranean operations that would contribute little to the quick defeat of Germany and his eagerness to restore the military power of France for questionable political reasons. Above all there was British history: the decades of anti-Bolshevism and the centuries of reliance on the bankrupt balance of power. Roosevelt believed that he could prevent this dangerous rivalry by convincing Stalin that the United States was an unselfish mediator interested only in preserving peace, and not an accomplice of Great Britain ready to "gang up" against Russia. Accordingly, the President suggested to Stalin that they meet alone for confidential talks free from the embarrassment of Churchill's presence. . . .

Although denied his meeting *à deux* with Stalin, Roosevelt continued until his death to seek a special personal relationship with the Soviet dictator and to court Russian approval by seeming to belittle his interest in Anglo-American ties. "The President's plan," an American diplomat who worked closely with Roosevelt has written, "was to make the Russians feel that the Americans trusted them implicitly and valued Soviet-American cooperation in war and peace above any other prospective alliance." Prime Minister Churchill described the same attitude as "a strong current of opinion in American Government circles, which seemed to wish to win Russian confidence even at the expense of coordinating the Anglo-American war effort."

*   *   *

One of the most somber aspects of the study of history is that it suggests no obvious ways by which mankind could have avoided folly. Would the postwar world have been a happier and more secure place for the United States and for all mankind if Roosevelt had behaved differently during the war? Possibly. It also might have been worse. Russia treated as an adversary rather than friend might, as men feared at the time, have reached a truce with Hitler. This seems unlikely, but the possibility was there. Or Stalin in the face of the type of opposition which Churchill recommended in 1945 might have acted with less rather than more restraint in Europe and Asia. Who knows?

The critic who denounced Roosevelt as a fool or worse and then says that such-and-such an alternative strategy in Europe and Asia, or both, would have altered the world for the better can never be convincing. In fairness to Roosevelt and his advisers, all that can be said is that they held too long to stereotypes about the United States and other nations and that they acted too often on the basis of hopes and illusion rather than ascertainable fact. If, as most men believed, it is usually wiser to base policies on as much fact as possible, then American leaders during the war were misguided. But even in saying this, one must be aware of the obstacles which stood in the way of finding facts and acting upon them during the war. Stereotypes are hard enough to avoid in ordinary times when men are free to reflect carefully about the world confronting them.

At the root of many American wartime stereotypes was a tendency to think about unfamiliar areas of the world in terms of historical analogies drawn from American experience. For example, Roosevelt knew very little about India but did not hesitate to suggest that Indians should imitate the history of the United States in the era of eighteenth-century struggle for independence from England. Similarly, the tendency to assume that other people and nations behaved like Americans prevented wartime leaders from understanding the depth of the internal disputes which plagued Poland and China. The facile transferral of American assumptions also led to serious miscalculations when Soviet leaders used words like "democracy," "freedom," and "independence." The next step was to ignore Russian history and Communist ideology and simply take it for granted that Soviet Russia and the United States, because they used the same words and because they both desired the defeat of the Axis, had identical expectations for the future.

Americans also held stereotyped views concerning the enemy. Unconditional surrender undoubtedly was the soundest policy to apply toward Hitler's Germany, but the simplicity of this phrase made it difficult to think of Germany in constructive ways. Hitler had brought misery to the world, but this did not lessen the fact that Europe would depend on the contributions of the German economy. Similarly, one could condemn Japan for her aggression in Asia and her sneak attack on the United States, but the simple application of unconditional surrender provided no answer to how Japan's positive role in the Asian economy would be filled. In the specific decision to drop the atomic bomb it would appear that Americans were convinced of the alleged suicidal fanaticism of the Japanese people and were prevented from seeing that Japan was close to surrender.

Perhaps the most persistent illusion of the war pertained to the probable future behavior of the United States. President Roosevelt and many others were obsessed by the unhappy national experience of 1917–1920 which seemed to prove that the American people would not tolerate permanent involvement in foreign affairs if that involvement required heavy expenditures or the risk of lives. This memory inhibited Roosevelt from contemplating postwar situations which necessitated sustained American involvement outside the Western Hemisphere. Under the general aegis of the United Nations, a cooperative Russia would maintain stability in Europe east of Germany. Britain would perform the same function in Western Europe where France was likely to cause trouble according to Roosevelt's stereotype. In Asia China might some day attain responsibility, but meanwhile much would depend, as in Europe, on the cooperative spirit of Russia.

Wilson's experience also stimulated a fervent dedication to the establishment of the United Nations, as a redemption of the ideal League of Nations and a painless instrument for lasting world peace. The naive enthusiasm generated throughout the United States for the United Nations during 1945 diverted the public's attention from the multiple unsolved problems facing the nation. Excessive faith in the United Nations may also have contributed to subsequent disillusionment and denigration of the many useful but limited tasks which the world organization is capable of handling.

Reliance on these stereotypes simplified the task of wartime leadership for President Roosevelt, but added immeasurably to the tasks of his successors. Two decades after Roosevelt's death American leaders still find it necessary to explain that the permanent solutions to international problems, which were implicit in the rhetoric of the Second World War, do not exist and that the preservation of peace and national security is onerous, never-ending, and expensive. That story, however, belongs to the historians of the cold war.

Diane S. Clemens

FDR AND COOPERATION WITH THE SOVIET UNION—THE COOPERATIVE RUSSIANS

The commonly held view of an uncooperative, paranoid Marshall Stalin has long been a staple of both traditional scholarship and American politics. No one has challenged that concept more directly than Diane Clemens, associate professor of history at the University of California at Berkeley. Although Clemens deals only with one small aspect of wartime diplomacy in her book Yalta, *which is the source of the following selection, her arguments have broad ramifications. She claims that Roosevelt, Churchill, and Stalin came to reasonable, amicable agreements during that famous wartime conference, but that domestic pressures and a general fear of Soviet expansion caused Churchill and Roosevelt to violate the bargains they had made. Instead of the greedy, grasping, ruthless Stalin usually pictured in books about the Yalta Conference, Clemens portrays him as firm, consistent, and concerned with assuring Soviet security through the establishment of a cooperative great-power system.*

The conclusions reached in this work differ from the conclusions reached by previous American diplomatic scholars—both of "orthodox" and "revisionst" persuasions—on the nature of several decisions made at Yalta. Here we will attempt, through a comparison with several representative and serious studies, to delineate these differences. After this, the negotiating positions of the three sides will be examined and charted. The points of discrepancy referred to in this chapter are illustrated graphically on the chart on page 286. [not reprinted]

John Snell, in *The Meaning of Yalta,* stated "the essential meaning of Yalta so far as Germany—and much of Europe—is concerned" was "how can the threat of German power be eliminated from Europe without leaving Soviet power dominant throughout the continent?" Snell intimated that this concern was reflected in the decisions of the conference. He argued specifically that "the Russians failed to win full satisfaction on a single one of the demands they raised at Yalta concerning Germany's future." Thus triumphed a "hard rock of Anglo-American solidarity" and a policy of "moderation toward Germany."[1]

[1] John Snell, "What to Do With Germany?" in John Snell (ed.), *The Meaning of Yalta* (Baton Rouge: Louisiana State University Press, 1966), p. 72.

Gabriel Kolko, in his recent book, *The Politics of War,* similarly viewed the decisions on Germany as a "substantial accomplishment for the Americans and English, who alone obtained tangible concessions, and above all secured Russian approval to the formal postponement of a German problem." Therefore, "Germany represented a success for the English and Americans."[2]

These conclusions about Yalta cannot be substantiated. The position of the President of the United States regarding Germany coincided in almost every instance with the Soviet position. In fact, as we have seen, America's, and to a lesser extent, Britain's, policy was the basis of Soviet policy itself. One can hardly visualize an Anglo-American "team," in this case: the conflict over Germany was as much between Churchill and Roosevelt as between Churchill and Stalin; Roosevelt and Stalin agreed. Certainly Roosevelt, who considered that he had made decisions on each one of the issues related to Germany, was not in this instance following a "policy of postponement." Further, Snell and Kolko assume a consistent Western anti-Soviet stance in the negotiations at Yalta. In fact, Yalta was more free of ideological content than has been supposed. The President did not follow a policy of "moderation toward Germany"; instead, he advocated harsh treatment of Germany. He sided with the Soviet Union *against* Great Britain on both dismemberment and reparations, with the result that Churchill acquiesced to a proposal on the first and agreed in principle to the second.

Snell, while citing the Soviet reparations plan as similar to the Morgenthau plan, hailed the Yalta reparations agreement as "a clear-cut rejection of the Morgenthau plan."[3] Yet the reparations agreement at Yalta, with only slight modifications, *was* the Soviet reparations proposal to which the United States agreed.

Snell claimed that Russia came out behind on reparations. Maisky, he wrote, weakened the concession received from Stettinius "by stating on February 10 that the proposed Russo-American draft 'did not commit the Allies to the exact figure'."[4] Since previous discussions and draftings of the protocol had always made clear that there was *no* exact figure, Maisky's remark must be seen as a restatement

---

[2] Kolko, *The Politics of War,* p. 356.
[3] Snell, "What to Do With Germany?" p. 58.
[4] Snell, "What to Do With Germany?" p. 61.

of the situation rather than a "weakening." The United States did not escape its responsibility; it endorsed the sum.

Snell concluded: "All in all, the reparations decisions were a thinly disguised defeat for the Russians." Roosevelt had "sidetracked the Soviet movement for American aid." He found that the "British and Americans put up a stiffer fight on reparations than on dismemberment," which was a victory for Roosevelt's policy, backed by Churchill, of "postponement."[5] This cannot be the case: the American delegation called the Soviet reparations plan reasonable and assured the Soviet Union that the United States supported it. Churchill and Eden disagreed but were unsuccessful in prying the Americans away from the Russians at Yalta. Their success in changing Roosevelt's policy came *after* Yalta. Further Soviet aid in other forms was hardly "sidetracked" at Yalta. The question was not officially raised by Stalin; however, Roosevelt did volunteer on February 8 that the United States intended to give substantial help to the USSR after the war.

The official Soviet history of the war made a blanket statement without qualifying the circumstances: "At Potsdam the United States refused to follow the Yalta 'agreement' on the establishment of a specific sum of German reparations ($20 billion), motivated by the fact that some parts of Germany suffered little destruction, namely, the parts occupied by the West." At Yalta this sum was agreed to as a basis of discussion or, in other words, it was agreed to establish it at a later date as a specific sum. As an indication of intention, the United States delegation did assure the Soviets that they found the sum equitable and intended to support it.

A harder look must be taken at the Soviet position on a French zone and French participation on the Allied Control Council. Herbert Feis, in *Churchill, Roosevelt, Stalin,* concluded that Russia resisted a zone for France "until the Conference was nearly over."[6] This is incorrect. On February 5, the first day France was discussed in tripartite session, Stalin at first followed Roosevelt's stand of the previous day and opposed a zone for France, but later that same day Stalin readily agreed to a French zone when Roosevelt did. Perhaps Feis had in mind the French role on the Allied Control Council, which was not decided until the final day of the conference. In this instance the

5 Snell, "What to Do With Germany?" pp. 57, 60.
6 Feis, *Churchill, Roosevelt, Stalin,* p. 532.

Soviet Union altered its position to harmonize with the Americans shortly after they learned what the President's position was.

In *The Politics of War* Kolko concluded, "Stalin was reluctantly prepared to let the English and American assign France an occupation zone." Stalin was a realist. He was prepared to grant the French a role; however, his reluctance was triggered by (and was perhaps entirely the result of) Roosevelt's stand. Kolko suggested: "The Allies resolved only one question pertaining to Germany at Yalta and that was France's role in the occupation." This is correct only in terms of *eventual* resolutions. In terms of the decisions made at Yalta, *two* questions were resolved—dismemberment and the role of France— and the basis of a third agreement—reparations—was created.

Forrest Pogue evaluated Stalin's strategy on the United Nations at Yalta in his essay, "The Big Three and the U.N." He found Stalin's policy "like Roosevelt's on Germany and Poland, one of postponement." In this framework he viewed Stalin's statement that he had not had time to study the Dumbarton Oaks proposals as a postponement tactic. Molotov "persisted in his postponement tactics" the next day in the foreign ministers' meeting. Finally Churchill, he claimed, adopted Stalin's postponement tactics.[7]

Although postponing agreement does of course entail a delay, this delay did not constitute a grand policy. Stalin's delay initially resulted from questions about applying the voting formula. Since the State Department had altered its proposal a number of times, both the British and Soviets (as well as Roosevelt before Yalta) were confused by it. Stettinius appeared to make a further last minute alteration in it the very day when Stalin allegedly implemented his strategy of postponement.

Stalin hesitated for two reasons. First, he sought assurance. He was perfectly willing to agree to the President's proposal provided it did not isolate or disadvantage the Soviet Union. Churchill's acceptance (hardly adopting Stalin's tactics of postponement) helped convince Stalin. *After* Stalin decided to announce his acceptance of the formula, Molotov remained quiet in the foreign ministers' meeting. At the plenary session acceptance of the voting formula was announced and it was linked to the Soviet proposal on Poland.

Second, there were two *quid pro quos* implicit in the United Na-

[7] Forrest C. Pogue, "The Big Three and the U.N.," in Snell, *The Meaning of Yalta*, pp. 176–178, 181.

tions issues. The first has already been mentioned above, i.e., Roosevelt's favorable response to the Soviet's Polish proposal in return for Stalin's acceptance of the voting formula. But there was also Britain's: the Soviet Union accepted the voting formula; in return Britain supported the admission of two (reduced from sixteen) Soviet Republics to the General Assembly. Molotov announced, "We paid much attention to what Churchill told us." Churchill cabled the War Cabinet that it was "due to our explanation that they had found themselves in a position to embrace the scheme whole-heartedly." He strongly urged the War Cabinet to authorize adding the Republics: "I should like to be able to make a friendly gesture to Russia in this matter."[8]

These *quid pro quos* have generally gone unnoticed. In fact, the whole change in the Soviet position is often ignored. For example, Feis dismissed the Soviet acceptance of the American formula with one sentence: "Of a sudden on the day after this discussion, the Soviet Government made a surprising change of front." After a paraphrase of Molotov's brief statement, Feis dropped the issue.

The decisions on Poland have generally been viewed unfavorably by American historians. A variety of reasons for the decisions have been provided, ranging from Roosevelt's "sell-out" to his ill-health, to his disinterest, to other such voluntaristic appraisals. Among deterministic evaluations there is that of Feis, who asserted, "They were paying the full price for coalition and Soviet military cooperation." Charles F. Delzell, in his essay in *The Meaning of Yalta,* concluded, "Obviously, it was not a question of what they would permit him to do but what they could persuade him to accept." Quoting Admiral William D. Leahy, he reminded his readers the Russians could take the "elastic" agreement and "stretch it all the way from Yalta to Washington without ever technically breaking it."[9] These deterministic accounts at least touch on the facts as they existed at the time of the conference.

Whatever the view one holds, another perspective must be considered in an appraisal of the Polish decision. The Soviet Union had been willing, for the sake of agreement with Britain, to come to terms with the Polish exile government, which was completely uncooperative and anti-Soviet. The London Poles had received verbal assur-

---

[8] Churchill, *Triumph and Tragedy,* pp. 359–360.
[9] Feis, *Churchill, Roosevelt, Stalin,* pp. 521, 553–554; Charles F. Delzell, "Russian Power in Central Eastern Europe," in Snell, *The Meaning of Yalta,* pp. 120, 124.

ances from President Roosevelt that led them to believe their cause and its anti-Bolshevistic aims would eventually triumph. But Roosevelt, playing with the London group for reasons of domestic politics, was unconcerned with Polish affairs. Believing they had American support, the London Poles would not negotiate; the Soviet Union finally turned to the Poles who *would* negotiate. The tragedy of Poland is less the agreement at Yalta than that no agreement was reached *before* Yalta. Further, when the United States decided to reject its own Yalta policy following Roosevelt's death, it virtually went to war—albeit a "cold" one—like Don Quixote fighting his windmills. Washington, not Moscow, prevented a settlement which might have left Europe intact rather than divided into blocs and camps. Both Churchill and Stalin were realists; Roosevelt was a moralist, with intermittent periods of realism. In terms of decisions, Yalta was a brief and reasonable interlude rather than a consistent feature of American foreign policy.

Gar Alperowitz, in *Atomic Diplomacy: Hiroshima and Potsdam,* advanced two hypotheses to which some exception must be taken. First, he suggested that Truman's foreign policy was basically a departure from Roosevelt's. Due to Roosevelt's ambivalence and vacillations, a case can certainly be made for this conclusion, especially if Yalta is taken as a typical example of Rooseveltian policy. However, Roosevelt in Washington and in conversations with his advisers demonstrated many of the views and attitudes that found a logical conclusion in the Truman Administration. It is hard to say in sum what Roosevelt's postwar policy would have been. Second, Alperowitz depicted the May 1945 talks between Harry Hopkins and Stalin as a new agreement or compromise. Actually, Hopkins's agreements with Stalin were Washington's *return* to the Yalta agreements, as Stalin well recognized. To some extent, there was before May a break between Truman and Roosevelt's Yalta policy. However, Hopkins' meeting with Stalin was not a compromise but an affirmation, albeit temporary, of the Yalta agreements. . . .

A study of these decisions as they were made at Yalta indicates that several conclusions can be made about the conference as a tripartite negotiating experience. Although the great powers differed in their initial viewpoints, a high incidence of consensus was reached at the conference. The Allied coalition, which had been primarily military in nature, produced at last an impetus to nonmilitary agreement among all three parties—on the assumption that consensus was in the best interest of each of the parties. Most importantly, each nation had an issue of prime importance to it, and each gained support from its other two Allies. Britain's insistence on reviving France in the creation of a Western bloc was agreed to by Roosevelt and Stalin; America's voting formula for the United Nations, the subject on which the United States spent much of its diplomatic effort during the war, did not meet the opposition Washington feared; the Soviet Union, which was determined to prevent another hostile Polish government on its borders, gained support for the Lublin Committee, although in a compromise form. But two Soviet desires, reparations and Poland's western frontier, remained unresolved, the former because of Churchill's instructions from the War Cabinet, and the latter because of an Anglo-American reluctance to make a frontier arrangement.

The conference functioned reasonably on the basis of balanced diplomatic interaction. Agreement between two parties tended to assure agreement of the third, even if the third party was reluctant: Stalin used Roosevelt's support for dismemberment and reparations, and his agreement to an expansion of the Lublin committee as the basis for the government of Poland, in order to force British concurrence. (In the case of reparations, only a two-way agreement resulted on the details, but a three-way agreement was achieved on the establishment of a Reparations Commission.) British support for admission of two Soviet Republics to the United Nations led Roosevelt (by his own admission) to accept that proposal. Stalin's acquiescence to a zone for France in Germany promptly followed a shift by Roosevelt to the same position. When it seemed apparent that Britain would accept the American voting formula in the United Nations, Stalin also concurred.

A review of the contents of original proposals, compared with subsequent proposals and final agreements, indicates that the Soviet Union in particular tended to incorporate compromises and suggestions in order to achieve agreement. During the conference the Soviet Union and the United States made six major proposals on prime topics and Britain made five. Of the five topics listed on the chart, the Soviet Union took the initiative on two issues, both on Germany and eventually a third, on Poland (although the first proposal came from Roosevelt). America took the initiative on one issue, and Britain on one. Considering the favorable military position of the Soviet Union as well as the disappointments of her earlier diplomatic encounters with the West, the Soviet Union showed a cooperative and conciliatory stance, which at the time of the conference was recognized by many participants.

Soviet "stubbornness" or "obstructionism" can be argued only if one accepts the hypothesis that the Soviet Union ought to have accepted as just and superior any proposal which differed from the Soviet position.

In retrospect, we see a diplomatic encounter in which all sides, not without misgivings and harsh words, struggled to achieve their aims, but an encounter in which they prized agreement by traditional negotiation as preferable to unilateral action which might undermine international stability. Herein lies the meaning of the Yalta agreements, which provided an alternative to a "cold war."

During World War II the United States was treading a path of expanding global "responsibility" and simultaneously fighting four wars to that end. The first was the military war against Germany, and the second the military war against Japan in the Pacific. The third was a struggle with Great Britain, allegedly to "defeat colonialism" (in American terms) but actually to determine which power would control Europe and Asia economically and politically. The last was the long-standing ideological struggle against "Bolshevist" Russia, which continued, though intermittently, during the war. That struggle increased in focus and intensity as the Soviet Union emerged from the war with great power status.

Although American policy reputedly rested on the high-minded priniciples of the Atlantic Charter, those principles were invoked mainly to ward off British or Soviet threats to American plans. During the war, cooperation, the cornerstone of wartime diplomacy, was sorely pressed. Roosevelt gave the Soviet Union several "opportunities" to demonstrate its cooperativeness. One critical "opportunity" came up in 1942, when the President invited Molotov to Washington to plan a second front for that year. Simultaneously Roosevelt encouraged the Soviet Union to drop the provision in the proposed Anglo-Soviet treaty which recognized the incorporation of the Baltic states into the Soviet Union. Molotov did so, and in return he received a written commitment for the invasion of France—which Roosevelt dropped when Churchill objected. At the same time the President seized the initiative on Stalin's request for a postwar guarantee of cooperation—Roosevelt began to plan the United Nations, a slightly updated League of Nations with its membership dominated by America's allies. (Russia, of course, had been expelled by the League after attacking Finland.)

By 1943, both Anthony Eden and Ivan Maisky were openly discussing the two policy alternatives which the Soviet Union would decide upon after the war: unilateral action, or cooperation with her Western Allies. Eden informed Washington that the Soviet Union preferred the latter course. Maisky emphatically affirmed this judgment. Washington hindered Great Britain from adjusting Anglo-Soviet policy and held out to the Soviet Union promises of postwar aid, cooperation, and amicable adjustments, while resolving nothing. The few tripartite negotiating experiences, such as the Italian surrender and the European Advisory Commission, raised serious questions about American intentions. On the other hand, the Soviet Union during the war remained basically cooperative. American officials complained of the frustrations of dealing with the Soviet central bureaucracy, but this did not constitute Soviet unwillingness to cooperate.

In the wake of Soviet military victories, Roosevelt at last decided it was time to resolve issues which he had postponed for three years. The Yalta Conference met with a sense of deliberation. It was to be a test of the ability of the three nations to resolve the issues dividing them. It was a moment when American ideology, normally submerged in moralistic phrases uncharacteristic of its actual behavior, was submitted to a traditional negotiating experience with binding results. Roosevelt and Churchill, when they met personally with Stalin, tended to treat the Soviet Union as the nation it was—an existing state with increasing influence in world affairs. The decisions at Yalta involved compromise by each nation, probably more by the Soviets than by the Western nations.

By abandoning the conference agreements after Yalta, America created a self-fulfilling prophecy. Believing that the Soviets intended to take advantage of any opportunity at the expense of the United States, Washington tried to renegotiate the zonal agreements and held Western troops in Soviet occupation zones as a political pressure tactic. Further, the American government changed its interpretation of the Yalta decisions on Poland. After deserting the original American-Soviet viewpoint, the United States accused the Soviet Union of breaking the Yalta agreements. Finally, the Allies decided, contrary to Yalta, not to support reparations. In doing so they abandoned the Soviet Union. These decisions, and many others, left the Soviet Union with no alternative than to substitute unilateral action for a policy of cooperation which they had hoped for, but which had never emerged —except briefly, at Yalta.

The Yalta Conference has been more condemned than commended by Western commentators. Under most of these condemnations lies the implicit and unexpressed premise that the Soviet Union is in essence evil while the West embodies the virtues of the ages; and, further, a belief that the Soviet Union has and can have no interests which the West considers legitimate. American policy during the war and afterward has been studied in terms of what the United States failed to do to foil Soviet aims, or else in terms of what the United States could have done to alter a decision acceptable to the Soviet Union. The policies based on this ideological bent attributed false motives to the Soviet Union and created a situation in which the Soviet Union increasingly defended herself from Western hostility.

Roosevelt's departure from America's moralistic and anti-Soviet bias, combined with Churchill's usually consistent realism, served diplomacy for the week the leaders met at Yalta. But the postwar world bears little resemblance to what these men worked to achieve. Broken promises, bad faith, misperceptions, and self-righteousness have forced new and different policies upon the nations. We are living with the problems of a world that did not benefit from the experience at Yalta.

It is perhaps relevant to ask what the world would have been like if the spirit of Yalta had triumphed.

Gabriel Kolko

FDR—ANTI-COMMUNIST CRUSADER

The differences between the interpretations offered in the four preceding selections are, to a great degree, a matter of emphasis. The four authors and the groups they represent generally accept a common body of factual knowledge and quarrel largely about the priorities to assign to the various goals and motives behind policy formulation. There are a number of scholars who work primarily outside the mainstream of most historical research. Many, including those whose work is reprinted in this and the following selection, use scholarly apparatus to justify their theses and conclusions, but they do not accept the same body of factual knowledge used by most other historians. Those on the extreme right and the radical left are usually accused, whether rightly or wrongly, of gross manipulation of evidence and overly selective use of data in order to make it fit preconceived themes. Of course, they claim that their critics are equally guilty of forcing the evidence to fit into the general structure of American liberalism. Even though the tendency among Americans is to split the difference between two extremes, both of these approaches have had a strong influence upon public and scholarly thought. Gabriel Kolko, professor of history at York University and an avowed radical, has studied recent American foreign policy extensively in three books; The Roots of American Foreign Policy (1969), The Limits of Power: The World and United States Foreign Policy, 1945–1954 (1972), and The Politics of War: The World and United States Foreign Policy, 1943–1945, from which the following selection is chosen. In it Kolko claims that American policy is based on three basic goals: suppression of the Left wherever it appeared, the maintenance of the Open Door for American trade and influence in Eastern Europe, and economic expansion at the expense of the British Empire.

To understand the role of the United States in World War II one must also understand that the American government had a series of immediate objectives, centered first of all around the desire to win battles and defeat the Axis, and an elaborate and highly sophisticated set of economic and political goals it defined as urgently desirable war aims. The interaction between the larger objectives of the United States and the world as the military and political leaders of the United States perceived it formed the vital context of the politics of World War II.

In considering World War II, and especially the years 1943–1945, there are three major issues, or themes, which subsume many, if not most, of the concerns of those in Washington who thought about the problem of American war and peace aims. First was the question of the Left, which is to say, the disintegration of the prewar social systems and the growth of revolutionary movements and potential upheaval everywhere in the world. Next was the problem of the Soviet Union, which at times appeared very much connected with the issue of the Left. Finally, there was the issue of Great Britain, invariably set in the context of the future of the world economy, and its present and future relationship to the United States. No facile dissection of these three elements is possible, and no priority or weighting is useful as a general rule. All three themes interacted so that a change in one area often affected policy and conditions in another, lowering the significance of one factor at one moment, posing new dimensions at another. Yet the reader must recall these intertwined components again and again, or else the events of the war will appear discrete and disconnected, and the politics of the war bewildering and confused. Moreover, the contemplated problems of the peace and military realities of the war meshed with each other with increasing frequency as the war wore on.

*   *   *

Churchill and Roosevelt were both flexible in the debate over Germany, shifting their weight in various directions during its course. Churchill in public statements assured the Germans that they would not be "enslaved or destroyed," but neither would they qualify for those rights specified in the Atlantic Charter.[1] It is significant that with the exception of a small group of socialist intellectuals and Labour Party members, no one of political consequence in either the United States or England advocated a far-reaching democratic social and economic revolution in Germany designed to destroy the critical alliance between the Nazi Party and big business and to make German imperialism impossible. The strengthening of the German Left as a counterbalance to reaction, which not even the Russians openly suggested, Washington implicitly rejected. The Free Germany Committee caused Hull much apprehension, and the OSS in mid-1944 anxiously charted the growing influence of the German Communist

---

[1] Holborn, *War and Peace Aims,* 465. See also *ibid.,* 466, 497.

party, utilizing its conservative United Front strategy, and allegedly having the strongest underground in Germany.

Lord Robert Vansittart, the Conservative, bitterly anti-Russian English political leader, advocated the most punitive occupation philosophy to receive public attention in 1944. He called for the total destruction of German industrial power, extensive trials of large numbers of German leaders, and a prolonged and stringent occupation. Many have erroneously identified Vansittart's widely discussed opinions with the views of Henry Morgenthau and Harry Dexter White of the United States Treasury Department, and in their common conservatism and specific control measures there is some truth to this analogy. Beyond that, however, it breaks down.

The Morgenthau-White view of what the Allies should do with Germany is the most interesting, the most complex, and surely the most misunderstood plan. Historians have called it anti-German, which is an accurate label but grossly misleading unless placed in its much-ignored context. It was in a most integral fashion also a plan for de-Bolshevizing Russia and of reintegrating it into a new capitalist world economy which Morgenthau, White, and the State Department discussed during 1943 and 1944. In this sense the Morgenthau plan was opposed to Communist internationalism—an abstraction which existed only in a few Leninist tracts and the minds of frightened Western politicians—and in favor of the creation of a world economy modeled after the ideal American image. The destruction of the German economy was not an end in itself or joined to a relatively isolated debate, but a part of a much larger and more ambitious design, a plan that can only be comprehended when the specifics of the Morgenthau-White proposals for the postwar role of the USSR in the world economy are analyzed and the pre-1944 position of White and Morgenthau on Russia considered in greater detail than has hitherto been the case.

Both Morgenthau and White were among the more anti-Russian executives in Washington, and their record in this regard extended back to at least 1940, when the Treasury Department froze funds of the Baltic nations in the United States in a manner that the Russians thought singularly unfriendly. White, for his part, suspected in October, 1940 that the Russians would soon damage United States interests in the Far East by signing a nonaggression pact with Japan, and several days after the German attack on Russia Morgenthau refused to initiate any steps to aid the USSR. "I am in no hurry to do anything about Russia," he informed his assistants. "It is six of one and seven of another, as far as I am concerned. One day it is the Ogpu [GPU] and the next day it is the—what is the German police?"[2] . . .

Morgenthau's scheme was not entirely original and merely applied in an extreme fashion proposals others had considered and rejected during 1943 and early 1944. It was a preliminary draft, one he deliberately made strong with the knowledge it would be watered down, and later modified several times, but as it first stood it called for total German disarmament and the destruction of all arms industry and related manufacturing facilities, allocation of East Prussia, the Saar, the area north of the Kiel Canal, and various Rhine areas to Germany's neighbors, and the remainder divided into two independent states. The Allies would make the Ruhr an international zone and not permit it to trade with Germany, and later Morgenthau added a proviso for the nearly total destruction of its plants and mines. The Draconian aspects of the plan, which White and lesser Treasury officials clearly had qualms about, Morgenthau always restricted to the Ruhr, with the enhanced export market for England serving as a major rationale for the scheme. He would permit Germany itself to maintain consumer goods and light industries. Reparations could not come out of current production, but only through dismantling and forced labor, and the occupation authorities could assume no responsibility for economic regulation, which would be left to the Germans themselves. No effort would be made to prevent chaos and famine. The plan demaned total denazification. The memo said nothing about what such a plan implied for future United States-Soviet relations, but it was obvious that the Russians could expect substantial reparations only if it came from current production, for it is in the nature of modern industry that machines in the hands of experienced men reproduce their own value many times over. The Russians would have to seek alternatives, and this, as we shall see, Morgenthau and White already clearly understood.

The State Department immediately reacted with near horror, not merely because, as Hull recalled, it "was a plan of blind vengeance," but because "in striking at Germany, it was striking at all of Europe."[3]

[2] *Morgenthau Diary*, 425. See also *ibid.*, 182, 190–192, 242; O.S.S., R. & A. Branch, "German Communist Party." R & A 1550. July 10, 1944. (N. P., 1944), *passim;* Dorn, *Political Science Quarterly*, LXXII, 485.
[3] Hull, *Memoirs*, 1606; *Morgenthau Diary (Germany)*, 415–448. See also *Morgenthau Diary (Germany)*, 461–475, 485–495, 505–506, 518.

There would be no recovery on this basis, and the door would be opened to communism and closed to American plans for economic reconstruction. The State Department wanted spontaneous partition, Hull insisted, but opposed imposing it in a form that would encourage nationalist irredentism. For the next several weeks there followed inconclusive, shifting debate among the Cabinet committee members, Roosevelt himself vacillating unpredictably. To Stimson, McCloy, and their allies, a subsistence economy in Germany would create new tensions, for the "speed of reconstruction is of great importance," Stimson wrote at the time, "if we hope to avoid dangerous convulsions in Europe."[4] Permitting Russia to share in the international control of the Ruhr caused McCloy to be "alarmed at giving this addition to Russia's power."[5] Stimson for his part saw the plan as giving Russia or Poland too much of East Prussia and Silesia. Morgenthau wisely sought out Roosevelt at Hyde Park, away from the counterbalancing pressures of the President's other advisers, and won a momentary endorsement by adopting the President's suggestions regarding a stronger policy on the Ruhr, and prohibitions of parades, uniforms, and airplanes, all of which struck Roosevelt as important. At the same time he had his staff prepare arguments on why his plan would help save the postwar British economy. The last word was yet to be heard.

On September 11 the Quebec Conference opened and Morgenthau was present while Hull, recovering from an operation, was not. Stimson too was absent. Churchill arrived on the scene after both the War Cabinet and Hull had strictly enjoined him to resist the Morgenthau plan. At this very time, in addition, the British were deeply worried about their future export position and earnings and were attempting to obtain a relaxation on Lend-Lease restrictions interfering with certain critical exports. The matter of Germany, which after the implementation of the Morgenthau plan would no longer exist as a British competitor, was set in this context, and according to Hull, Morgenthau threw out the bait of possible postwar credits totaling over $6 billion. Churchill at first reacted violently, but soon saw the logic, and according to his memoir he agreed, without first consulting Eden, to "consider" the plan. On September 15 he and Roosevelt initialed a significantly watered-down version which reduced the

---

4 Memo in Stimson Diary, September 5, 1944, HLS Mss. See also *Morgenthau Diary (Germany),* 517ff.
5 Stimson Diary, September 7, 1944, HLS Mss.

question to the metallurgical, chemical, and electrical industries, the "war-making industries in the Ruhr and in the Saar," and the conversion of Germany "into a country primarily agricultural and pastoral in its character. . . ."[6] Eden was furious at this concession, but when they returned to London the War Cabinet rejected the plan outright. Hull saw Morgenthau trading away Lend-Lease and important levers for British acceptance of his trade program. Stimson now bitterly complained that the plan was irrational, and Morgenthau "so biased by his Semitic grievances that he is really a very dangerous adviser to the President at this time."[7] But Roosevelt, so it seemed, had been firmly converted to the Morgenthau plan.

Morgenthau regarded the Quebec meeting as "the high spot of my whole career in the Government," a complete triumph.[8] In fact it only forced Hull and Stimson to intensify their efforts and led to an even more acrimonious renewal of the controversy. Stimson immediately drafted a memo to Roosevelt, pitched on the highest level of morality, and in the meantime the Cabinet continued to haggle. Hull, who claimed "stupefaction" over Roosevelt's decision, joined with Stimson to ask how he might arrive at such critical decisions before consulting the Russians, a consideration that had not occurred to them prior to that time. Reinforcing this line was the fact the British were still deeply divided among themselves on the issue of Germany, and in fact remained split at least until Yalta. A firm American policy, therefore, would be in the nature of a unilateral decision damaging to the alliance. Hull then directed his appeal to Roosevelt along these lines, also lecturing the President on the responsibility of the State Department, especially after years of effort on this question, for the conduct of foreign policy.

*   *   *

Roosevelt was naturally unable to resist the combined pressures of his advisers. Added to this, on September 24 the press described an exaggerated version of the Morgenthau plan and the Cabinet split, strongly supporting Hull and Stimson. Two days later Roosevelt dis-

---

6 *Morgenthau Diary (Germany)*, 621. See also *ibid.*, 593–594, 601–602, 612–613, 619–620; Stimson Diary, September 5, 1944, HLS Mss; Stimson, *On Active Service*, 570–575; Hull, *Memoirs*, 1606–14; Woodward, *British Foreign Policy*, 472–73; Churchill, *Triumph and Tragedy*, 134; *Yalta Papers*, 135, 138.
7 Stimson Diary, September 14, 1944, HLS Mss.
8 *Morgenthau Diary*, 1234.

solved the Cabinet committee and on the 29th publicly described the problem of Germany as still under study. On the 29th the President also wrote Hull that "No one wants to make Germany a wholly agricultural nation again," much less completely eradicate the industry of the Ruhr and the Saar, but he insisted that they did not have to consult the British nor, especially, the Russians regarding the issue, for "In regard to the Soviet government, it is true that we have no idea as yet what they have in mind, but we have to remember that in their occupied territory they will do more or less what they wish."[9] The same day the Cabinet committee informed Roosevelt that they did not endorse the Morgenthau plan, that the United States should postpone all decisions on the partitioning of Germany, and that other than the destruction of military industry incapable of reconversion, basic economic objectives in Germany should be to reintegrate it into the world economy by eliminating self-sufficiency, preventing rearmament, and reducing the power of the large industrialists and landowners. They took no firm position on reparations, save to argue that the United States itself had no desire to collect any. Thus challenged, Roosevelt backed down altogether. He only signed the Morgenthau memo, he now insisted, to prevent the British from going bankrupt. On October 3 Stimson saw Roosevelt and noted he appeared "very tired and unwell."[10] The President admitted that the provisions of the plan, to which he had not given "much thought," had "staggered" him. "Henry Morgenthau pulled a boner," the President observed in burying the scheme.[11] But Roosevelt erred as well, and from this point on he carefully heeded the as yet not altogether unified proposals of his other advisers.

*   *   *

There is no doubt that Hull, Stimson, Forrestal, and most of official Washington feared that chaos in Germany and elsewhere would open the door to Bolshevism, and this was hardly a well-kept secret.[12] There was a direct correlation between those advocating leniency in Germany and fear of the spread of the Left. The State Department's desire to save Germany for a renovated world capitalism reinforced

9 *Yalta Papers*, 155. See also *Morgenthau Diary (Germany)*, 673.
10 Stimson, *On Active Service*, 580. See also *Yalta Papers*, 155–58.
11 Memo of Conversation, October 3, 1944, HLS Mss.
12 Forrestal to Robert Strausz-Hupé, November 23, 1944, JF Mss, box 24: *Yalta Papers*, 175; Hammond, "Directives for the Occupation of Germany," 405–406.

this position. Yet surely there was nothing radical or pro-Soviet about the Morgenthau plan. On January 20, 1945, Maisky and Harriman discussed Germany's future. Though the Russian stressed security as their first consideration, which they might attain by an overall 25 percent reduction of Germany's industrial capacity, far less than most of Washington's estimates, much less Morgenthau's, he emphasized the extent and form of Soviet reparations demands in far greater detail. The Morgenthau plan, for reasons indicated below, would have deprived Russia of the level of reparations it had in mind and later presented at Yalta. The basic psychological assumptions of Morgenthau and White on Germany were entirely conservative, stressing the irredeemability of German character in a manner any radical, seeing the critical role of a reactionary social system in the formulation of politics, would have rejected. In fact the Treasury group shared the prevailing view in Washington that one had to control the effects and consequences of a moribund social order rather than restructure it to prevent both chaos and the reemergence of reaction. The Morgenthau plan would merely have introduced new dynamics for destabilizing Europe, and only Roosevelt's personal susceptibilities made such hastily devised proposals possible in the first place.

*　　　*　　　*

The coalition against the Axis was born of necessity rather than deliberation or choice, and only the common need to defeat a common enemy bound it together. Great Britain, the Soviet Union, and the United States shared no single set of objectives other than this preeminent reality, no unifying political and economic peace aims—save, in the case of Britain and America, the negative one of containing Russia and the Left—and when Germany and Japan lay in smoking ruins the wartime Allies turned from a tenuous coalition to open conflict. That incipient struggle grew in importance throughout the war, until no later than the end of 1944 it necessarily became the defining obsession of the Western members of the coalition. That conflict has shaped the contours of modern world history, and we have yet to feel or know its full meaning and ultimate consequences.

No major power sacrificed less of its blood and material wealth during World War II than the United States. If one considers military potential in terms of overall industrial and technological capacity to sustain modern warfare over a period of time, in August 1945 only the United States had that power and only the United States emerged from the bloodiest conflagration in human history stronger than ever before. The war ultimately drained Britain more than even Russia, relative to its limited manpower and resources, transforming that small island into a power of the second tier. The United States was incomparably the greatest single nation in the world, with sharply articulated global political and, primarily, economic aspirations equal, even much more than equal, to the role.

The leaders in Washington were above all else fully aware of their own physical strength as well as their political and economic objectives, and they always viewed the problem of future relations with the USSR or Great Britain, or the nature of the world, with these critical goals in clear perspective. For how to advance its peace aims and apply its directing power to the inordinately complex and unpredictable realities of the broken, war-torn world colored every specific American response and assumption, and it was these expansive premises that were to define the postwar structure of relations—and conflict—between great states.

The problem of Soviet power gradually subsumed the other great wartime challenge to American diplomacy: the emergence of the Left and its threat to securing American economic and political war aims. In Eastern Europe, perhaps more than any other single region, American leaders found evidence of what they interpreted to be the dangers of Soviet expansionism that might undercut the attainment of their nation's largest postwar goals. The war utterly and finally destroyed the traditional Eastern European political and economic structure and nothing the Russians might do could alter that fact, for not the Soviet Union but the leaders of the Old Order in Eastern Europe themselves made that collapse inevitable. The Russians could work within that new structural limitation in a variety of ways, and in practice they did explore many political options, but they could not transcend the new socioeconomic reality. More aware than anyone else of their own weaknesses in the event of a conflict with the United States, the Russians pursued a conservative and cautious line wherever they could find local non-Communist groups willing to abjure the traditional diplomacy of the cordon sanitaire and anti-Bolshevism. They were entirely willing to restrain equally the militant Left and militant Right, and given the complex political admixtures of the region they showed neither more nor less respect for an unborn functional democracy in Eastern Europe than the Americans and British evidenced in Italy, Greece, or Belgium. For neither the Americans, British, nor Russians were willing to permit democracy to run its course anywhere in Europe at the cost of damaging their vital strategic and economic interests, perhaps also bringing about the triumph of the Left or the restoration of prewar clerical fascism. In fact we now know that the Russians lost control of the revolutionary forces in Yugoslavia and Greece, and that they had no intention of Bolshevizing Eastern Europe in 1945 if—but only if—they could find alternatives.

For the United States, Eastern Europe was a question of economic war aims to which political realities had also to conform to satisfy American aspirations, and quite apart from the local leaderships' policies toward Russia, that was hardly possible in nearly all the Eastern European nations. Even where the United States had yet to develop all of its objectives in specific detail, it was imperative that it prevent any great power from totally dominating Eastern Europe or any other region of the world for that matter, because the United States considered all political and economic blocs or spheres of influence that it did not control as directly undermining its larger political, and especially economic, objectives for an integrated world capitalism and a political structure which was the prerequisite to its goals. For this reason America opposed Britain's control over French affairs and set itself against an Eastern European reality which neither it, nor in the last analysis, the Russians, could fully shape according to a plan or desire.

Given the pervasive, chronic Russian conservatism on political questions during the war, one best reflected in the United Front tactics of accommodation which caused the Russian-disciplined Left to submerge its distinctive socialist character at all costs, the failure to reach agreement over Poland or Czechoslovakia—and Eastern Europe in general—reflected the effort of the United States to disengage Soviet influence in Eastern Europe and to create states ready to cooperate with a postwar economic program compatible with American objectives and interests. To the Russians during the war, Eastern Europe was a question of preventing the resurrection of traditionally hostile conservative leaders, and in this they had the total collapse of much of Eastern European society working on their behalf. To the Americans it was a matter of putting together a perhaps somewhat reformed version of the social and political sources of Eastern Europe's alliance with atavistic forces of imperialism and nationalism during two wars and reintegrating the region into a traditional prewar European economy in a condition of semicolonialism. That task was beyond the power of the United States or Russia, but it was a failure of American policy for which Washington was ultimately to hold Russia responsible. This exacerbation of world politics over Eastern Europe was a result of American expansion into the historically hopeless imbroglio and mire of Eastern European affairs.

In the last analysis both the Soviet Union and the United States could only partially control the uncontrollable—the Left—and could seemingly inhibit it only in Western Europe. For World War II brought to fruition a whole spectrum of internal crises inherent in the civil war in society, which was a by-product of different admixtures within each nation of industrial capitalism, World War I, and the continued weakening of world capitalism and colonialism after 1939. America, with some significant aid from Russia, might retard that collapse, yet it could not stay its irresistible momentum, and all the issues were joined during the period 1942–1945 that were again to break out with renewed force after the war to define the direction of modern world diplomacy and conflict. The Old Order of prewar capitalism and oligarchy with which the United States identified, with reservations, and which it hoped to reform and integrate into a transformed world capitalist economy, was dying in the colonial world and a dependent China; it committed suicide in Eastern Europe, and the United States could refurbish it in temporarily acceptable ways only in Western Europe. The impact of these changes on the conditions and structure of world power ultimately were to be more far-reaching than the Bolshevik Revolution itself, in part because—after 1947—the protective existence and support of Soviet power was a cushion between success and failure in many, but by no means all, socialist or revolutionary nations.

By 1945 the war itself delivered the *coup de grâce* to the prewar sturcture of European politics and economics, for which there was now but slight social backing, and therefore slight resistance to change. Only external intervention saved what remained of European capitalism, and it is this attempted unilateral great power definition of the internal affairs of other nations that became the defining fact of wartime and postwar politics. The Americans and British set the precedent in Italy, and formalized it in Europe when the United States also extended the principle elsewhere by preventing the emergence of a truly collaborative forum in the European Advisory Commission in the hope that occupation forces might contain potentially revolutionary changes via a controlled "democracy" whose limits and outcome the West might determine.

The larger instability in European economics and politics required the United States to aid the resuscitation of cooperative conservative elements of Europe and to attempt to prevent a total collapse of the Old Order in Europe and Asia that might open the door to Soviet predominance in a region or even the complete transformation of whole nations. For this reason the United States did not advance a truly permanent stern peace for Germany or Japan, since toward the end of the war many important American leaders accepted the need to reintegrate and reform German and Japanese power to create a balance to Soviet predominance and to advance American objectives. And this deliberate ambiguity, which permeated all their wartime considerations of the future role of the defeated Axis, implied that it was not the total destruction of Axis power, but the advancement of American global interests that soon became the preeminent concern in American planning. In this sense World War II was a tragic error to the American government in that even before the war was over it understood that perhaps a less imperialist Germany and Japan would be preferable to the USSR as allies in the future.

Indeed, this perceptible shift in priorities ultimately became the basis of American postwar policy, reflecting a shift in tactical goals all along the line, one that also significantly downgraded initial American hostility to British political aims in Europe, and more particularly in France, on behalf of a far deeper commitment to the objectives of containment and stability—containment of the dual menace of the Left and the Soviet Union, and stability for the essential social and economic system of prewar European capitalism and colonialism.

Although the United States undertook a task that was insuperable in many places, it was still possible in much of Europe, and in any event the American government had no option but to resist as best it could those destabilizing political and economic conditions which brought revolutionary movements of every shape and variety into existence, and attempt to compensate for their subversive effect on American interests and postwar objectives by containing, redirecting, or destroying them. There was no other recourse for the United States but to undertake the difficult, and in many places, the impossible, for the consequence of inaction might have been the unchallenged triumph of the Left in numerous countries. Only the United States had the power to engage fully in international counterrevolution and sustain the forces of conservatism for prolonged periods of time, and it was this militant intervention into the affairs of literally every area of the world that set the pattern for postwar world politics. By 1945 Washington's decision to undertake that role was an unquestioned postulate in America's plans for the future of its power in the world.

The Russians understood the American intention and the risks of any covert aid to the Left, and they gave precious little of it during and immediately after the war, when they discovered that even an obviously conservative policy failed to blunt the American belief that behind all the world's social and economic ills, somehow, and in some critical fashion, a Russian plot and device existed. From this viewpoint United States policy-makers saw Russia and the Left as the cause rather than the reflection of the collapse of capitalism, and responsible for the failings of a system that began to commit suicide in vast areas of the globe no later than 1914. Still, it was Soviet conservatism on revolutionary movements everywhere that gave Western European capitalism the critical breathing spell during which it might recover, though the caution of the Western European Communist parties became a permanent and willingly self-imposed fact of political life. This desire to opt into the existing order where possible, and the correct realization that the American and British armies would certainly not permit a triumph of the Left either by the ballot or a takeover in the streets, shaped the political conduct of the Communist parties wherever there were Western troops. And the USSR demanded and assiduously enforced this strategy where it controlled local Communist parties and, through them, the Resistance. It brought an end to the illusions of possibilities and national renovation that inspired the European Resistance. Yet where the Soviets could not control the armed opposition, or the Right was too rigid to absorb the armed Left—as in China, Greece, and Yugoslavia—the end result was revolution and international crisis.

These crises were not a by-product of Soviet policy, but reflected a lack of Russian control over the Left and the response of the British and, preeminently, the United States to the irresistible tides of change. Outside Western Europe the Americans could recognize, in moments of clarity, the total breakdown of existing societies, but they bent every energy—via dollars and ultimately force of arms—to avoid the political and economic consequences of a perceptible reality for which they could have no sympathy. In Western Europe both dollars and guns succeeded, but where the Americans could not undo disintegration resulting from the war and economic collapse, they often limited and shaped the character of change. American resistance to social and revolutionary upheavals from diverse sources and causes, whether Communist or revolutionary nationalist, polarized change in the world, denying pluralism and options which were natural to radical and humanist movements unable and unwilling to risk survival along with diversity and social exploration. Successful movements of social transformation, due in some degree to ideology but necessarily because of the external pressures, became monolithic and anti-American as a precondition to success. Counterrevolution in this manner defined the course of revolution and history for decades and imposed on the remnants of the tortured men and women seeking to create a new life for themselves in Asia and elsewhere the American problem as the constant threat to social renovation and survival.

With each new success in confining British power in the Middle East or British financial freedom to pursue an independent course, or in its ability to define the future contours of the postwar world economy, the United States downgraded the relative importance it attached to bringing Great Britain into complete conformity with postwar American economic and political objectives. As time revealed the full extent of British weakness, and as the common denominator of anti-Communism made what the two states shared more important than ever before, the problems of the Soviet Union in the postwar world and the international movement of social change altered, but by no means eclipsed, the previous weight Washington assigned to its relations with the British Empire.

The initial Anglo-American rivalry was based on the interwar world economic experience, and on the basis of that period the United States defined its postwar economic objectives with an unusual precision unequaled in other fields. Nearly all important leaders in Washington assumed and hoped that the United States would revive and reform capitalism everywhere in the world, but pre-eminently in the British Empire, and that there would not be a collapse of world capitalism so deep or profound as to raise the fundamental question of the inherent viability of the system on an international level in any form. Only toward the very end of the war did the enormity and social impact of the event begin impressing many in Washington so that they understood that the needs of reconstruction in Europe might necessarily precede the creation of a liberal international economy modeled after late-nineteenth-century British free trade. In the meantime the Hullian theory of American economic objectives was less significant than its specific goals, and these showed more practically what it was the United States sought to attain for itself in its ideal world economy. At least in the short run the accumulated privileges of the British in the Middle East, and their unique challenge to United States hegemony over the foreign trade sectors of other Western Hemispheric nations, presented the major obstacles to attaining these goals. In the theory of a world economy which Cordell Hull propounded on behalf of the government, the United States would have enjoyed a competitive advantage over all the other industrialized nations; in the practice of applying American power to specific interests, in particular oil, the British were certain their wartime ally was bent on a course of economic imperialism which might also result in the eclipse, even demise, of British power. Rhetoric aside, expedient references to the Open Door in the international economy functionally meant American economic predominance, ofen monopoly control, over many of the critical raw materials on which modern industrial power is based. Oil revealed the theory and reality of American economic war aims.

The rivalry between the United States and Britain over oil and the postwar world economic structure added to the inevitable weakening of Britain during the war to create a vacuum in world power which the Americans quickly and gladly filled in the Middle East and Latin America. This new role was not unplanned or accidental, but was sought with a compulsion and desire the British perceived as the creation of an American equivalent of the form of spheres and blocs Washington attributed to the British. The elimination of Britain's power in large areas of the world, and the American entry into the wake, carried with it the enormous political and strategic responsibilities which unavoidably befell those who wished global profit, and that new burden was as much a by-product of an American desire for world economic expansion as it was a response to the emergence of the Left everywhere, much less the growth of Russian power. It was inherent in the clear vision of the type of world order the Americans wished to create, and inevitably the American defeat of Britain for predominance in the Middle East also predicated the task of policing ever-growing regions of the world. America's foreign policy at the end of World War II necessitated the ability and desire to employ loans, credits, and investments everywhere, to create a world economic order according to its own desires. In this the United States did only what was functional to its own needs and objectives, as the British had done before it in an earlier era.

It is this deliberate quality, this articulate set of economic and political goals which ultimately set the United States at the end of World War II against the Soviet Union, against the tide of the Left, and against Britain as a coequal guardian of world capitalism—in fact, against history as it had been and had yet to become. That there was something accidental or unintended about the American response to the world is a comforting reassurance to those who wish to confuse the American rhetoric and descriptions of intentions with the realities and purposes of operational power, but given the society and its needs American foreign policy could hardly have been different. For the United States emerged from the war with a sense of vast power, and indeed, as the most powerful single state in the world, anxious to attain a highly organized world economic and political community as a precondition to the realization of its vital peace aims. But as strong as it was, the United States, even when the Soviet Union worked with it for its own reasons and toward its own ends, was too weak to mold the destiny of mankind everywhere on earth. It might limit and shape that fate, but it could not control the world by creating its desired political and economic order modeled after American aspirations.

At times the key decision-makers in Washington fully appreciated America's possible inadequacy and need for allies, as in their enigmatic attitudes toward the future of Germany in Europe and Japan in the Far East. Everywhere in the world America could deploy material power in various forms, and at the conference table it spoke with a weight beyond that of any other state. Estimating this strength in relation to that of other states, Washington fully intended that at the end of the war America could, and would, determine the basic character of the postwar world. For this reason Roosevelt and his aides throughout 1943 and 1944 opposed the desire of the British Foreign Office to meet Soviet aims in Eastern Europe at the bargaining table, for the leaders of the United States fully expected—and this was as true of Roosevelt as of Truman—to employ American power to define the political and economic outcome of the war when their allies were relatively weak. The problem, which it was impossible for anyone in Washington to sufficiently perceive and appreciate, was that the kind of world emerging from the war required power beyond the factory and army, the kind of resources and inspiration that only revolutionary movements in villages and mountains can possess and generate.

For insofar as world conflict was transformed from wars between states into ideological and civil wars for social transformation and liberation, the political arithmetic of insufficiency of numbers made it impossible for the Americans to be everywhere at once, and to employ vast technological power—in bases and ships the Americans planned to have throughout the world—against sheer mass. To succeed in that situation one had to be neither American, English, nor Russian, but to be present in every village in the hungry world, or, as in the case of the Russians, to endorse an inevitability that they could neither initiate nor prevent.

It was in this context of vast material might and yet greater ambition that World War II ended for the United States and defined the manner in which the postwar period began. There was nothing qualitatively unique about this goal or the tools that the United States employed, for the reliance on the state to attain the domestic and international objectives of private American business interest, or to advance a broader "national interest" on behalf of an allegedly new internationalism which scarcely concealed the imperial intent behind it, much less the consequence, was a characteristic of American life and had been for many decades. What was new was the vastly more destructive technology which now accompanied the expansion of states—of which the United States was both the most powerful and first after 1943—and the human consequences of international conflicts.

The United States has yet to construct the international political and economic system modeled after the images and goals which it carefully formulated during World War II, and to make its creation the test of a stable and ideal postwar order, or to compensate for the political and economic frustrations of only one nation of the world, set the stage for an endless series of international crises. In this sense the quality and purpose of modern American diplomacy—in principle and form—we may see in microcosm during the years 1943 to 1945. No nation could build such a world and the efforts of the United States to do so almost consistently revealed its weaknesses. It attempted to apply its strength while refusing to see the limits of American capabilities and ideology in a world that, given its inherently decentralized nature and problems, was moving beyond the mastery of any one nation or alliance of states. For nowhere were the long-term political and economic objectives that the United States formulated during World War II fully realized, save in the replacement of Britain in certain areas by a lesser American influence.

World War II was a prelude to the profound and irreversible crisis in world affairs and the structure of societies everywhere which is the hallmark of our times.

For the war had come to an end, but the world was still aflame.

Anthony Kubek

FDR—COMMUNIST DUPE

At the other extreme of the political spectrum lie right-wing critics such as Anthony Kubek, professor of history and political science at the University of Dallas and author of How the Far East Was Lost: American Policy and the Creation of Communist China, 1941–1949 *(1963). Kubek, a student of Charles C. Tansill's, has elaborated upon the themes put forth by his mentor. Kubek, like the radical-left historians, sees Roosevelt as merely the spokesman for other interests and hence can discount statements and actions by the President which do not fit his thesis. Kubek claims that the Treasury Department and Secretary Henry Morgenthau, Jr., exercised extensive influence over American foreign policy, and that because the Treasury Department had been widely infiltrated by Soviet agents, it meant that American foreign policy was all too often made in Moscow. Kubek has developed that theme in his book and in two lengthy introductions to portions of the Morgenthau diaries published by the Senate Internal Security Subcommittee—a holdover from the days of Senator Joseph McCarthy. Kubek rises above the mean accusation that Roosevelt was a conscious agent of the Communist conspiracy, but does condemn him for holding leftist sympathies and for permitting himself to be duped by Stalin's promises and foreign agents.*

These data not only serve a historical purpose regarding events prior to and during the Second World War, but also indicates the serious problem of a Cabinet department exceeding its jurisdiction by presuming to make foreign policy as a result of unauthorized, uncontrolled, and often dangerous power exercised by nonelected officials.

In the formulation and execution of the foreign policy of President Roosevelt, the chief collaborators were, naturally, the secretaries of state, war, and navy. To these must be added, for the period under consideration, the efficient, urbane, bespectacled secretary of the treasury, Henry Morgenthau, Jr., who served in the Cabinet from January of 1934 to July of 1945. Before Morgenthau was appointed secretary of the treasury, he had lived near Roosevelt's home at Hyde Park, N.Y., for two decades and could be counted as one of his closest and most trusted friends. His appointment was clearly the culmination of twenty years of devotion to, and adoration of, his

From Anthony Kubek, "Introduction" to *Morgenthau Diary (Germany),* prepared by the Subcommittee to Investigate the Administration of the Internal Security Act and Other Internal Security Laws of the Committee on the Judiciary, U.S. Senate (2 vols.; Washington, D.C.: U.S. Government Printing Office, 1967), vol. 1. Footnotes omitted.

neighbor on the Hudson. According to his official biographer, Morgenthau's "first joy in life was to serve Roosevelt, whom he loved and trusted and admired."

The conduct of American foreign policy today consumes such a large share of the annual budget that the secretary of the treasury and his financial experts automatically become involved in diplomatic decisions of all kinds. In Roosevelt's time, however, Secretary Morgenthau's deep involvement in questions of international significance sorely annoyed other Cabinet members and created considerable friction with the State Department. In certain instances in American history, of course, the secretary of the treasury has played a significant part in the shaping of foreign policy. Our first Secretary of the Treasury, Alexander Hamilton, had perhaps a greater influence in formulating and controlling foregin policy than did Secretary of State Thomas Jefferson. Usually, however, the Treasury Department has concerned itself exclusively with the economic aspects of foreign policy. Our early interest in China, for example, was almost wholly economic; but as American traders expanded their activities, they sought and obtained protection from that department which was responsible for international relations—the Department of State.

In the case of the Treasury Department under Secretary Morgenthau, one can question many functions that went beyond anything in that department's history. The Morgenthau diaries reveal that the Treasury presumed time and time again to make foreign policy. In his *Memoirs* Secretary of State Cordell Hull described it in these terms: "Emotionally upset by Hitler's rise and his persecution of the Jews, Morgenthau often sought to induce the President to anticipate the State Department or act contrary to our better judgment. We sometimes found him conducting negotiations with foreign governments which were the function of the State Department. His work in drawing up a catastrophic plan for the postwar treatment of Germany, and inducing the President to accept it without consultation with the State Department, was an outstanding instance of this interference."

Elsewhere in his *Memoirs* Hull acknowledges that Morgenthau was an able administrator with an "excellent organization . . . ably headed by Harry Dexter White." Actually it was Dr. Harry Dexter White, Morgenthau's principal adviser on monetary matters and finally assistant secretary of the treasury, who conducted much of the important business of the department. The diaries reveal that White's influence was

enormous throughout the years of World War II. Shortly after Morgenthau became secretary in 1934, White joined his staff as an economic
analyst on the recommendation of the noted economist, Professor
Jacob Viner of the University of Chicago. Then forty-two years old,
White had been teaching at Lawrence College in Appleton, Wisconsin,
and was about to receive the doctorate in economics from Harvard
University, where he previously had taught as an instructor. In 1938
the position of Director of Monetary Research was created for him,
and in the summer of 1941 he was given the additional title and
duties of "Assistant to the Secretary." Articulate, mustachioed, and
nattily dressed, he was a conspicuous figure in the Treasury but remained unknown to the public until 1943 when newspaper articles
identified him as the actual architect of Secretary Morgenthau's
monetary proposals for the postwar period.

The diaries reveal White's technique of domination over general
Treasury affairs by submitting his plans and ideas to the secretary,
who frequently carried them directly to the President. It is very significant that Morgenthau had access to the President more readily
than any other Cabinet member. He ranked beneath the secretary of
state in the Cabinet, but Hull complained that he often acted as
though "clothed with authority" to project himself into the field of
foreign affairs and inaugurate efforts to "shape the course of foreign
policy in given instances." Morgenthau, Hull felt, "did not stop with
his work at the Treasury."

Over the years White brought into the Treasury, and into other
branches of government, a number of economic specialists with
whom he worked very closely. White and his colleagues were in a
position, therefore, to exercise on American foreign policy influence
which the diaries reveal to have been profound and unprecedented.
They used their power in various ways to design and promote the so-
called Morgenthau Plan for the postwar treatment of Germany. Their
power was not limited to the authority officially delegated to them;
rather it was inherent in their access to, and influence upon Secretary Morgenthau and other officials, and in the opportunities they had
to present or withhold information on which the policies of their
superiors might be based. What makes this a unique chapter in
American history is that Dr. White and several of his colleagues, the
actual architects of vital national policies during those critical years,
were subsequently identified in congressional hearings as partici-

pants in a network of Communist espionage in the very shadow of the Washington Monument. Two of them, Frank Coe and Solomon Adler, have been for some years working for the Chinese Communists in Asia. From the Morgenthau diaries we can glean many details of extensive political espionage operations by this group, especially in the area of policy subversion.

The record of Harry Dexter White has been of continuing interest to the subcommittee during all the sixteen years of existence. In the course of its investigation of the Morgenthau diaries, the subcommittee may be able to shed additional light on the strange career of Dr. White. If ever fully unveiled, his record undoubtedly would furnish hitherto hidden links in the chain of evidence respecting conspiratorial Communist activities within the government which were first intimated by Elizabeth Bentley and Whittaker Chambers in testimony before the House Committee on Un-American Activities in the summer of 1948.

In the hearings before the Senate Internal Security Subcommittee on the operations of a Communist group within the Institute of Pacific Relations, White's name came up repeatedly with the result that his role in the field of Far Eastern affairs was disclosed. Subsequently, when the subcommittee dealt with interlocking subversion in government departments, its hearings revealed additional data on White's activities and his connection with members of a conspiratorial Communist group operating within the government. Dr. White was the center of all this activity. His name was used for references by members of the espionage ring when they made application for federal employment. He arranged their transfer from bureau to bureau, from department to department. He assigned them to international missions. He vouched for their loyalty and protected them when exposure threatened.

When the former Communist courier Elizabeth Bentley appeared before the subcommittee in 1952, she painted a startling picture of the fundamental design of Communist penetration. One of the two espionage groups that she "handled in Washington" was headed by Nathan Gregory Silvermaster, an official of the Treasury Department. Concerning the avenues for placing people in strategic positions, she said: "Two of our best ones were Harry Dexter White and Lauchlin Currie. They had an immense amount of influence and knew people, and their word would be accepted when they recommended someone." Currie, a Canadian-born Harvard economist, fled the United States after testifying one time before the House Committee on Un-American Activities. He has lived for years in Colombia, but once had enjoyed access to the inner circle of the Roosevelt Administration. He came to Washington in 1934, first to the Treasury and then to the Federal Reserve Board. In 1939 Currie was appointed as one of the six administrative assistants to the President, with special duties in economics. After Pearl Harbor he was active in the area of "economic warfare," functioning for a time as deputy administrator of the Board of Economic Warfare and the Foreign Economic Administration. As a representative of the Executive Office of the President, he attended many interdepartmental meetings to consider postwar international economic problems and policies. With Currie in the White House and White in the Treasury, the stage was set for the development of what Secretary Hull has called the "catastrophic" program for the postwar disposition of Germany which came to be known as the Morgenthau Plan.

Stated in its simplest terms, the objective of the Morgenthau Plan was to de-industrialize Germany and diminish its people to a pastoral existence once the war was won. If this could be accomplished, the militaristic Germans would never rise again to threaten the peace of the world. This was the justification for all the planning, but another motive lurked behind the obvious one. The hidden motive was unmasked in a syndicated column in the *New York Herald Tribune* in September 1946, more than a year after the collapse of the Germans. The real goal of the proposed condemnation of "all of Germany to a permanent diet of potatoes" was the Communization of the defeated nation. "The best way for the German people to be driven into the arms of the Soviet Union," it was pointed out, "was for the United States to stand forth as the champion of indiscriminate and harsh misery in Germany." And so it then seemed, for in a recent speech Foreign Minister Molotov had declared the hope of the Soviet Union to "transform" Germany into "a democratic and peace-loving state which, besides its agriculture, will have its own industry and foreign trade." Did Russia really plan on becoming the savior of the prostrate Germans from the vengeful fate which the United States had concocted for them? If this was indeed a hidden motive in the Morgenthau Plan, what can be said of the prinicipal planner? Was this the motive of Harry Dexter White? Was White acting as a Communist but without specific instructions? Was he acting as a Soviet agent when he drafted the plan? There is no confession in the Morgenthau diaries in which White admits he was either ideologically a Communist or actively a Soviet agent. But it is possible, given an understanding of Soviet aims in Europe, to reconstruct from the diaries how White and certain of his associates in the Treasury worked assiduously to further those aims. From the diaries, therefore, it is possible to add significant evidence to the testimonies of J. Edgar Hoover and Attorney General Herbert Brownell that Harry Dexter White was ideologically a Communist and actively a Soviet agent from the day he entered the service of the United States government.

Before the entrance of the United States into World War II, Secretary Morgenthau's principal efforts were directed at arming the Allies against Japan and Germany. Perhaps no individual in Washington was more committed to assisting the Allies or more ardent in furthering national defense than Morgenthau. At times Secretary Hull was fearful that Morgenthau's crusading fervor might provoke the Axis nations too far. The diaries show sharp disagreements between the State and Treasury Departments in administering export controls and foreign funds on deposit in the United States. Morgenthau early initiated a struggle to wrest from the State Department its traditional authority over exports and imports of war materiel in the hope of bringing the Office of Arms and Munitions Control under his department. The secretary of the treasury had a strong personal taste for diplomatic bargaining and was frequently engaged in discussions with ambassadors or in correspondence with foreign statesmen—activities which, of course, were properly the function of the secretary of state. Hull warmly resented what he regarded as unwarranted interference in the field of foreign affairs. The voluminous records kept by Morgenthau provided unmistakable proof of the Treasury's constant projection into the domain of the State and the resulting administrative duel between these two Cabinet departments. "Despite the fact that he [Morgenthau] was not at all fully or accurately informed on a number of questions of foreign policy with which he undertook to interfere," Secretary Hull writes, "we found from his earliest days in the Government that he seldom lost an opportunity to take long steps across the line of State Department jurisdiction."

The extent to which the staff of the Treasury would go to acquire information not related to its jurisdiction, and in fact restricted to only a few ranking officials of the State Department, is clearly indicated in the following bizarre episode. In 1943 the Treasury requested from State a copy of a cable from Ambassador Leland Harrison in Bern, Switzerland, concerning the plight of the Jews in Europe. The State Department turned down the request, advising that the cable did not "relate to any matters that concerned the Treasury," that few people at State had seen it. Josiah E. DuBois, Jr., an assistant to the secretary of the treasury, telephoned Donald Hiss, brother of Alger Hiss and an assistant to the legal adviser in the State Department, and asked him to get a copy of the cable. Hiss told DuBois that he himself was having "considerable difficulty" obtaining a copy. Later Hiss was able to acquire a copy, but had to tell DuBois that the cable was really "none of Treasury's business" and that "in no event" should it be shown to other Treasury officials. He added that if it were known that he had shown this cable he might lose his job. He was sure that his telephone was being tapped, and that unfriendly ears had listened in on his conversations with Treasury officials. Donald Hiss was subsequently identified by Whittaker Chambers, as a member of a Communist cell, a charge which he denied.

The diaries also reveal sharp differences between Morgenthau and the Secretary of War, Henry L. Stimson, regarding the selection of personnel for postwar planning. Late in 1943 Morgenthau asked the President to name Lauchlin Currie as a representative to the European Advisory Commission meeting in London. The commission was charged with drafting surrender terms, defining zones of occupation, and formulating plans for Allied administration of Germany. Morgenthau told the President that Currie "would work well with the Treasury" and that "we could surround him with three or four men" to advise him. When John J. McCloy, assistant secretary of war, informed Secretary Stimson of Morgenthau's recommendation of Currie, Stimson became "mad as a boil." He did not want Currie, he said, and would not take Currie unless the President ordered him to do so. Moreover, Stimson was "quite angry" that Morgenthau should have spoken to the President about Currie before speaking to Stimson about him. At a meeting in Morgenthau's office on January 3, 1944, McCloy remarked that Currie was "doing a poor job" in the Foreign Economic Administration, and that he was going to be dismissed from that position. Morgenthau, however, insisted that Currie was a "first-rate, top man in the field of money and finance," and the Treasury would be glad to give him a job. He explained that the position on the European Advisory Commission was very important because it "would help shape monetary, economic, and financial developments throughout Europe possibly for the next decade," and hence it was "important that men not be sent who would not represent the President's views." Currie was not appointed to serve on this important commission; the United States was represented by John G. Winant, the American Ambassador in London. According to the testimony of Elizabeth Bentley, Lauchlin Currie was not, as far as she knew, a member of the Communist Party, but he was "very close to various members of the Silvermaster group. . . ." He was used not only to "bail out" other Communist members "when they were in trouble," but also to steal White House secrets for the Soviets. On one occasion, according to Miss Bentley, Currie sent word through George Silverman and Harry Dexter White that the United States was about to break a Soviet code.

The diaries established that in April, 1945, Morgenthau was impressed by the "good things" he had heard about Nathan Gregory Silvermaster. "We may want him over here," Morgenthau told the Treasury lawyer John Pehle, instructing him to talk with another Treasury official, Frank Coe, about Silvermaster because "I have a special assignment in mind for him." The name of Silvermaster had been given to Miss Bentley in 1941 by Earl Browder, General Secretary of the Communist Party in the United States, as "a man working for the United States Government, who was interested in helping in getting information to Russia and who could organize a group of other Government employees to help in this work." Silvermaster organized the group and collected its dues for the Communist Party. According to the testimony of Elizabeth Bentley, White brought documents from the Treasury to Silvermaster, who photographed them in his basement and passed them on to Miss Bentley. In his testimony before both the House Committee on Un-American Activities and the Senate Internal Security Subcommittee, Silvermaster invoked the fifth amendment regarding his Communist activities and affiliations. Yet in 1945 Morgenthau offered Silvermaster an important post in the Department. . . .

In the realm of foreign policy Silvermaster was likewise active.

He sent Morgenthau a memorandum on June 19, 1945, advising that the immediate problem was "the establishing of solid Soviet-American friendship." The man to become the next secretary of state, he said, should be "a liberal" and "someone not 'anti-Soviet'." President Truman had been "arduously preparing himself" for the forthcoming meeting at Potsdam with Stalin and Churchill. Because of his intimate knowledge of the American economy and his understanding of the postwar problems it would face, President Truman doubtless would "favor the establishment of solid and friendly relations with the Soviet Union." Because the President's "way of thinking" and "his desire to see things for himself and his tremendous capacity to receive and absorb factual material," it would be extremely desirable if the chief executive could "take a trip through the big industrial plants, mines, and devastated areas of the Soviet Union." This visit would enable the President to acquire the "actual facts of the Soviet economy and a realistic perspective of Soviet-American trade." Moreover, a trip through the Soviet Union and Siberia would enable the President to return "from the Big Three meeting with more intimate personal knowledge and direct personal relationship with the key people having a better knowledge than any other American and any Briton."

Anyone who studies the Morgenthau diaries can hardly fail to be deeply impressed by the tremendous power which accumulated in the grasping hands of Dr. Harry Dexter White, who in 1953 was identified by J. Edgar Hoover as a Soviet espionage agent. Following the Munich crisis in the spring of 1938, Secretary Morgenthau invited White, then chief of the Division of Monetary Research, to become a regular member of the "9:30 Group," made up of his principal advisers. A week after Pearl Harbor the secretary, in a departmental order, announced that "on and after this date, Mr. Harry D. White, Assistant to the Secretary, will assume full responsibility for all matters with which the Treasury Department has to deal having a bearing on foreign relations . . . ." The wording of this order is of the greatest significance. White's full responsibility included not only all foreign matters in which the Treasury was specifically engaged, but also any matter "having a bearing" thereon. To a Communist agent, the opportunities this position offered were incalculable. . . .

Morgenthau seemed very confident that the President would not waver in his support of a punitive program for postwar Germany. Any effective plan, however, would have to be executed within the next six months, or otherwise the Allies might suddenly become "soft." The best way to begin, Morgenthau advised, was to have American engineers go to every steel mill in Germany, every coal mine, every chemical plant, and every synthetic gas factory, and dynamite them or "open the water valves and flood [them]." Then let the "great humanitarians" simply sit "back and decide about the population afterwards." Eventually the Ruhr would resemble "some of the silver mines in Nevada," Morgenthau said. "You mean like Sherman's march to the sea?" asked Dan Bell. Morgenthau answered bluntly that he would make the Ruhr a "ghost area."

Such was the character of Secretary Morgenthau's views on the treatment of postwar Germany. Never in American history had there been proposed a more vindictive program for a defeated nation. With the Treasury exerting unprecedented influence in determining American policy toward Germany, such fallacies of logic, evasion of issues, and deliberate disregard of essential economic relationships were manifested in the postwar plan as finally adopted. As it resulted, no paper of any importance dealing with the occupation of Germany could be released until approved by the Treasury. The State and War Departments became virtually subservient to the Treasury in this area of their responsibility.

* * *

The plan for postwar Germany as presented at the Quebec Conference was precisely that which was outlined in the Black Book of Harry Dexter White and his associates. This plan called for a repudiation of the Atlantic Charter signed by Roosevelt and Churchill three years before. The Atlantic Charter had pledged that the United States and Great Britain would "endeavor . . . to further the enjoyment by all states, great or small, of materials of the world which are needed for their economic prosperity." The Treasury plan now would deprive millions of Europeans of such basic economic rights. It was Morgenthau's difficult task at Quebec to justify the plan to Churchill, who thought it far too drastic. According to Morgenthau's recollection, the Prime Minister was "violent in the most foul language." He declared that the American proposals were "like chaining his body to a dead German," and were "cruel, unchristian."

As Morgenthau hammered on the idea that the destruction of the Ruhr would create new markets for Britain after the war, Churchill gradually changed his attitude. When Anthony Eden objected strenuously to Churchill's reversal, the Prime Minister retorted: "If it gets down to the question of whether I am for the German people or the English people, I am for the English people, and you can be for whomever you want." The he added this warning: "And I don't want you to tell the War Cabinet about [Morgenthau's proposal] until I get home."

What prompted Churchill to change his mind and accept the Treasury plan? Is it because Harry Dexter White had intimated to Lord Cherwell, who was at Churchill's side at Quebec, that if the Prime Minister approved the American plan the British could have the large loan they were seeking? Morgenthau felt that some kind of guarantee of continuing financial aid, even beyond the end of the war, was "uppermost" in Churchill's mind. The diaries reveal that Morgenthau himself talked with Cherwell and asked him to "speak to Churchill" which he did, and the next morning Churchill "changed his mind." Moreover, the diaries show that Churchill was promised a loan of $6.5 billion to tide Britain over during the period from the end of the war in Europe to the surrender of Japan. Later, in a meeting with Secretary Stimson, Morgenthau denied that he had dangled such an inducement before the Prime Minister. When Stimson asked which had come first, the Treasury plan or the proposal for a loan, Morgenthau replied that Churchill "came across" before "we agreed" on the loan. White, who was present, remained discreetly silent, but later he reminded Morgenthau that Churchill had given his oral approval to the Treasury plan only after receiving a pledge of continuing American financial support. This was their conversation:

> White: *Of course . . . what they are promising to deliver [support of the Treasury Plan] . . . was quid pro quo for this up in Quebec—*
> Morgenthau: *What part?*
> White: *Their attitude on Germany was in your mind—*
> Morgenthau: *That isn't what I told Stimson in your presence. He tried to make it quid pro quo and I told Stimson that they came across on the German business before we agreed to this.*
> White: *I didn't want to say anything, but that wasn't quite true. They did that before they signed the document, but the oral agreement was made before. But in any case, in your mind they were tied together.*

> Morgenthau: *Are you sure now?*
> White: *Yes.*
> Morgenthau: *Can you prove that to me?*
> White: *I will have to reconstruct by sequence of events.*
> Morgenthau: *Didn't I go over that with you coming down on the plane?*
> White: *You put special stress on when they signed the document, but if I may remind you, what Churchill said to the President when he was trying to get the President to agree on the document [loan], you remember, he said, "What do you want me to do, stand up and beg like Fala?" And the document was signed on the Lend-Lease after, but there practically was an oral commitment before then. It was just to be put in writing.*

By White's own admission, therefore, Morgenthau did offer Churchill a loan in exchange for his approval of the Treasury plan for postwar Germany. But more important are these questions: Did White advise or encourage or prompt Morgenthau on how to deal with Churchill, whom he must have known would present an obstacle? What discussions did White have with Cherwell behind the scenes? What was the precise role of White at the Quebec Conference? At present these questions cannot be answered because the official papers of the conference have yet to be published.

Although foreign affairs and military matters were discussed in depth at the Quebec Conference, neither Hull nor Stimson was in attendance. The Treasury Department took precedence over State and War in negotiations regarding Germany. The commitments made by Roosevelt and Churchill were of greatest importance to White and his associates, who from the very beginning advocated the total destruction of Germany. To make certain that the British would fulfill their commitments under the Treasury plan, White recommended his long-time Treasury associate Frank Coe to act as secretary of the U.S. delegation in future Lend-Lease negotiations with Britain. (Coe, identified by Elizabeth Bentley as having been a member of the Silvermaster cell, subsequently fled the United States and now resides in Communist China where he writes 'agit prop' for the Chinese Communists.) The position was a critical one, since in it Coe would have control of the formulation of policy on all matters of future British Lend-Lease.

Thus the influence of White and his associates upon the President, indirectly through Morgenthau, was of major importance in the planning of policy toward postwar Germany. Morgenthau's own admission of the enormous help of his subordinates is clearly indicated in this summary of his successes at Quebec:

> *The thing up at Quebec, all together, was unbelievably good. And as far as I went personally, it was the high spot of my whole career in the Government. I got more personal satisfaction out of those forty-eight hours than with anything I have ever been connected with. The thing that we have been working with here, with regard to the attitude towards Germany—the Treasury viewpoint was wholly accepted, and so it was, that thing that everybody here worked on so hard was accepted, and the President put it this way: He said he had been groping for something, and we came along and gave him just what he wanted. But I don't know how they are going to announce it or what they are going to do about it. . . .*

The effects of Mongenthau's victory at Quebec were quickly felt in Washington. At a luncheon with Undersecretary of War, Robert Patterson, Morgenthau brought up the Quebec agreement. Patterson said jokingly: "To degrade Europe by making Germany an agricultural country, isn't that offensive to you?" Morgenthau replied: "Not in the case of Germany."

Morgenthau's frequent opportunities to talk to the President informally gave him a great advantage over other Cabinet officers in whose departments German affairs belonged far more formally than in the Treasury. The Quebec agreement caused an irreparable division among policy-makers in Washington. The old cleavage between Hull and Stimson on the one side, and Morgenthau on the other, became hopelessly deep when the President bypassed both the State and War Departments by asking the secretary of the treasury to present his plan at Quebec. Hull later wrote:

> *This whole development at Quebec, I believe, angered me as much as anything that had happened during my career as Secretary of State. If the Morgenthau Plan leaked out, as it inevitably would—and shortly did— it might well mean a bitter-end German resistance that could cause the loss of thousands of American lives.*

Hull felt strongly that Morgenthau should have been kept out of the field of general policy, and so did Stimson. When Stimson heard of the President's endorsement of the Treasury plan at Quebec, he quickly drafted another critical memorandum, though it must have seemed to him a waste of time to do so. Yet this refutation of the "pastoral plan" for Germany remains the most powerful ever presented to the President:

> My views have already been submitted to you in other memoranda. I merely wish to reiterate briefly that I still feel that the course proposed by the Treasury would in the long run certainly defeat what we hope to attain by a complete military victory, that is, the peace of the world, and the assurance of social, economic and political stability in the world.
>
> The point of difference is not one of objective—continued world peace—it is one of means. When we discuss means, the difference is not whether we should be soft or tough on the German people, but rather whether the course proposed will in fact best attain our agreed objective, continued peace.
>
> If I thought that the Treasury proposals would accomplish that objective, I would not persist in my objections. But I cannot believe that they will make for a lasting peace. In spirit and in emphasis they are punitive, not, in my judgment, corrective or constructive. They will tend through bitterness and suffering to breed another war, not to make another war undesired by the Germans nor impossible in fact. It is not within the realm of possibility that a whole nation of seventy million people, who have been outstanding for many years in the arts and sciences and who through their efficiency and energy have attained one of the highest industrial levels in Europe, can by force be required to abandon all their previous methods of life, be reduced to a peasant level with virtually complete control of industry and science left to other peoples.
>
> The question is not whether we want Germans to suffer for their sins. Many of us would like to see them suffer the tortures they have inflicted on others. The only question is whether over the years a group of seventy million educated, efficient and imaginative people can be kept within bounds on such a low level of subsistence as the Treasury proposals contemplate. I do not believe that is humanly possible. A subordinate question is whether, even if you could do this, is it good for the rest of the world, either economically or spiritually. Sound thinking teaches that prosperity in one part of the world helps to create prosperity in other parts of the world. It also teaches that poverty in one part of the world usually induces poverty in other parts. Enforced poverty is even worse, for it destroys the spirit not only of the victim but debases the victor. It would be just such a crime as the Germans themselves hoped to perpetrate upon their victims—it would be a crime against civilization itself.

*   *   *

The acceptance of the Treasury plan by Roosevelt and Churchill at Quebec greatly strengthened Morgenthau and his colleagues during subsequent interdepartmental negotiations. They won many concessions. After the adverse press reaction, the President kept a judicious silence. He did not publicly repudiate the Treasury plan just as he never publicly announced it, but he dissolved the Cabinet committee and appointed Robert D. Murphy to serve with the rank of ambassador on Eisenhower's staff as political adviser on German affairs. Careful to give no affront to Morgenthau in his campaign speeches, the President did not commit himself beyond promising that the German people were "not going to be enslaved." "Enslaved" was a word one could take as one chose.

How the Treasury officials were able to integrate basic features of their plan into the military directive, originally prepared by the Joint Chiefs of Staff and known as JCS 1067, is fully disclosed in the diaries. White saw to it that many elements of his thinking were embodied in JSC 1067. Previous directives for guidance of American troops upon entrance into Germany, which already had undergone six or more revisions of a stylistic nature, were now brought more in line with the punitive thinking of Morgenthau and White. A new directive, which called for a more complete de-Nazification, was, with some modifications, the spirit and substance of the Treasury plan. This directive, an elaborate memorandum of twelve large column printed pages for the guidance of American Military forces upon entrance into Germany, became the core philosophy of JCS 1067 which General Eisenhower received upon entering Germany and which legally controlled American activities there after the surrender. However it might be read, JCS 1067 reflected the harsh philosophy of quarantine and revenge, devised and advocated by Morgenthau, White, and the Treasury staff. It is very important, therefore, to grasp the fact that the revised directive of September 22, 1944, became *an official but diluted version of the Morgenthau Plan,* and remained formally in effect until supplanted by a new policy directive from the Joint Chiefs of Staff in July 1947.

In the two full years that JCS 1067 was the cornerstone of American policy in Germany, Communist infiltration into the American military government was a very serious problem. The harshness of the army directive made it possible for Communist infiltration to succeed. As Germany was punished and substantially dismantled in accord with the basic tenets of the Morgenthau Plan, the American zone of occupation enabled the Communists in the military government to influence policy in the direction of Soviet desires. The directive was largely negative in character. It articulated the idea that the

German people could not escape responsibility for what they had brought upon themselves. It forbade fraternization by American personnel with the Germans, ordered a very strict program of de-Nazification extending both to public life and to business, prohibited American aid in any rebuilding of German industry, and emphasized agricultural rehabilitation only. Under its philosophy the Germans were regarded collectively as guilty of crimes against humanity and as a menace to the world, and as such they were to be dealt with very firmly. Punishment was to be meted out to the German people as a whole by reducing their standard of living drastically. Measures were to be taken to make sure that former Nazis were not used in the military government, regardless of administrative necessity; there were to be absolutely no German parades, "military or political, civilian or sports." No oil or rubber was to be manufactured; no merchant ships were to be built; and there was to be no aircraft of any kind. All in all, the program was punitive to the point that it showed the United States and the rest of the world as shortsighted, motivated largely by revenge, and with little appreciation of the fundamental problems of occupation.

*   *   *

How was it possible for the United States to embrace a myopic postwar policy which, in effect, induced economic retrogression in the heart of Western Europe? It is hard to believe, as one looks back upon the White-Morgenthau program, that large numbers of Americans could have been gullible enough to subscribe to this unrealistic proposal to de-industrialize one of the most highly industrialized countries of the world. The Treasury plan for Germany aimed at quarantining the entire population of the defeated nation and reducing its people to abject misery. It was the absolute negation of every democratic principle the United States held dear, and for which it had gone twice to war in one generation. Had it been carried out in its original form, it surely would have constituted the greatest act of genocide in modern history. The totalitarianism and barbarism of the Nazis were certainly enough to convince even the most charitable of Americans that only a tightly restrictive program would effectively eliminate Germany as a threat to peace in the future. But the vision of a completely prostrate Germany with her people "stewing in their own juice," so captivated the vindictive planners of the Treasury that economic fact and fiction were inextricably confounded. And, since the Departments of State and War were made virtually subservient to the Treasury in planning for the occupation, the Government's most knowledgeable specialists on German affairs were consistently bypassed or overruled.

After all this has been said, an implicit question haunts the historian. It is this: if the Morgenthau Plan was indeed psychopathically anti-German, was it also consciously and purposefully pro-Russian? To date, historical scholars have failed to answer, or even to ask, this vital question in their otherwise comprehensive studies of American diplomacy during and immediately following World War II. Yet this is a question of such profound historical importance that someday it must be answered definitively. The Secretary of the Treasury never denied that his plan was anti-German in both its philosophy and its projected effects, but no one in his department ever admitted that it was also pro-Russian in the same ways. In his book, *And Call It Peace,* Marshall Knappen suggested in 1947 that the Morgenthau Plan "corresponded closely to what might be presumed to be the Russian wishes on the German question. It provided a measure of vengeance/*and*/left no strong state in the Russian orbit." What were the Soviet aims in the summer of 1944, when White was putting the plan into final form, and which of these would the plan have fulfilled or furthered? Is it possible that the plan was a response to some sudden, unexpected obstacle to Soviet aims? These questions are basic, but they defy answers. Can it be said finally that the Morgenthau Plan was Soviet-inspired? The Morgenthau diaries alone do not yield enough incontrovertible evidence to permit an absolute pronouncement, but some of the documents published for the first time in this volume certainly point to an answer in the affirmative.

The original draft of the Morgenthau Plan, as first presented at Quebec, contained no intimation of the enormous benefits which might accrue to Soviet Russia as a result of its joint endorsement by President Roosevelt and Prime Minister Churchill. Yet the very timing of that draft suggests that Russophilia may have been foremost in the mind of Harry Dexter White, its principal draftsman. By the end of the summer of 1944 Russia's military position was vastly improved, and Soviet leaders were at last able to foresee the eventual collapse of German forces on the eastern front. At the same time, however,

American and British intelligence reports indicated the possibility of Germany surrendering unconditionally "within a matter of weeks or even days." The moment was ripe, therefore, for the urgent presentation of a scheme for the postwar treatment of Germany which, when made known to the Germans, would stiffen their resistance, forestall immediate surrender, and thus leave the door open for oncoming Russian armies of occupation to move en masse into the vacuums of war-ravaged Europe.

That Harry Dexter White was the actual architect, as well as the master builder, of the Morgenthau Plan can no longer be seriously disputed. In document after document the diaries reveal White's abiding influence upon both the formative thinking and the final decisions of Secretary Morgenthau. Innocent of higher economics and the mysteries of international finance, the secretary had always leaned heavily on his team of experts for all manner of general and specific recommendations. White was the field captain of that team, and on the German question he called all the plays from the start. As a result of White's advice, for example, the Bureau of Engraving and Printing was ordered in April, 1944, to deliver to the Soviet government a duplicate set of plates for the printing of the military occupation marks which were to be the legal currency of postwar Germany. The ultimate product of this fantastic decision was to greatly stimulate inflation throughout occupied Germany; and the burden of redeeming these Soviet-made marks finally fell upon American taxpayers to a grand total of more than a quarter of a billion dollars. White followed this recommendation with another, in May of 1944, which again anticipated the emerging plan. This time he urged a postwar loan of 10 billion dollars to the Soviet Union. White doubtless reasoned that if Moscow could be assured of such direct financial aid from the United States, the Russians would then have to ask for nothing more than a little land, a few slave laborers, and some industrial equipment as their reparations from defeated Germany!

The documents in this volume demonstrate that the so-called Morgenthau Plan might more properly be remembered in history as the "White Plan," for the contriving brain and tireless hand of Dr. Harry Dexter White who produced it. But a disturbing question remains: Who or what inspired or guided the brain and hand of White? The striking similarities in both concept and detail between the Treasury plan and Soviet designs for postwar Germany may, of course, have been merely coincidental. It can be said, on the other hand, that a program sponsored by the U.S. government would be far more palatable to the people of the Western democracies than anything emanating from Moscow. The diaries, of course, do not tell the story of machinations behind the scenes on the part of White and his colleagues Glasser, Coe, Ullmann, Silvermaster, and others who have sought refuge in the Fifth Amendment. Perhaps some day additional documents, as yet unavailable, may shed more light on their activities. It is clear, however, as the diaries indicate, that White and his associates were constantly coming up with recommendations on Germany for the sensitive ears of Morgenthau, and that the secretary in turn was carrying these very recommendations directly to President Roosevelt for his personal and irreversible stamp of approval. Was there some person or some group behind White? The diaries reveal that in 1943 the mysterious Robert McConnell wrote what seems to have been the first memorandum on postwar control of Germany which eventually was incorporated into the plan. Did the deeper objectives of the plan originate beyond the confines of the Treasury, with White on the inside acting as the technician and the catalyst? In her testimony before the subcommittee in 1952, the confessed Communist courier Elizabeth Bentley charged that White was the inside man who prepared the plan for Secretary Morgenthau, and "on our instructions he pushed hard."

If in fact Harry Dexter White was himself an active agent of Soviet espionage, as J. Edgar Hoover of the FBI has charged, the implications are indeed profound. There can be no denial of the fact that White had wide contacts with individuals, inside and outside the government, who had in common their admiration of Marxian philosophy. Nor can it be denied that White had direct access to much of the top-secret data of the American government. He had persuaded Morgenthau to exchange information with other departments, and by the spring of 1954 at least seven agencies were trading their confidential papers with the Secretary of the Treasury. Many of these papers inevitably crossed White's desk.

The concentration of Communist sympathizers in the Treasury Department, and particularly the Division of Monetary Research, is now a matter of record. White was the first director of that division; those who succeeded him in the directorship were Frank Coe and

Harold Glasser. Also attached to the Division of Monetary Research were William Ludwig Ullmann, Irving Kaplan, and Victor Perlo. White, Coe, Glasser, Kaplan, and Perlo were all identified in sworn testimony as participants in the Communist conspiracy. Coe, Glasser, Kaplan, and Perlo consistently invoked the Fifth Amendment when questioned by congressional investigators. In his one appearance before the House Committee on Un-American Activities in 1948, White emphatically denied participation in any conspiracy. A few days later he was found dead, the apparent victim of suicide by sleeping pills. Notes in his handwriting were later found among the "pumpkin papers" on Whittaker Chambers' Maryland farm. In a statement before the Senate Internal Security Subcommittee in 1953, Attorney General Herbert Brownell declared White guilty of "supplying information, consisting of documents obtained by him in the course of his duties as Assistant Secretary of the U.S. Treasury, to Nathan Gregory Silvermaster. . . ." Silvermaster passed these documents on to Miss Bentley after photographing them in his basement. In his testimony before both the House Committee on Un-American Activities and the Senate Internal Security Subcommittee, Silvermaster invoked the Fifth Amendment.

Never before in American history had an unelected bureaucracy of furtive, faceless, "fourth floor" officials exercised such arbitrary power or cast so ominous a shadow over the future of the nation as did Harry Dexter White and his associates in the Department of the Treasury under Henry Morgenthau, Jr. What they attempted to do in their curious twisting of American ideals, and how close they came to complete success, is demonstrated in these documents. But that is all which is known for sure. What priceless American secrets were conveyed to Moscow through the tunnels of the Communist underground will probably never be known—and how much actual damage these sinister men did to the security of the United States remains, at least for the moment, a matter of surmise.

III THE ROOSEVELT FOREIGN POLICY —AN OVERVIEW

Willard Range

FDR—A REFLECTION OF AMERICAN IDEALISM

Willard Range, professor of political science at the University of Georgia, is one of the few scholars who have attempted to examine the intellectual attitudes toward foreign relations held by Franklin Roosevelt. His view is that Roosevelt personified American ideals and hopes. By emphasizing peace, disarmament, moral leadership, and international cooperation, the President typified the approach of the general public to foreign policy. Although Range recognizes Roosevelt's practical side, he places the President within the mainstream of what Range considers American postwar intellectual attitudes; that is, peace through a sort of Wilsonian world order. Range sees nothing to apologize for in American foreign policy goals and by identifying Roosevelt with them argues strongly for labeling him as a great moral leader.

No student of Roosevelt is likely to deny that the President was something of an intellectual jumping-jack and was often guilty of hopping helter-skelter in several directions at once with the same problem. But it is wrong to assume, I think, that because Roosevelt was at times inconsistent in the way he went about affairs, that underneath there lay no basic aspirations, attitudes, or purposes. It was in his means and methods that Roosevelt was inconsistent and opportunistic, not in his ends, his aims, his goals. It is my conclusion, in fact, that Roosevelt's conduct was largely guided by a set of assumptions, principles, and values which he clung to with remarkable consistency throughout most of his life. I would reject categorically the argument that he did not know where he was going or wanted to go. Assuredly, he did not always know how he would get there and he was everlastingly willing to try almost any available means of reaching his goal. But his objective was rarely in doubt. When in 1938 he published the papers of his first term he was frank to admit that they revealed many inconsistencies, but he insisted that they also showed consistency of purpose. "There were inconsistencies of methods," he wrote, "inconsistencies caused by ceaseless efforts to find ways to solve problems for the future as well as for the present. There were inconsistencies springing from the need for experimenta-

From Willard Range, *Franklin D. Roosevelt's World Order* (Athens, Ga., 1959). Reprinted by permission of the University of Georgia Press. Footnotes omitted.

tion. But through them all . . . there also will be found a consistency and continuity of broad purpose." And that claim can, I think, be borne out regarding his ideas on international relations.

Most of the writers who charge Roosevelt with being an intellectual madcap, moreover, have not yet given much attention to his thinking during the war years—the period in which he did the major part of his thinking about international relations. And when that period is examined sufficiently, I believe his tendency toward consistency will be more apparent.

*   *   *

The spiritual and moral transformation of international relations required not only the ridding of the world of the evils of fascist totalitarianism and excessive armaments, thought Roosevelt; it required also that the world be rid of imperialism in all its forms; that the exploitation of one group of people by another be stopped; and that in the place of such things as colonialism and spheres of influence, a system of tutelage and international trusteeship be instituted for peoples not yet ready to govern themselves; and *bona fide* independent states based on the principle of self-determination be established for those people able to stand on their own political feet.

Here also Roosevelt experienced something of a conversion; for in the early years of his public life he was a humanitarian imperialist. Like Theodore Roosevelt and many other moralistic liberals of the Progressive Era, he believed it quite justifiable for a good, just, Christian democracy like the United States to impose the blessings of her civilization on more backward and less fortunate peoples, even by the use of force. . . .

But the humanitarian, paternalistic, missionary spirit of the imperialism of the liberals of the Progressive Era kept their imperialism from being sordid; and that spirit Roosevelt had in abundance. The promotion of democracy, the ending of internecine violence and perpetual revolution, the establishment of order, the advancement of education and health and general welfare of the natives, and the raising of standards of living were invariably major objectives, and often the only objectives of Roosevelt and those who thought as he did, in every imperialistic adventure. And it was in the achievement of these objectives that Roosevelt took the greatest pride and boasted until the end of his life.

*   *   *

It was sometime during the war, however, when Roosevelt began a vigorous attack on colonialism everywhere. It would probably be going too far to say that Roosevelt's trip to Casablanca in January-February 1943 was the turning point. If the President's son Elliott is correct, the President had made up his mind by the time of the Atlantic Conference not to help England hold on to her colonial peoples. But it is quite clear that the President's trip to Casablanca had a profound effect on his attitude toward colonialism. In British Gambia he saw what he believed was colonial exploitation at its worst, and the sight was so unforgettable that he talked repeatedly about it during the remaining two years of his life. It was the most horrible place he had ever seen, he declared: it was 5,000 years behind American civilization, with the people working in rags for less than 50¢ and a half cup of rice a day and with ignorance, poverty, and disease rampant. "For every dollar that the British have put into Gambia," he charged, "they have taken out ten. It's just plain exploitation of these people." The people were treated worse than livestock, he concluded, and there could be no effective organized peace in the world with such conditions. And while he agreed that the United States had not lived up to her responsibilities in Liberia (where he stopped also) his greatest irritation was reserved for the British.

In French Morocco the colonial rule he saw was more enlightened; and while he was quite interested in the various types of colonization in West Africa, his general conclusion regarding the whole area was that "it hasn't been good," a conclusion he passed on to Churchill. Shortly after his return from Casablanca he declared publicly that the day of the exploitation of one country for the benefit of another was over. And three weeks after that he recanted to President Benes of Czechoslovakia his earlier desire to see France recover her empire. He expressed to Benes his personal disappointment in France in general, criticized her regime of her colonies as he had seen it in North Africa, and expressed doubt of France's ability ever to recover and develop her colonies. By that time he seemed also to have developed a grudge against France's handling of Indo-China and, as he told Lord Halifax later, he had decided it certainly should not go back to France. France had held Indo-China and her thirty million inhabitants for more than a hundred years, he went on inaccurately, "and the people are worse off than they were at the beginning." France had "milked" Indo-China for a hundred years, he wrote Hull, and the people there "are entitled to something better than that."

Meanwhile Roosevelt also publicly refuted Churchill's contention that the Atlantic Charter applied only to Europe. It applied to the entire world, Roosevelt declared on several occasions; and when queried about Churchill's remark to the effect that he, Churchill, had no intention of presiding over the liquidation of the British Empire, Roosevelt told the press off the record that "dear old Winston will never learn on that point." For by the latter part of the war the liquidation of the British and all other empires was one of Roosevelt's ambitions. Not only should India be given her independence, he thought, but the British should also renounce their claims to Hong Kong, Shanghai, and Canton. "Exploitation everywhere" should be opposed, he told the International Labor Conference in May 1944, and again he referred to the horrible conditions of Gambia. A few months later he told the American people that hundreds of millions of people in the Pacific area were stirred with a desire for the right to work out their own destinies, and he implied that they ought to have that right.

But if there was no place in Roosevelt's new world order for colonialism neither was there any place in it for spheres of influence. Unfortunately for the student of the theory of international relations, Roosevelt said very little about spheres of influence, but what little he did say was almost all negative. Spheres of influence, he seemed to think, were simply another means for one people to dominate another and they were incompatible with the kind of postwar world he wanted. If Roosevelt ever favored spheres of influence during the war, Hull implied, he meant for them to apply only to military operations. At Casablanca military spheres were agreed upon; but there was no intention on Roosevelt's part, thought Hull, for economic or political matters to be included although the delineation was not made clear and much effort was necessary to convince the British to that effect.

When the question of spheres of influence arose again in the fall of 1944 and some decisions regarding Eastern Europe had to be made, Roosevelt steadfastly resisted all attempts by Britain and Russia to make political agreements with implications that each would have postwar positions of dominance there. Finally he approved purely military spheres of influence for a three-months period; but even that was done with reluctance; for there was a tendency, he feared, for such military arrangements to develop into political and economic arrangements and he wanted no such development in the Balkans.

There have been charges that Roosevelt believed Stalin's desire for a Russian dominated Poland as a bulwark against future aggression was quite justifiable; and there have been allegations that at Yalta the President approved such arrangements. There is much evidence, however, that regarding Poland and at Yalta Roosevelt did all he considered reasonably possible to insure the establishment of governments in Eastern Europe that would be friendly to but not dominated by Russia. As we shall see later, his demand for free elections in that area was persistent. On his return from Yalta he told Congress that not only had much confusion and unrest developed in the liberated areas of Eastern Europe, but "worse than that, there actually began to grow up in some of them vaguely defined ideas of 'spheres of influence' which were incompatible with the basic principles of international collaboration. If allowed to go unchecked, these developments might have tragic results." No one nation was to blame, he added, but that kind of development is inevitable unless the major powers should cooperate and assume "joint responsibility" for problems of the area; and fortunately, they had decided to cooperate.

*   *   *

Thus far we have seen that Franklin Roosevelt dreamed of a world purged of totalitarianism, relieved of the burden of excessive armaments, and freed of the political domination of one group of people by another. A logical implication is that in the coming world thus reformed, democracy and individual liberty would flourish universally as never before. And that is exactly what Roosevelt wanted.

It must be remembered that during a large part of Roosevelt's public life totalitarian dictatorship was the major alternative to libertarian democracy and Roosevelt's thinking was conditioned by that fact. There is little evidence that he ever gave much consideration to gradations between these two extremes. In his view, therefore, the peoples of the world had only these two alternatives and there was never any doubt in his mind as to which they ought to choose.

It is well to remember also that all during Roosevelt's presidency libertarian democracy was on the defensive throughout the world, challenged by totalitarianism of both right and left; and it was this particular challenge that Roosevelt was forced to meet.

Roosevelt readily conceded the obvious merits of modern dictatorships. They had brought capital and labor together, he agreed, had achieved a substantial utilization of all their material and human resources, had solved at least temporarily such problems as unemployment and idle capital. But he abhorred the methods of dictatorship. . . .

Since Roosevelt saw an almost total correlation between democracy and individual liberty, he was just as interested in promoting a new world order of freedom as he was in promoting a new world order of democracy. When sending Welles to Europe and Myron Taylor to the Vatican early in 1940, the President told both that in their peace discussions they should keep in mind that a morally justifiable peace should give recognition to the various freedoms of which the common man had been deprived in the Axis states. Both publicly and privately throughout the war Roosevelt stressed the desire for a world consecrated to human liberty. A life of freedom and justice, he declared "are the inalienable rights of every man." And "we and our associates in the great alliance of the United Nations are determined to establish a new age of freedom on this earth." One of the ultimate objects of the United Nations, he declared, was to build a world in which human beings can think and worship freely and associate with friends of their own choice. And toward the end of the war he put this in only slightly different words, asserting that the United Nations was fighting to make "a world based on freedom. . . ." After the 1944 election he wrote Henry Wallace that one of the reasons he and the Democrats won again was that the people had faith in them to carry forward the fight "for freedom on this earth. . . ."

*   *   *

In addition to the reforms discussed above Franklin Roosevelt also had many suggestions for what might roughly be called a global New Deal. In general, his suggestions represented a desire to export to all the world the economic and social gains and techniques that had done so much to raise standards of living, cultural as well as material, in the United States throughout her history in general and during the Roosevelt Administration in particular. As would be expected, Roosevelt's suggestions were highly impregnated with the concept of social justice which to him seemed to mean the opening of opportunities and the bestowing of benefits to all individuals in society regardless of class. A richer cultural and material life for every man, woman, and child on the globe seems to have been his objective, and there is no doubt that he gave much thought to it. . . .

The first point to notice is that Roosevelt seemed to believe that the primary responsibility for improving the well-being of the world's peoples rested with the peoples themselves and their own national governments, or in the case of dependencies, it rested with the mother country or trustee. Roosevelt had little patience with governments unresponsive to the needs of their people and it was his great hope that after the war governments everywhere would act vigorously to solve internal economic and social problems and to raise standards of living.

He seemed to have no fear of, or even objection to, the spread of the milder types of socialism and seemed to feel that in many countries socialism would be the best thing. In 1934 he praised slum clearance programs that Germany, Austria, and England had undertaken, and regarding the cry that such action was socialistic he answered that socialism "has probably done more to prevent Communism and rioting and revolution than anything else in the last four or five years." And by way of example he noted that Vienna had done a "grand job" of practically clearing out her slums. According to Mrs. Roosevelt, the President felt that the world was going to be considerably more socialistic after the war and he indicated no regrets about it. Near the end of the war he told the Conference of the International Labor Organization that the promotion of the well-being of their peoples must be the aim of national governments after the war or there was no hope for the success of the great international goals.

But as a convinced believer in the interdependence of all nations, Roosevelt was aware that there were limits to what each national state could do for herself. National efforts would have to be supplemented, therefore, by international cooperative efforts at many points. . . .

Although the evidence is extremely fragmentary, it seems quite likely that Roosevelt would have been favorable to both foreign aid and technical assistance programs to further his global New Deal.

During the thirties he showed interest in the beginnings of a technical aid program in Latin America, supporting the projected Pan-American Highway project from 1933 on, and favoring such projects as aid to improve Nicaragua's agriculture, improve the channel in the San Juan River, and provide a director for Nicaragua's military academy. At the same time he also revealed interest in helping Liberia get back on her feet and he suggested that the United States might be able to send her technical experts in the fields of agriculture, public health, and geology.

His Lend-Lease program, almost entirely his own idea, was eloquent testimony of his belief in the interdependence of nations and the necessity of aiding one another. At Casablanca when enchanting the Sultan of Morocco with his vision of developing North Africa's resources, the President suggested that engineers and scientists could be trained for the job by some kind of reciprocal education program with some leading American universities. As the war neared its end the President also made it clear that he favored the use of at least technical assistance during the period of reconstruction to restore war-damaged highways, bridges, and communications. We know also that Roosevelt was in favor of helping the Soviet Union get into the shipping business and expand her foreign trade; and at both Teheran and Yalta he offered to sell Stalin some of the cargo ships that would be surplus after the war. He told Stalin that while the British never sold anything without interest, he (Roosevelt) had some new ideas regarding surplus property disposal; and he proceeded to describe a method of selling the ships to Stalin that would make the sale equivalent to a gift. Henry Morgenthau has testified also that Roosevelt planned to keep the Lend-Lease programs going after the war to lay the foundations for world recovery, and that had that been done, the Marshall Plan and other similar programs might not have been necessary.

Here we have only hints as to what Roosevelt might have done in the postwar world to achieve his global New Deal, but they are enough to justify guesses at the direction his foreign policy might have taken.

*   *   *

Another guiding principle Roosevelt seemed to apply in his thinking about a global New Deal was that there must be in it only a relatively small amount of altruism, but no exploitation, and a great deal of reciprocity. Here again the evidence is only fragmentary, but what evidence there is supports the above statement.

His opposition to economic exploitation of one people by another was long standing. Even in the years of his youthful imperialism he had opposed dollar diplomacy and the protection of merchants who took advantage of backward peoples. The era of exploitation was over, he said many times during his presidency; and one day in 1943 he told the press that when the President of Bolivia had visited him recently he apologized for the past behavior of some Americans who in the twenties had forced loans on Bolivia at exorbitant interest rates and extortionate commission fees. When in 1944 he sent Donald M. Nelson to China to find out what needed to be done to shore up that war-torn country's economy, the President told Nelson he was "particularly anxious that the Generalissimo and his advisers in the economic field understand that we are not going in there as exploiters and yet I feel sure we have a proper function, to help put China on its feet economically."

To prevent exploitation he repeatedly urged the leaders of backward areas to take care to maintain control over their resources and development projects, as in his advice to Arab leaders to maintain control over their oil resources and to get enough revenue from them to develop their countries. He was especially anxious to promote domestic ownership and control in Latin America. Early in 1940 he gave the press a long background sermon on the resentment many Latin Americans felt regarding the foreign ownership of their utilities, farms, and business firms. President Vargas of Brazil had recently asked Roosevelt how the people of the United States would like such foreign ownership and Roosevelt answered that such a situation in the United States would provoke a revolution. This situation in Latin America, the President went on, tended to give Latin Americans an inferiority complex and he favored a method of financing development there that would overcome such an attitude. He proposed, he said, a financing method that would enable the Latin Americans themselves to own the enterprises after twenty-five or thirty years; and he thought a good place to try the scheme would be with those many British-owned enterprises that Britain would be forced to sell during the war. The United States might buy them and then refinance them so as to achieve eventual local ownership in Latin America.

In 1944 Roosevelt came back to the subject while considering a policy regarding Latin American airline investments. He wrote Hull that while he was not opposed to United States investments in or technical aid to Latin American airlines, "I do not believe that it makes for good relations for American capital to dominate or control . . ." lines there. He much preferred that the lines be owned at least largely by Latin Americans with United States investors in a minority.

Evidence that Roosevelt's postwar New Deal would contain some altruism is only circumstantial, but the character of his domestic New Deal and of his aid to the Allies during the war suggests that he probably intended some of his postwar development programs to have an altruistic basis. Since he intended keeping the Lend-Lease program going during the period of reconstruction after the war, there is no evidence known to this writer that Roosevelt ever seriously expected more than a nominal repayment for Lend-Lease aid. His proposal to sell Russia surplus merchant vessels in a way that virtually made the ships gifts indicated a willingness to use the "give away" method of promoting development. His comment that his ideas on helping Iran would not cost the American taxpayer much money suggests that they would, however, cost the American taxpayer some money. But just as the altruism of his domestic New Deal was greatly exaggerated by his critics, so the degree of altruism intended in his global New Deal might easily be exaggerated. It seems safe to conclude that outright gifts to raise standards of living elsewhere were to play a relatively small part in Roosevelt's plans.

Reciprocity was the principle on which he seemed to depend the most. His major means of expanding trade was to be by reciprocal agreements. He wanted all nations to have a balanced trade with favorable and unfavorable balances of trade made things of the past. He approved the most-favored-nation principle in trade agreements but wanted even the United States to apply it only with other states which granted us the same privilege. Thus in the thirties when Germany and Australia discriminated against our products, the most-favored-nation clause in treaties with them was canceled. In 1944 he wrote Hull that regarding postwar foreign trade "while we shall not take advantage of any country, we will see that American industry has its fair share in world markets."

He also seemed to believe that the development of backward areas such as those in North Africa and the Middle East and Latin America could be carried out in a way that could be called an investment rather than a "give away." As already noted, he wanted new enterprises in Latin America developed in a way that would provide local ownership, but they would not be gifts. American investors were entitled to a reasonable profit on their development loans or investments, he thought, even in Arabian oil. Roosevelt simply opposed what might be called exploitation in the unfair sense of that word and he opposed the use of foreign investments to produce economic colonialism. After his return from Teheran he wrote his old schoolmaster, Endicott Peabody, about the poverty, disease, and barrenness of North Africa and the Middle East and then added, "But we can help those countries in the days to come—and with proper management get our money back. . . ." Thus his global New Deal was to produce mutual benefits, and not necessarily only indirect ones.

*   *   *

Franklin Roosevelt's final proposal for a new world order was that the whole new system of international relations must be held together by a collective security system under the guardianship of the five Big Powers.

We have already noticed that Roosevelt originally looked upon the plan for a League of Nations as a utopian dream and that he was not converted to either the League or to the principle of collective security until the latter part of 1919. Once converted, however, Roosevelt favored the principle of collective security—although not always the League—for the rest of his life; and he spent no little time during the following twenty-five years in a search for the proper vehicles and methods to apply the principle.

Characteristically, Roosevelt never made any detailed analysis of the principle of collective security. His great interest was in achieving the chief objective of the principle: cooperative action by states for the maintenance of peace. Despite the interest he showed occasionally in the details of international organization, especially from the beginning of 1943 and on, he seems to have had few deep convictions regarding the details or structure of the machinery of collective security. He was willing to accept almost anything in the way of machinery so long as it produced cooperative action; and during the thirties when he felt his objective could not be achieved through the League, he seemed willing to work without any machinery at all other than the traditional facilities of conference and diplomacy.

*   *   *

The major development in Roosevelt's thinking in this matter during the year after the Atlantic Conference (1942) was that the Soviet Union and China must be included among the world's policemen. Roosevelt had concluded by then that all other nations, including France, should be disarmed after the war. But for a variety of reasons the President concluded during 1942 that the Soviet Union and China could not be excluded from the international policing force. The major task of the policemen, the President asserted, would be to see that no disarmed nation secretly rearmed. If caught doing so, the culprit would first be threatened with quarantine; and if that did not work, she would be bombed. Inspection would go on continuously.

On occasion Roosevelt stated that the Big Power policing system he had in mind was designed only for a transition period after the war, until a more permanent security system could be established and made strong enough to take over the policing function. At the time of the Atlantic Conference, however, that transition period was envisioned as of such an indefinite length of time that the President seemed unable to see beyond it to the day when a comprehensive international organization would take over. Thus his refusal to accept any more than a very weak statement on a future international organization in the Atlantic Charter was due not only to fear of alarming American opinion, but to lack of interest on his own part as well.

It was this idea of a Four Power Condominium or a sort of new Holy Alliance that Roosevelt had firmly fixed in his mind early in 1943 when he began his many discussions with Hull, Welles, and others on plans for the United Nations, and it is doubtful if Roosevelt ever gave up this vision. According to Welles, the President gradually saw that his Big Power policing scheme would not work, that Britain would be too weak after the war to help much, that great new revolutionary forces were at work in the world and that even the United States would not be able to cope with them.

But Roosevelt clung to his idea of Big Power guardianship until the day of his death. When British Foreign Secretary Anthony Eden visited Washington in March, 1943 the President emphasized to him his desire for Big Power control not only of policing but of all important postwar decisions. It was the Big Powers that were going to have to write the peace treaties, he told Eden, and he did not want to have to do a lot of bargaining with the small states about it. The smaller states had all sorts of conflicting ambitions and any attempt to satisfy them would get nowhere. The important thing was to make settlements conducive to world peace. With regard to security, he told Eden, the Big Powers would have to maintain troops in the defeated Axis states and in such strong points as Tunisia, Bizerte, Dakar, and Formosa; and regardless of what kind of a general international organization existed, the Big Four would have to make the decisions regarding security and police the world for many years to come.

In September, 1943, he was again expressing the same view, although he declared that he was advocating a Big Power Condominium for only a transition period of three or four years. He told the press one day, however, that if the experiment of the Big Powers keeping the peace looked good to other nations, they all might want to keep it even after the transition period was over. To George Norris he likened the Big Four police to "sheriffs" who would maintain world order while the world's people recovered from the shell-shock of the years of fear and violence they had gone through. And again he justified his idea by the argument that a large group of nations could not handle security problems effectively. Where military matters would be involved, he told the press in October, 1943, the Big Four simply would not have time to consult thirty-two other nations. On matters about which there was "time to turn around," such as deciding ultimate objectives, all nations should have a place in the "picture." But not on a "military thing."

At Teheran the President again talked a great deal about his Four Policemen idea; but this time it was to be a permanent part of a full-fledged international organization, not a temporary arrangement for a transition period. His concept of the future international organization, he declared, included a worldwide assembly, an executive committee of about ten members to deal with such *nonmilitary* matters as economy, food, and health, and an enforcing agency which he called "The Four Policemen." The Four Policemen would have power, he said, to deal with any sudden emergency, such as

Italy's 1935 attack on Ethiopia. Had such an agency existed then, he asserted, it could have blocked the Suez Canal and prevented Mussolini's attack. Minor threats to the peace by revolution or civil war in a small country could be dealt with by the quarantine method. Major threats such as aggression by a larger power, could be met by an ultimatum from the Four Policemen, by bombardment, and even by invasion if necessary. According to Sherwood, there is no evidence of any discussion of the possibility of aggression by one of the Four Policemen. Among themselves the policemen would work out the problem of the future location of strong points for stationing military forces in such a way that they would not start arming against each other.

But this Big Four guardianship of the world did not mean Big Four domination of small nations, said the President after his return from Teheran. The rights of every nation large and small were to be respected and guarded as jealously as were the rights of individuals in the United States. The doctrine that the strong should dominate the weak was an Axis doctrine and the Big Four rejected it. The only objective of the Big Four was to keep the peace and to do it by force "for as long as it may be necessary."

Until such materials as the Hull papers are made available it probably will be impossible to trace what happened to Roosevelt's Four Policemen idea after Teheran. The Dumbarton Oaks proposals give the impression that the idea was modified considerably. But Roosevelt himself probably was not overly displeased. The provisions granting the Big Powers a predominant position in the Security Council of the United Nations, of assigning security matters to the Security Council, of having the council meeting continuously so it could act quickly, and of providing for a military staff committee composed of the Big Five might have looked enough like his police proposal to satisfy him. After the Dumbarton Oaks Conference, at any rate, he again referred to the contingents of world "policemen" who were going to be available to the Security Council and he wanted the council to have power to use them quickly and decisively to keep the peace. A few months earlier he had announced that the members of the coming UN would be asked to provide military contingents according to their capacities; but unless he had by then changed his mind about the capacity of other nations to maintain armaments, the chances are that he expected only the Big Powers to furnish contingents, with the other nations supplying facilities for the use of the forces of the Big Powers.

At Yalta the President indicated again, although in a somewhat different context, that the idea of Big Power guardianship of the world had not been disspelled from his mind. He agreed with Stalin, for example, that it would be ridiculous to give small nations like Albania equal power with the great nations in postwar affairs, and he agreed that the Big Powers should write the peace treaties. At a press conference after his return from Yalta the President also talked in a very paternalistic tone about the small nations, declaring that one of his objectives was to provide machinery to protect the "many little nations," and to give them a chance to be heard. He hoped, he said, that all nations would eventually become members of the UN Assembly. Little countries like Saudi Arabia ought to have a place where they could tell other nations of their needs. But it was awfully difficult to handle matters of importance in a large body, and he implied that important matters should be left to the major powers.

Although his Four Policemen concept was modified in the evolution of the United Nations Charter, the fact that the security system of the UN is based on Big Power unity and control is probably due in large part to the President's tenacity in clinging to his concept.

*   *   *

Although from 1917 until after the Nazi attack on Russia in 1941 Roosevelt blew hot and cold regarding the Soviet Union, he never ceased being intrigued by the social and political experiment going on there. William C. Bullitt, the President's first ambassador to Russia, has stated that Roosevelt's recognition of the Soviet Union in 1933 was inspired largely by the President's disgust with Europe and Japan and a faint hope that he might get Russia's cooperation to maintain peace in Europe and Asia. Russia's failure to live up to her 1933 commitments, however, produced a mild reaction, promoted reservations about Soviet trustworthiness and caused the President considerable disappointment. When he sent Joseph E. Davies to Moscow in 1937, therefore, he instructed Davies to make the President's disappointment clear and to leave it up to the Soviets to make overtures. He still hoped for Soviet cooperation to stop aggression, however, and in January, 1938, directed Davies to explore the possibility of Russian help to check Japan. But nothing came of the effort.

It was not until Russia's attack on Finland in late 1939, however, that the President publicy condemned the Russians with vigor. In February, 1940, he told the American Youth Congress that in the early period of the Soviet experiment he had possessed the "utmost sympathy" for the effort of the Russian leaders to bring better health, education, and opportunities to Russia's millions and he had hoped that in time the reign of terror and irreligion of the regime would pass and Russia would begin evolution toward a democratic, peaceful, and respected member of the family of nations. But the attack on Finland shattered all that hope and the USSR stood revealed as "a dictatorship as absolute as any other dictatorship in the world," and as an aggressor also. Meanwhile he suggested to Hull that the State Department consider retaliation for the repeated minor irritations promoted by the Soviets for such things as searching consul's luggage and regulating telephone calls from Moscow.

But after the Nazi attack on Russia in June, 1941, and particularly after the Soviets revealed unsuspected power and endurance, Roosevelt expressed many reasons why Russia should be accepted as one of the guardians. It is quite likely that, as one observer said, Roosevelt always looked on the idea as a calculated risk; he once told Polish Premier Stanislaw Mikolajczyk that "in all our dealings with Stalin we must keep our fingers crossed." But he had a strong hunch, reports Bullitt, that his gamble would pay off. When Bullitt presented Roosevelt with a strong memorandum against cooperation with Russia, the President argued that while Bullitt's facts and logic made sense, nevertheless "I just have a hunch that Stalin is not that kind of man. Harry [Hopkins] says he's not and that he doesn't want anything but security for his country, and I think if I give him everything I possibly can and ask nothing from him in return, *noblesse oblige,* he won't try to annex anything and will work with me for a world of democracy and peace."

But Roosevelt seems to have begun with the assumption that he had little choice in the matter, for he considered Russian cooperation *necessary* for peace. As early as May, 1939, he implied this to President Benes of Czechoslovakia; Welles got the same impression; and so did Churchill. Thus as Roosevelt saw the matter, he had the choice of cooperating with Russia for peace or of having no peace at all.

As Roosevelt saw the Soviet Union reveal the muscles of a super-power he seems also to have accepted the idea that the interests of both the United States and Russia had become worldwide and the two giants would have to cooperate whether they wished to or not. This was the reason, Hopkins told Stalin after Roosevelt's death, why the President had gone to such great lengths to arrange conferences with the Russians and to put their relations on a workable foundation.

Roosevelt also argued optimistically about the prospects of co-operating with Russia. Relations with her would not be a bed of roses but their differences could be worked out.

In the first place, the Soviet record regarding peace was good, with the exception of her attack on Finland. After joining the League in 1934, she had worked conspicuously for peace and the President believed she would function in the UN as she had in the League. Her record of cooperation as an ally during the war had also been good, no important point of friction developing until the Dumbarton Oaks Conference. Dissolution of the Comintern in 1943 had raised hopes of an even better record to come.

The President's second reason for being optimistic about Russian cooperation was his belief, despite the attack on Finland, that the Soviets had no aggressive ambitions. Immediately after Hitler's attack on Russia the President wrote Admiral Leahy that he did not think "we need worry about any possibility of Russian domination." A few weeks later he wrote the Pope that while the Soviet Union was under as rigid a dictatorship as Germany, the only weapon the Russians were using outside their borders was propaganda, and while that caused a certain amount of harm, the Russians were not even in the same class with the Germans who menaced the world with *both* propaganda and military aggression. At Cairo Roosevelt told General Stilwell that he had little fear of the Russians trying to get Manchuria from China. "Stalin doesn't want any more ground. He's got enough," said the President; "he could even put another hundred million people into Siberia." In 1944 Roosevelt publicly said the same thing, declaring that the Russians were not trying to "gobble up all the rest of Europe or the world." They did not have "any crazy ideas of conquest," he asserted; and especially since Teheran he did not think there was anything in the fear that the Russians were going to dominate Europe. "They have got a large enough 'hunk of bread' right in Russia to keep them busy for a great many years to come without taking on any more headaches," he said.

A third reason for Roosevelt's optimism regarding Russian co-operation stemmed from his idea of progress and theory of history, which held that the course of history is ever upward and onward toward a better, more democratic, more libertarian society. And it was this theory of history which convinced Roosevelt that no society was static and that Russia was bound to undergo evolutionary changes away from tyranny and dictatorship and toward freedom, tolerance, and peace. In his talks with Litvinoff in 1933 Litvinoff had told him he thought that although the United States and Russia had been poles apart in 1920 they had come much closer together in the ensuing thirteen years. "Perhaps Litvinoff's thoughts of nine years ago are coming true," he told a friend in 1942. The two nations might never get closer together than in a 60–40 ratio, he once told Welles, but that would provide a workable relationship. Since 1917, he argued, the USSR had moved a long way toward a modified state socialism while the United States had gone in much the same di-rection in her progress toward political and social justice. Thus con-flict between the two was not inevitable, provided Russia abandoned her doctrine of world revolution, and that, he thought, was receding also. If, therefore, a head-on clash between the two giants could be prevented until the new international security system had a chance to strengthen itself, he believed Russia's standards of living would rise, her foreign trade would increase, her walls of isolation would go down, her cultural and intellectual ties with the West would multi-ply, and the Russian people would eventually obtain freedom of in-formation about the outside world. Then Russia would be so trans-formed that cooperation with Russia would not be difficult. The big question was whether or not the necessary time for these develop-ments would be available, for the whole thing would require years.

Admiral McIntire has reported that in shipboard bull sessions on the way to Teheran the President showed no fear of not being able to bridge the gulf between the United States and Russia. The Presi-dent argued that the Kremlin's leaders had already discarded or modified many Marxist tenets, the Communist philosophy was too materialistic to have lasting appeal for the minds and souls of men, and he expected the trend in Russia to swing toward nationalism and old Czarist imperialism. He implied, supposedly, that that was a system with which we could get along.

A fourth reason for Roosevelt's optimism regarding Russion cooperation was his great confidence in his personal ability to win Stalin over to the idea of working in harness with the other powers. One reason for his repeated efforts to arrange his first meeting with Stalin, despite the latter's elusiveness, reports his son, was that he wanted to turn his personality on Stalin and gain the dictator's confidence. He looked on his first meeting with Stalin at Teheran as a challenge, his wife reported, because the Russians were so suspicious; and while he was not certain when he came home that he had dissipated any of Stalin's distrust, he showed no sign of giving up the campaign.

A final reason for Roosevelt's optimism regarding Russian cooperation was his belief that cooperation in keeping the peace was so obviously in Russia's best interest that she could be made to see it and would act accordingly. Welles claimed that by August, 1943, the President was convinced that the Soviet Union would recognize that her security and legitimate objectives could best be achieved by cooperating fully with the United States and an international organization. Stettinius testified to the same point, declaring that Roosevelt emphasized many times that although Russia might be difficult to get along with, the United States must continue trying with patience and determination to get the Soviets to realize that it was to their own selfish interest to win the confidence of the rest of the world, that cooperation would be to their advantage, and it was the only hope for peace. Even after Soviet intransigence began to cause him concern in the last few months of his life, the President continued to feel that Russia needed peace and opportunity to develop her resources to raise her standards of living so badly that he still had faith Stalin could be brought around by appeals to reason and self-interest.

It was the United States, however, that Roosevelt most wanted to be one of the guardians of the postwar collective security system; and he wanted the United States to be not only a guardian, he wanted her also to be the leader of all the others.

The idea that the United States should lead the world was such a strong conviction with Roosevelt from at least 1920 on that one is somewhat puzzled by his refusal to assume that role during the thirties. Preoccupation with domestic affairs, fear of isolationist opposition, and the timidity of the politically almost indispensable Hull are obviously part of the answer; but anyone going over the material on Roosevelt is very likely to get the feeling that they are not the whole answer.

In his 1920 acceptance speech Roosevelt called for American leadership of the world, declaring that "America's opportunity is at hand." He called for membership in the League of Nations with his argument that the United States should join the League because it would give the country a vehicle for world leadership and a forum to spread her doctrines of liberty and representative government.

United States leadership was imperative, he often argued, because of all the Big Powers she was the only one with a disinterested point of view. She had no traditional enemies, had no territorial desires, was interested only in peace and the advancement of civilization, and was, therefore, the only Big Power the world was willing to follow.

He argued repeatedly also that United States leadership was essential for promoting better standards of international morality and goodwill. Throughout her history, he wrote in 1928, the United States had been influencing the world is these respects. The Monroe Doctrine, her relations with Canada, the peaceful methods used by her in the Far East with the Perry Expedition and Townshend Harris, the Alabama Claims and Bering Sea Fisheries cases, her final decision to reject imperialism and prepare the Filipinos for self-government, and her help to the people of Cuba had all helped establish the United States as a moral leader. The Hay Open Door policy, the Boxer indemnity, aid in helping to organize the Hague tribunal, aid in the Treaty of Portsmouth and the Algeciras Conference, and Wilson's diplomacy had all helped lead the world toward more international goodwill. The only blots on "our liberal leadership" he could then think of were the seizure of Panama, Taft's dollar diplomacy, interventions in the Caribbean, and the Panama tolls legislation. But Wilson's diplomacy had made up for most of those mistakes, he asserted, and had shown the way to a new relationship among nations. The goodwill and high moral purpose of the United States had already had much influence on the world, he concluded, and this influence could continue. The moral power of the United States, he asserted near the end of World War II, was even greater than her political, economic, and military power; and he implied that she should continue to wield it.

Another reason for United States leadership of the world, in Roosevelt's mind, was his belief that as Europe disintegrated into chaos, Western culture might disappear unless the United States preserved it and assumed leadership in perpetuating and restoring it. Here was another idea that Roosevelt might have gotten from Mahan in his youth, for as early as 1894 Mahan had expressed the view that the Anglo-American peoples must be the protectors of modern civilization, a civilization based on indvidual freedom and respect for law. By the time of Munich, Roosevelt felt that Europe already disintegrated so much that in the years to come it would be up to the United States to "pick up the pieces of European civilization and help them to save what remains of the wreck. . . ." The United States was the heir of European culture, he declared a year later, and it was up to her to keep that civilization alive. In 1940 he asserted again that the United States (along with the other American republics) must become the "guardians of western culture, the protectors of Christian civilization," and he implied that United States leadership was essential for that task.

Roosevelt also seemed to think that peaceful relations among the guardians might also be dependent on United States leadership. It would be her task to serve as moderator in the conflicts that must inevitably arise among Britain, the Soviet Union, and China, all of whom were suspicious of each other, and all of whom would need a referee.

A final argument Roosevelt presented for United States leadership among the guardians was that the postwar world would offer the United States a large opportunity to shape the kind of world she wanted, and unless she took hold of the opportunity this time, she might never have another chance. "It is the destiny of this American generation," he said in the 1940 campaign, "to point the road to the future for all the world to see. It is our prayer that all lovers of freedom may join us—the anguished common people of this earth for whom we seek to light the path." Late in 1944 he reminded the country that after World War I the United States had failed to organize the kind of world conducive to peace. "Opportunity knocks again," he added. But "there is no guarantee that opportunity will knock a third time." A few weeks before his death he reiterated this idea, arguing that the United States had a rendezvous with destiny. Ahead lay both promise and danger. The world could go forward toward unity and a widely shared prosperity or it could go backward and break up into competing economic blocks. The decision was in the hands of the United States, or at the very least the United States could influence that decision mightily. If, therefore, the American people wanted the world to go in the direction conducive to their way of life, they had better lead the way.

It is obvious that Roosevelt's conception of a collective security system under the guardianship of the Big Powers led by the United States was very paternalistic and clearly placed all the medium and small powers in the position of children in the family of nations. It seems likely that Roosevelt finally agreed to accept some small powers on the Security Council of the United Nations only on the assumption that their role would be minor and their participation would be of only the "ostensible" type he had told Welles in 1941 might be acceptable. He was willing, however, to have an assembly or some sort of forum wherein the lesser powers could express their views. His hopes for a global New Deal and a good neighbor climate of opinion had great bearing on the problem of security; and while his attitude toward smaller nations was that of a father, it was the attitude of a good father and a twentieth-century, somewhat democratic and benevolent father who had the best interests of the children at heart; and if he could not quite bring himself to let the children have a vote in important family decisions, he nevertheless wanted them to express their views, be treated with decency, and be made to feel important.

*   *   *

It is very doubtful that Roosevelt believed that power politics could ever be abolished completely and it is quite likely that the comments he made to that effect in a few of his speeches were inserted by the State Department and delivered without much thought. The weight of the evidence indicates that Roosevelt was entirely too practical to believe that his ideals could ever be more than aimed at and approximated. Even though, therefore, Roosevelt's goal was a world order in which the struggle for power was far more restrained than in the nineteenth century and in which a cooperative attack would be made on the problems of ignorance, disease, and poverty surpassing any previous effort ever known, it is doubtful that he expected the transformation of international relations to involve more than modest progress toward his goals.

Roosevelt's major objective was simply to turn the world around, to stop the trend toward more hell and chaos, and to get the world going again in the right direction. Unfortunately, his psychotherapy was not sufficiently effective to prevent the cold war. But is it not possible that his psychiatric approach was a sound one and that the major problem of international relations—of all politics—lies in the attitudes of men, as the UNESCO thesis holds, and that the problem can be much ameliorated, even if not solved, by the thesis that a good neighbor approach will, if pursued long enough, produce a good neighbor response from all except a small group of incurables?

William A. Williams

FDR—A REFLECTION OF AMERICAN POLITICAL ECONOMY

William A. Williams, currently professor of history at Oregon State University and author of a number of provocative books and articles on American foreign policy, also claims that Roosevelt reflects basic American goals and aspirations. In Williams' view, however, those goals are materialistic and restricting rather than idealistic and uplifting. In his The Roots of the Modern American Empire *(1969), Williams emphasized the significance of the need for foreign markets for agricultural goods as a determinant of American policy during the nineteenth century, and the tragedy referred to in his essay,* The Tragedy of American Diplomacy, *excerpted below, is that American success in following a policy of ever-expanding industrial markets in the twentieth century completely negated any more humane and idealistic facets of that policy. In short, Williams finds that the economic and political demands of our liberal-capitalist system have, in the long run, superseded other more lofty impulses. Williams hints that Franklin Roosevelt showed signs of breaking that pattern but the pressure of events soon forced American policy into the old pursuit of the Open Door; that is, the creation of a world in which American political, economic, and social institutions could flourish and spread.*

While the initial necessity to grapple with the domestic crisis temporarily de-emphasized the foreign policy that was an integral part of that outlook, the New Deal did not signify any fundamental change in the traditional policies of economic and ideological empire. Even in the depths of the depression, and increasingly so in subsequent years, the overseas expansion of the American corporate system was considered a basic means of recovery and further development. Franklin Roosevelt quickly reasserted, moreover, the kind of aristocratic *noblesse oblige* that his cousin Theodore had infused into American diplomacy. He also revealed a good bit of the crusading fervor for the extension of American ideas and ideals that had characterized the outlook and actions of Woodrow Wilson. . . .

But thinking of the New Deal so narrowly (or wholly) as a reform movement tends to blind both its critics and its defenders to the way that it steadily drew more and more of its leadership from the community of large, established corporation executives, their counsels, and their economic advisors. This does not necessarily mean that the New Deal became less reformist. It does mean, however, that the reforms were of a certain kind; namely, they rationalized the system as it existed, and did not lead to significant modifications of its character.

This aspect of New Deal leadership offers an important insight into the developments in American policy specifically toward Latin America, but also more generally, between 1937 and 1941. It helps explain, for example, the gradual willingness (after mid-1939) to grant a loan to Bolivia on the basis of a gentleman's agreement that Standard Oil would then be given prompt satisfaction on its claims. This slow and halting process of change was brought about by four principal factors. On the basis of the available evidence, they can be ranked in the following order of importance.

There was first a general reassertion during and after the sharp and serious recession of 1937–1938 of both central themes of American diplomacy as it evolved during and after the Crisis of the 1890s: that vigorous overseas economic expansion was essential to the functioning of the system; and that, as stated so explicitly by Secretary of State Root in 1906, policy had to be formulated so "that the door, being open, shall lead to something." This feeling, and the new urgency behind it, was manifested by government spokesmen and also by leaders of the corporate system who did not hold public office. Official policy-makers like Lawrence Duggan, Eric Johnston, and Nelson Rockefeller, for example, advanced this view with great vigor. But corporation leaders outside the government shared the same outlook. A group of them meeting in 1939 under the auspices of *Fortune* magazine agreed that it was important to "provide adequate economic opportunities to the so-called 'have-not' countries."

Secondly, American private and official leaders were by 1939 very disturbed by German and Japanese economic competition in Latin America (as well as in Asia). It may be, indeed, that this factor was most important of all. On the other hand, there were many important Americans who felt as late as 1940 that it would be possible to work out some kind of economic compromise with the Axis powers. Two things, however, are certain: Axis competition worried a significant number of men in policy-making positions after 1938, and that concern served to convince some of them that it was necessary to modify some of the existing practices of America's overseas economic expansion in order to protect the expansion itself. Sumner Welles offers a good example of the way that kind of interaction altered earlier attitudes and actions.

The third consideration was the determination on the part of some of the larger Latin American countries, such as Mexico, to stand firm in their efforts to reform, control, and restrict American business activities in their countries. This resistance unquestionably speeded up the modification of American policy.

Fourth, the humanitarian idealism of American policy-makers affected their decisions. Never absent in the making of American policy, it enjoyed a renaissance in the late 1930s. This is no doubt partly explained as a reaction against Axis domestic and foreign policies whose nature was growing more obvious and more disturbing after 1936. But it was also the result of a few strong and even assertive reformers having positions of some authority, probably the best example being Josephus Daniels as Ambassador to Mexico. He not only softened some of Hull's outbursts to the Mexicans, but also enjoyed a direct correspondence with Roosevelt. More significant, however, the existence of a growing crisis by nature involved Roosevelt more directly in all relations with Latin America. And that brought his sense and spirit of *noblesse oblige* more actively into the policy-making process.

*   *   *

Considered alone, the combined economic and strategic challenge from the Axis could, and might well, have prompted the United States to maintain its intransigence (and even to increase its economic pressures). That was, after all, the course followed in dealing with Argentina. Such a might-have-been proposition is useful primarily to help clarify the reason that it did not occur. And that seems clearly to have been because Roosevelt was reached and persuaded by those policy-makers who insisted upon the need for a sophisticated reform in the methods of America's overseas economic expansion. The Duggan-Rockefeller-Johnston group had worked out a broad tactical conception which, as Professor Lloyd Gardner has described it, amounted to modifying the laissez faire system of Adam Smith so that separate national economies rather than individuals were defined as the entrepreneurs.

Now it is true, at least in one sense, that this was not so much an adaptation of Adam Smith as simply a decision to honor in practice the precepts of the theory as originally stated. Smith did lay great emphasis on the international division of labor, and that one point could be (and was) interpreted to mean that raw-material producing countries remained raw-material producing countries even though they became more efficient. But Smith also stressed freedom of enterprise where the resources existed, and many nations which in 1939 were still raw material producers enjoyed human and material resources that were capable of building and sustaining far more diversified economies. *To a certain extent, and one still to be controlled and structured by the economy and the policies of the United States, this latter interpretation of Smith is the one advanced by the sophisticated American reformers.* The idea was to create somewhat more diversified political economies under the direction of the United States. The economic objectives were more markets and more efficiently produced raw materials. The political objective was middle-class government stabilized in a pro-American posture. . . .

As they devoted more of their attention and energy to the challenge of extending the new American frontier, many economic leaders became enthusiastic converts to the mission to reform the world. The convergence of a sense of economic necessity and a moral calling transformed the traditional concept of Open Door expansion into a vision of an American Century. In this fashion, the United States entered and fought World War II. Americans were convinced that they were defending an anticolonial democracy charged with a duty to regenerate the world. They also had come firmly to believe that their own prosperity and democracy depended upon the continued expansion of their economic system under the strategy of the Open Door.

*　　　*　　　*

Politicians become statesmen, not by honoring pious shibboleths, nor even by moving men to action with inspiring rhetoric, but by recognizing and then resolving the central dilemmas of their age.

When measured against this demanding standard, Franklin Delano Roosevelt's performance after 1940 poses a difficult problem in judgment for the historian. On the one hand, he seems clearly enough to have sensed the contradiction between his intellectual, emotional, and policy commitment to America's traditional strategy of the Open Door, and the new circumstances arising out of World War II which called for the acceptance of limits upon American expectations and actions, and for the working out of a concert of power with other major nations. Though it was not in any sense unique, Roosevelt's recognition of that new reality does entitle him to a place of honor within the community of American policy-makers. It also explains and justifies the praise of his partisans.

On the other hand Roosevelt did not resolve the dilemma posed by that contradiction between tradition and reality. He occasionally spoke candidly of the problem. He offered a few very general ideas about the kind of things that could be done to adapt American thinking and policy to the new conditions. And he even suggested a few concrete proposals for dealing with specific aspects of the developing crisis. But he never worked out, initiated, or carried through a fresh approach which combined necessary domestic changes with a fundamental reevaluation of American foreign policy. He did not resolve the dilemma. At the time of his death, he was turning back toward the inadequate domestic programs of the New Deal era, and was in foreign affairs reasserting the traditional strategy of the Open Door Policy.

Explorations into the forest of conditional history are sometimes fruitful, for they occasionally suggest new insights into what did occur. This is perhaps the case with the debate over what would have happened if Roosevelt had lived. The most sympathetic interpretation explains Roosevelt's ambivalence as a result of his declining health. But while his fatigue was a relevant consideration, there is little evidence that Roosevelt seriously entertained even the idea of initiating a reevaluation of America's conception of itself and the world. For the further such an inquiry is pushed, the more it becomes apparent that Roosevelt had not abandoned the policy of the Open Door; and that, even if he personally had been on the verge of trying to do so, few of his advisors and subordinates had either the intention or the power to effect such a change. . . .

Supported by a thoroughly bipartisan assortment of liberals and conservatives, this reassertion of the traditional Open Door strategy guided the community of American policy-makers throughout the war and on into the cold war era. Ultimately it became, in the best tradition of the Open Door, and in the words of G. L. Arnold, a sympathetic British observer, a view of the world resting "upon the expectation of a prolonged era of peace, Anglo-American hegemony (with the aid of China) in the United Nations and in the world generally, free trade outside the Soviet Orbit and gradual liberalization within, a weakened and profoundly pacific Russia far behind the Western powers in the utilization of atomic energy." The assumption of virtuous omnipotence, implicit in the Open Door Notes and formulated explicitly on the eve of American entry into World War I, reached full maturity in that image of an American Century. As with Theodore Roosevelt's concern to save civilization and Wilson's crusade to make the world safe for democracy, however, the urge to give the future a New Deal was powered by a persuasive sense of the necessity to expand economically in order to sustain democracy and prosperity in the United States.

In keeping with this outlook, the United States declined in the winter of 1941–1942 even to consider the Soviet Union's bid to settle the postwar boundaries of Eastern Europe on the basis of the situation as it existed just prior to Hitler's attack. Russia raised the question in conversations with the British during November and December 1941, at which time Soviet spokesmen made clear and pointed references to being left out of the Atlantic Conference discussions of August, 1941, between Churchill and Roosevelt.

Stalin suggested five major areas for agreement: (1) the boundaries of the Soviet Union should be guaranteed largely as they existed just prior to Hitler's assault in June, 1941 (including the Curzon Line in Poland); (2) Austria should be restored as an independent nation; (3) Germany's industrial and military base should be weakened by splitting off the Ruhr manufacturing complex, by incorporating East Prussia into Poland, and perhaps by breaking off one other large province; (4) Yugoslavia and Albania should be reestablished as independent countries, and Czechoslovakia and Greece should have their prewar boundaries reaffirmed; and (5) Russia should receive reparations in kind from Germany.

These proposals pose a fascinating "iffy" question: what if Russia had been committed to those conditions, and they had been honored by both sides? Certainly the postwar era would have developed in a significantly different manner. Another consideration is more relevant to what did happen, because the Soviets continued in large measure the emphasize their proposals of 1941 during the war and on into the subsequent period.

At the time, however, the American response was wholly negative. Hull considered it "unfortunate" even to discuss such "commitments," and simply refused to agree to them. He first put strong pressure on the British to delay and then spurn the Soviet offer. There is no particular mystery about his adamant. In the most general sense, American leaders did not want to negotiate any settlements until they were in the strongest possible position, and they thought that would be at the end of the war. More specifically, their guiding attitude was that of the Open Door Policy, and they had neither the desire nor the intention to negotiate away any equality of opportunity in Eastern Europe. . . .

In order to bypass all the misunderstanding that it is possible to avoid, let these points be stated as simply and as directly as possible. As Stalin made clear in the winter of 1941–1942, the Soviet Union fully intended to reestablish what it considered to be its minimum natural and desirable frontiers in Eastern Europe. He further concluded that the United States and England would resist that effort. His opposition raised in the minds of Soviet leaders the very natural question as to whether or not they did not need an even firmer security perimeter.

Hence the problem for American leaders was one of developing an attitude and a broad set of proposals involving such security and economic aid for the Soviet Union that would enable them to negotiate some kind of modus vivendi with the Russians. The failure of American leaders to do that is the central theme of American diplomacy after the abortive negotiations of 1941–1942. If studied and written as a critique of Soviet policy, the emphasis involved in treating these matters would be different. In that case, the story might very well focus on the way that the breakdown of the talks of 1941–1942 strengthened those Soviet leaders who laid primary stress on extending communism as the Red Army moved westward. That might very possibly be the real tragedy of Soviet diplomacy. But since this essay is about American diplomacy, and—even more—since it was the United States that refused to offer any clear and unequivocal basis for such fundamental negotiations, the essay has to concentrate on America's actions and the ideas behind them.

*   *   *

There is at least one account, moreover, which suggests that Roosevelt's position was very similar to those who wanted to use Russia's needs to win major political and economic concessions. The story is told by James Byrnes in his second volume of memoirs, *All In One Life.* He reports that Leo Crowley, who was to terminate Lend-Lease shipments to the Soviet Union as soon as Germany surrendered, told him of a conversation with Roosevelt that took place about April 1, 1945, shortly before the President died. "Crowley told me that . . . he told the President about a rumor that our government was considering a loan to the Soviets of $10 billion, and that he [Crowley] thought it wise to refrain from making any loan until more was known of their postwar attitude. He said the President agreed." This account should not be taken as full proof of Roosevelt's attitude. But it does, even when evaluated with caution, support the main point at issue. It is simply not possible to account for the continuance of the Open Door Policy by blaming Roosevelt's successors, for the President did not carry through on persistent Russian overtures for major economic assistance to help them rebuild their shattered economy.

Had Roosevelt done this, it would be more meaningful to charge his successors—or the Russians—with sabotaging his plan for the future; for it is quite true that the small group around Nelson favoring some rapprochement with the Russians was opposed by a much larger number of America's corporate leaders. It seems likely that Averell Harriman, one of the many wealthy industrial and banking leaders who supported Roosevelt, and who was one of the President's top advisors, was one of the more influential leaders of the anti-Russian group. Harriman's natural antagonism to the Soviets was reinforced by his vigorous belief in the necessity of Open-Door expansion, a belief that may have been heightened even more by an unhappy experience with the Russians in the 1920s, when his attempt to control a sizable segment of the world's manganese market by developing Russian supplies ended in mutual dissatisfaction. Harriman was but

one of many corporate leaders, however, who had gone into the
Roosevelt Administration with anti-Russian views. Others included
James B. Forrestal and Bernard Baruch. All of these men were skep-
tical of Nelson's approach to dealing with the Soviets and were sup-
ported in their view by State Department experts such as George F.
Kennan (who was in Russia much of the time with Harriman).

*   *   *

Roosevelt's attitude, which so clearly reflected the traditional outlook of the Open Door Policy, was revealed even more vividly in the
spring of 1944, when the Soviet Army began to advance into Eastern
Europe. Confronted by Churchill with the need to come to some clear
arrangement with the Russians, Roosevelt at first agreed to the idea
of a clear and precise division of authority. Then, in an abrupt turn-
about, he asserted that he must have "complete freedom of action,"
whatever the agreement arranged by Churchill and Stalin. After considerable effort, Churchill and Stalin worked out an understanding—
"a good guide," said Churchill, "for the conduct of our affairs"—
whereby Russia would exercise predominant authority in southeastern
Europe, Great Britain would do so in Greece, and the Allies would
share responsibility in Yugoslavia. Roosevelt reluctantly accepted this
division of power on the basis of a three-month trial.

During subsequent months, the British intervened to crush a revolution in Greece and prepare the way for the installation of a government they wanted and could control. Though he urged the British to
take a more liberal line, Roosevelt went along with Churchill on the
need to control affairs in Greece and acquiesced in the Prime Minister's action. *Both in fact and in the eyes of the Russians, that committed Roosevelt on the eve of the Yalta Conference to the agreement
worked out between Churchill and Stalin.* For his part, Stalin refrained
from attacking or blocking the British move in Greece. Churchill reported that Stalin "adhered very strictly to this understanding." Stalin
also initiated his efforts to forestall trouble with the Western Allies
arising from foreign Communist agitation and revolution. He advised,
and apparently even warned, Tito and Mao Tse-tung to abstain from
revolutionary action in their nations and instead to accept subordinate
positions in coalition governments led by pro-Western parties.

Against this background, and in the context of Germany's imminent defeat, Roosevelt met Churchill and Stalin at Yalta in February,

1945. In addition to their knowledge of the Churchill-Stalin agreement, and of Stalin's self-containment during the Greek episode, American leaders were aware that the Chinese Communists, after a long debate, had concluded in September, 1944, that they preferred to work with the United States rather than with Russia in the future development of China. Thus it is absolutely clear that Roosevelt and his advisors knew that the Soviet Union was prepared to negotiate seriously about the character of postwar relations with the United States and that America had an equally fruitful opportunity in Asia. But during the conference American leaders were not concerned to push such negotiations. They were not prepared to abandon, or even seriously to modify, the traditional strategy of American expansion.

Disturbed by America's ambivalence and Churchill's increasingly open opposition, which increased the difficulty Stalin had in controlling the doctrinaire revolutionaries within his own camp, Stalin went to Yalta with two approaches to the postwar world. One was based on receiving a large loan from the United States. His overtures in this direction were answered with vague and unrewarding replies. Stalin's alternative was to obtain, by agreement or by self-exertion, economic reparations from Germany and a strong strategic position in Eastern Europe, the Black Sea area, and the Far East. America went to Yalta, on the other hand, guided by little except a sense of mission to reform the world, a growing fear of postwar economic crisis, and an increasing confidence that Russian weakness would enable America to exercise its freedom and solve its problems by further Open-Door expansion.

Commentators have criticized President Roosevelt very severely on the grounds that he was naive in believing that he could persuade Stalin to cooperate with the West after the war. Such attacks are weak and misdirected in several important respects. In the first place, it is almost absurd to think—or charge—that a man with Roosevelt's mastery of political infighting was naive. He may have overestimated his power or his skill, but he was not naive. Significantly, too, Roosevelt had *not* abandoned, at the time of his death, the intention of reasserting American power and influence in Eastern Europe. It was suggested to him that the United States should file a vigorous protest over the Soviet action early in 1945 of reconstituting the Rumanian government along pro-Soviet lines. Roosevelt did *not* reply that the basic issue should be forgotten. His position was quite different. *He said merely that the Rumanian episode, because it involved supplies for the Red Army that was still fighting Germany, did not offer the best kind of ground upon which to take a stand.*

Roosevelt's idea of reaching an accommodation with Stalin was not based on some utopian dream of perfect and everlasting agreement on any and all issues. However, Roosevelt simply did not understand the nature and workings of a modern, complex industrial economy. The result in domestic affairs was that his political acumen and skill were never focused on the central and vital issues of getting the political economy into some kind of fundamentally dynamic balance. The same weakness plagued him in dealing with the Russians. He never got his priorities straight. Short of war, economic aid was the one effective tool he had in negotiations with the Soviets. But he never used it.

Roosevelt's successors understood and used that lever, but they treated it as a weapon to force the Soviets to accept American policies. The conflict over affairs in Eastern Europe which developed out of that attitude is usually stressed in discussing the origins of the cold war. Yet it may be that the issues of German reparations and American expansion in the Middle East were equally important as determining factors. Failing to obtain a loan from America, Stalin had to decide between three possible courses of action.

He could give way and accept the American interpretation of all disputed points, abandoning foreign Communists to their fate and attempting to control the extremists in his own nation. He could respond with an orthodox revolutionary program throughout the world. Or, relying on large economic reparations from Germany, he could continue the effort to resolve his dilemma in a conservative manner even though he did not have any formal understanding with the United States. This approach would also do much to keep Germany from becoming a threat to Russia in the immediate future. It left him, however, with the need to effect some basic settlement concerning Eastern Europe, the Far East, and the Black Sea region.

Stalin was able to reach such an understanding with the United States in but one of those areas. This was in Asia, where he traded American predominance in China (and Japan) for strategic and economic rights in Manchuria. Concerning Eastern Europe, however, Stalin accepted an ambivalent proposal on the Polish issue which represented America's unwillingness to acknowledge his agreement with Churchill as much as it did Russia's security needs. He was no more successful in the Middle East, where American oil companies had moved back into Iran in 1943. Supported by the State Department and special emissaries, the companies were well along in their efforts to obtain extensive concessions. Roosevelt was "thrilled" by the chance to work along with the oil companies and make Iran an example of what America could do for underdeveloped areas of the world, an attitude which helps explain why the United States was not willing to allow the Russians to obtain oil rights in northern Iran. Stalin gave way on the issue at Yalta and also refrained from pushing his desire to gain more security for Russia in the Black Sea area.

Despite his failure to get any positive response from the United States on the question of a postwar loan, or a clear understanding on other vital issues, Stalin still hoped to effect a conservative resolution of his dilemma. Throughout the first half of 1945, for example, *Izvestia* stressed the vitality of the American economy (in striking contrast to the fears being expressed in congressional hearings), emphasized the importance of resolving outstanding issues by negotiation, and reiterated the fruitfulness of economic cooperation. The British press attaché in Russia reported that Soviet comment remained restrained and hopeful until America initiated a campaign of vigorous criticism and protest aimed at Soviet predominance in Eastern Europe.

But the most significant indicators of the predisposition to work out some modus vivendi with the United States, and then to concentrate on internal recovery and development, came in the debates within the Soviet hierarchy, and in the relatively restrained policies followed in Eastern Europe after the Nazis were defeated. . . .

Soviet officials who later chose to live in the West often offered the same kind of evidence bearing on Russian policy at the end of the war. One of the American experts who interviewed many such men offered this general judgment about Soviet policy in Germany. "The paramount consideration was not the extension of the revolution to Germany and the establishment of a Soviet Government there, but the rehabilitation of the Soviet Union's war-ravaged industry and transportation . . . regardless of the effect this policy might have on . . . establishing a Soviet Germany." For that matter, the Red Army's railroad lines across Poland into Germany were ripped up in 1945. And in Eastern Europe, the Soviet approach was modeled on the popular front governments of the 1930s rather than upon the existing Soviet system.

The point of these examples (and there are many more) is not to suggest, let alone try to prove, that Stalin and other Soviet leaders behaved either as Western democrats or as men uninterested in exercising influence in Eastern Europe. The point is to indicate and to stress the importance of three quite different things: first, the very significant extent to which Soviet decisions from 1944 through 1947 were based on domestic Russian conditions; second, the degree to which the Soviets were assuming that capitalism would stabilize itself around the great and undamaged power of the United States; and third, the way in which those two factors pointed in the mind of many Russians—including Stalin—to the need to reach some kind of agreement with America. They never defined such an understanding on the basis of abandoning Russian influence in Eastern Europe or acquiescing in each and every American proposal just as it first emanated from Washington. But neither did they emerge from World War II with a determination to take over Eastern Europe and then embark upon a cold war with the United States.

James MacGregor Burns

FDR—"BOTH FIXER AND PREACHER"

The title of this selection, taken from one of the chapters in James Mac-Gregor Burns' study of Roosevelt: The Soldier of Freedom, 1940–1945 *succinctly sums up Burns' appraisal of Franklin Roosevelt's foreign policies. Burns, who is professor of political science at Williams College and the author of a number of books and articles including* Roosevelt: The Lion and the Fox *(1956), reflects what is the most widely held view of Roosevelt's approach to international affairs during World War II. Essentially, he asserts that the President articulated high and inspiring ideal goals, but lacked the means by which to achieve them. In spite of a realistic and practical analysis of international power relationships, Roosevelt consistently raised false hopes among Americans about his ability to solve postwar problems in accordance with the principles of self-determination, political freedom, and international cooperation. Unable to reconcile such things as spheres of influence for the Soviet Union with democratic liberties, Roosevelt came under attack at home and abroad. What he tried to do was to walk a tightrope between sheer power politics and utopian idealism. Burns can only admire the goals and the attempt while criticizing the impracticality of the policy.*

Since Pearl Harbor, Roosevelt had been pursuing two aims in China: to strengthen it as the central base for the final attack on Japan, and to treat it as a great power that would be a bulwark of Asian stability and democracy after the war and a focus of American cooperation with Asia. While the first aim was a matter of military need and the latter of long-run hopes, the two goals meshed. By sending men, munitions, and money to China he was strengthening its postwar as well as its war role; by including China as one of the Big Four, by bringing it into summit conferences such as that at Cairo, he was bolstering Chungking's legitimacy, giving it a greater claim on war supply and on participation in military decisions.

Roosevelt sharply modified his first goal during 1944. As Chiang's armies melted away before the Japanese ground attack, as Chennault not only failed to break up that attack but also lost his advance air bases, as Chiang refused to undertake drastic reforms of his government and army command, and—most important by far—as American amphibious forces hopped across the Pacific with ever-growing

FIGURE 6. The second front: a political or military issue? (1943) (Courtesy, *The Washington (D.C.) Star-News*)

power and momentum, the President lost hope that China would constitute the main springboard for the climactic assault on the home islands. Stalin's promise to take on the Japanese armies in Manchuria sometime after Hitler's fall, along with the anti-Japanese and pro-American attitude of the Yenan Communists, made Chiang's role even less vital. In telling the Generalissimo twice in October that the ground situation in China had deteriorated so sharply that he no longer wanted an American officer to take command of Chiang's forces under the Kuomintang, Roosevelt was not only venting his frustration, but he was signaling his changed military policy, and he was demonstrating once again that essentially military considerations dominated his basic strategy.

The shift in military policy, however, was not accompanied by a shift in political. Faced with his failure in China, Roosevelt had a choice of only two fundamental alternatives. He could continue or even accelerate his military effort in China and try to persuade or compel Chiang to produce basic reforms, thus giving the government the military basis for its aspirations as a great power; or he could scale down his political goals for China at the same time he scaled down his military ones. In fact, the President tried to do both and ran the risk of succeeding in neither. He kept talking to and about China as a great power even while he was giving higher and higher military priorities to other theaters.

This separation of strictly military and operational from broad political or strategic considerations in Asia exemplified Roosevelt's approach to the European situation, too. Europe First had been his firm priority from the start, regardless of political-military implications for Asia. And in planning strategy in Europe he and Stimson and Marshall had put it to the more politically minded British that the invasion of France was the quickest, cheapest, and surest means of defeating Germany. Churchill had struggled to plant Allied influence in the Balkan area, only to give in to Roosevelt's insistence on nourishing the invasion of France even at the expense of the Allied effort in northern Italy. In the fall of 1944, as Allied troops pressed to the border of Germany, the American emphasis on a focused, massed military effort, regardless of political considerations, seemed vindicated.

Other examples of Roosevelt's setting military over political priorities could be cited—his cautious approach to rescuing the Jews of Europe, his handling of the occupation zones in Germany, his withholding of atomic information from the Russians—but his absolute insistence on unconditional surrender seemed to some at the time and to many in retrospect as the clearest example of his subordination of long-run political concerns to immediate military ones. The practical purposes of unconditional surrender were to allow the Allied commands to concentrate on winning a total military victory over Germany, to strengthen the anti-Hitler military coalition by insuring that neither Russians nor Anglo-Americans would negotiate for a separate peace, and to help insure that the Russians would live up to their promise to join the war against Japan. Neither Churchill nor Stalin supported the doctrine with Roosevelt's determination, but each gave it lip service while seeking to modify it to meet particular situations.

If military strategy, in Samuel Morison's words, is the art of defeating the enemy in the most economical and expeditious manner, Roosevelt must rate high as a military strategist. As Commander in Chief he husbanded military resources in both the Atlantic and the Pacific until the enormous power, industrial and technological, of the nation could be brought to bear on the military scene. Despite endless temptations to strike elsewhere he stuck firmly to an overall strategy of Atlantic First, and in Europe, despite the diversions of Africa and Italy, he and his military chiefs finally delivered the full weight of the Anglo-American effort into France. He helped gain a maximum Soviet contribution to the bleeding of German ground strength and brought Allied troops into the heart of Germany at just the right time to share in and claim military victory; he found the right formula for getting the most militarily from the Russians without letting them, if they had so wished, occupy the whole continent. And if he was deliberate and single-minded in Europe, where victory demanded consistency and continuity of effort, he was opportunistic and flexible in the early stages of the Pacific war. He shifted from a strategy of depending on China and Formosa as huge bases for ground forces to stepped-up island-hopping by amphibious forces. Compared with Soviet, German, and even British losses, and considering the range and intensity of the effort and the skillful and fanatical resistance of the enemy, American casualties in World War II were remarkably light.

He had been an architect of military victory. Well could the Commander in Chief boast in his Navy Day campaign talk in Philadelphia on October 27, 1944, that, since Navy Day a year before, the army, navy, and air force had participated in no fewer than twenty-seven landings in force on enemy-held soil and that "every one of those 27 D-Days has been a triumphant success." Until the final days of 1944 Roosevelt never met a major military defeat after the setbacks of Pearl Harbor, the Philippines, Kasserine Pass, and in the Pacific during the first fifteen months of the war.

But grand strategy—achieving the nation's broad and enduring goals by marshaling its full military, diplomatic, economic, and psychological resources—puts a much harsher test to a commander in chief.

Grand strategy requires not only putting ends before means, political goals before military, long-run aims before immediate success. It is not merely, in the Clausewitzian sense, the subordination of war to diplomacy, and diplomacy to politics. It is the marshaling of a series of plans and decisions in every relevant area of a nation's life—war, diplomacy, economics, popular opinion, domestic politics —in such an order that power and action can be mobilized persistently and widely behind a people's enduring principles and goals, that the instrumental ends and means—governmental policies, military decisions, institutional patterns—be continually readapted in the light of the wider purposes being served, and that the goals and principles be reassessed in the light of those ends and means. The language of grand strategy is the language of priorities. The priorities serve and structure a nation's ideology.

It has become conventional to see Roosevelt as a master pragmatist or opportunist or improviser who waged war without political ends in mind, or who at least subordinated his ends to his means and made a mess of the former, or even of both. The dichotomy was not this simple.

Roosevelt had political goals; few leaders in history, indeed, have defined them with more eloquence or persistence. He expressed these goals most broadly and simply in the Four Freedoms—freedom of speech, freedom of religion, freedom from fear, freedom from want— a bit more extensively in the Atlantic Charter, and at great length in a host of pronouncements, campaign speeches, press releases, fireside chats, letters, and conversations. The Four Freedoms, he said, were the "ultimate stake," perhaps not immediately attainable throughout the world, "but humanity does move toward those glorious ideals through democratic processes." Those freedoms would be realized through the more specific aims of the Atlantic Charter—the end of territorial aggrandizement, the right of all peoples to choose their own form of government, the free and fair sharing of raw materials, international collaboration to raise living standards, abandonment by nations of the use of force. Serving these goals in turn were a host of still more concrete policies and institutions: Big Power unity and cooperation, the complete eradication of Nazism, general disarmament, a United Nations with power to enforce the peace, and a variety of international agencies and arrangements for specific purposes in education, transportation, relief, refugees, and many other fields.

It is said that while Roosevelt stated noble ultimate ends and appropriate instrumental ends and generally believed in them, he ignored or compromised them when an immediate purpose or advantage could thereby be achieved, that he was supremely subject to what Alfred Vagts has called the vice of immediacy. He decided in favor of the invasion of North Africa, for example, without fully grasping its inevitable effect of delaying the cross-channel attack on Germany; and he "walked with the devil" in the person of Darlan and Franco and Badoglio without seeing the implications for democratic principle and morale. Too, in 1942 he could urge on Smuts that the United Nations not adopt a hard-and-fast strategic policy for 1943 until 1942 operations were concluded. And he could tell Churchill, in perhaps the most revealing phrase of all, that the "political considerations you mention are important factors, but military operations based thereupon must be definitely secondary to the primary operations of striking at the heart of Germany."

The sharpest indictment of Roosevelt on this score concerns unconditional surrender. It has been ably argued that this policy, on which he insisted to the end and which was gleefully exploited by Goebbels, may well have hardened the resistance of the German people and the Wehrmacht, discouraged the resistance to Hitler inside the armed forces and without, prolonged the war, and caused unnecessary loss and bloodshed, and that all of this was at variance with Roosevelt's goals. Yet unconditional surrender is a prime example of how the standard indictment of Roosevelt can be turned around and can require a closer look at his grand strategy.

Unconditional surrender flatly contradicts the usual argument that Roosevelt was pragmatically and opportunistically concerned with immediate specific results at the expense of the more general and long run. It was fully apparent to the President, as to his friends and critics, that the Nazis could exploit unconditional surrender to stiffen resistance to the Allies. Indeed, the President's own Chiefs of Staff had advised him to modify the doctrine for military reasons. The Commander in Chief not only insisted on unconditional surrender, but he also resisted Machiavellian notions that he modify the doctrine publicly and later apply it in fact. Roosevelt's ultimate insistence on a direct attack on Germany, whatever the military cost, as compared to a strategy of encirclement or attrition, his decision to recover the Philippines largely for symbolic reasons despite practical military arguments for bypassing them, his own warning to senators that there could be no sharp division between political and military matters are other examples of his willingness to subordinate immediate military advantage to broader goals.

The real point is less Roosevelt's simple separation of political ends and military means than his capacity to marshal his means of all kinds—military, institutional, propagandistic, diplomatic, and indeed political—in support of his most fundamental objectives. His failures lay in linking the ends and the means. Thus he was banking on Soviet popular as well as governmental confidence in the willingness of the Big Four to share and sacrifice together, yet he agreed to a long delay in the coss-channel attack. He wished to recognize the potential role of the several hundred million Chinese people but made Chungking a poor third in the allocation of military assistance, and he was unwilling to apply the political pressure that was the only conceivable way to bring about military and possibly political and economic reforms in China. He was deeply concerned about colonialism and expressed strong views to the British about India in particular, only to draw back when Anglo-American collaboration seemed threatened. Even when Churchill appealed to him in 1944 for some ships after an ammunition ship had exploded in Bombay Harbor sinking vessels loaded with 36,000 tons of grain, Roosevelt refused to divert shipping from military needs.

Roosevelt was a practical man who proceeded now boldly, now cautiously, step by step toward immediate ends. He was also a dreamer and sermonizer who spelled out lofty goals and summoned people to follow him. He was both a Soldier of the Faith, battling with his warrior comrades for an ideology of peace and freedom, and a Prince of the State, protecting the interests of his nation in a tumultuous and impious world. His difficulty lay in the relation of the two. The fact that his faith was more a set of attitudes than a firmly grounded moral code, that it embraced hope verging on utopianism and sentiment bordering on sentimentality, that it was heavily moralistic, to the point, at least in the view of some, of being hypocritical and sanctimonious—all this made his credo evocative but also soft and pasty, so that it crumbled easily under the press of harsh policy alternatives and military decision.

Roosevelt's moral credo was a patchwork of attitudes and instincts about honor, decency, good neighborliness, *noblesse oblige.* It was often hard to translate these attitudes and instincts into clear directives, operative programs, specific policies. His mind rejected comprehensive plans and long-run programs. He shrank from set institutional arrangements because these tended to freeze rather than invigorate end-means relations. Trumbull Higgins has said of Roosevelt that when his "dichotomies" could not be resolved by the great political magician himself, they were left to circumstance." But Roosevelt's lofty dreams and his parochial compromises not only collided with one another; they also inflated the importance of each other, for the higher he set his goals and the lower he pitched his practical improvisations, the more he widened the gap between the existing and the ideal and raised men's expectations while failing to fulfill them.

Roosevelt's views of atomic secrecy are a case in point. All his instincts were toward trusting people, toward sharing, toward fostering the community of learning. Churchill had aroused his fears and suspicions at Hyde Park about the Soviet quest for atomic information, but when members of the scientific community became less alarmed about the German threat and more alarmed about the dangers of secrecy, and when scientists brought influence to bear in the White House during the fall of 1944, the President may have drifted back toward his original instinct of putting some trust in the Russians and restricting the use of the bomb. Alexander Sachs got in to see him in December and claimed later that Roosevelt agreed that the first step should be a nonmilitary demonstration of the bomb observed by international scientists and clergymen, following which a warning would be given, specifying the time and place of an imminent nuclear attack, thus permitting civilians to escape. But he never did instruct Stimson to carry out such a plan, and he took no step toward sharing the secret with the Russians. He talked about the global brotherhood of science and the ability of all peoples to work together for peace, but between the idea and the reality, between the conception and the creation, fell the shadow.

If Roosevelt was both realist and idealist, both fixer and preacher, both a prince and a soldier, the reason lay not merely in his own mind and background, but also in his society and its traditions. Americans have long had both moralistic and realistic tendencies, the first strain symbolized by Wilson, the second by the tough-minded men—Washington, Monroe, the two Adamses—who directed the foreign policy of the republic in its early years. No modern American statesman could fail to reflect this dualism. If Roosevelt's values were a bit overblown and vaporous, they were developed against a background of liberal values and internationalist impulses so widely shared and diluted as to provide little ideological support for politicians and parties. To some extent Roosevelt succumbed to the classic dilemma of the democratic leader: he must moralize and dramatize and personalize and simplify in order to lead and hold the public, but in doing so he may arouse false hopes and expectations, including his own, the deflation of which in the long run may lead to disillusionment and cynicism.

American foreign policy in particular has been shaped by two diplomacies, as Russell Bastert has argued—one diplomacy of short-run expediency and manipulation, of balance of power and sphere of interest, of compromise and adjustment, marginal choices, and limited objectives, and another diplomacy—almost an antidiplomacy —of world unity and collective security, democratic principle and moral uplift, peaceful change and nonaggression. Then, too, the institutional arrangements in Washington—the separation of decision-making between the State Department and the Pentagon, and in their lines of access to the President, the absence from the White House of a staff that could integrate diplomacy and military policy, the institutional gaps in Congress among legislators specializing in military, foreign, and domestic policies, and indeed the whole tendency in Washington toward fragmented policy-making—all reinforced the natural tendency of the President to compartmentalize.

All great nations, all world leaders exhibit such dichotomies; everything depends on the actual combinations. Stalin, for all his ruthless opportunism, was so consistently intent on the long-run, or at least middle-run, goal of postwar Soviet security that in the darkest days after Hitler's assault he would not barter or gamble on matters relating to that security. He was, like Roosevelt, a brilliant tactician, an actor and even a dissimulator; like Roosevelt he was a master of timing, of the art of "dosage"—measuring out pressure to what the traffic could bear—and of waiting and watching as well as striking out quickly; like Roosevelt he was superb in playing his adversaries off against one another. But Stalin far more than Roosevelt linked his wartime decisions to a strategy for long-run security, a strategy to which he adhered with steel-like tenacity. He had in abundance the defects of his virtue. Insecure, suspicious, parochial, he was so imbued with an essentially old-fashioned and brutal *Realpolitik* that he could never claim the impact on mass opinion and ideals of a Lenin, a Gandhi, or even a Roosevelt.

As a grand strategist Churchill was a more subtle study. Not lacking in his own canons of honor and responsibility, he embodied a diplomatic and military tradition that had helped Britain, in protecting its tiny isles against the colossi on the Continent, to practice all the black arts of diplomacy deplored by Hull and the other Wilsonians. He was, in truth, the Whig aristocrat of the eighteenth century that Harold Laski called him during the war. He had the aristocrat's saving compassion for the miserable, but he also had the Whig's fatal incomprehension of the tumultuous forces gushing out of the revolutions in Russia and China and elsewhere. Compared with Roosevelt's, his vision was long but narrow; he could see the relation between wartime strategy and postwar balances of power in Europe, but he could not imagine the surge of masses of people in Asia or Africa. Like Roosevelt he was an opportunist and improviser in his approach to grand strategy, but he lacked the comprehensive principles that gave at least a general direction and focus to Roosevelt's day-to-day decisions. He himself, as he once wrote admiringly of Lloyd George, "surveyed the problems of each morning with an eye unobstructed by preconceived opinions, past utterances, or previous disappointments and defeats," and in the wartime kaleidoscope of shifting values and prodigious events, his strategy drew from intuition and insight rather than long-run purpose and settled goals. Versatile, fertile, vigorous, he lacked the steadiness of direction, the comprehensiveness of outlook, the sense of proportion and relevance that mark the grand strategist. And his strategy was Western-oriented; Roosevelt at least glimpsed the explosive energy lying dormant in the billion people of Asia, especially when that energy was released and focused by the call of freedom that the antifascist leaders were trumpeting throughout the world.

*   *   *

Roosevelt, like Lincoln and Wilson, died fighting for his ideals. It might have been more dramatic if he had been assassinated by an ideological foe or had been stricken during a speech. But his decisions to aid Britain and Russia, his daring to take a position before the 1944 election against the Senate having direct power over America's peace-enforcing efforts in the proposed Council of the United Nations, his long, exhausting trips to Teheran and Yalta, his patient efforts to win Stalin's personal friendship, his willingness to go out on a limb in his belief that the United States and the Soviet Union could work together in the postwar world—all this testified to the depth of his conviction.

Yet he could believe with equal conviction that his prime duty was to defend his nation's interests, safeguard its youth, win the war as quickly as possible, protect its postwar economy. With his unconquerable optimism he felt that he could do both things—pursue global ideals and national *Realpolitik*—simultaneously. So he tried to win Soviet friendship and confidence at the same time he saved American lives by consenting to the delay in the cross-channel invasion, thus letting the Red Army bleed. He paid tribute to the brotherly spirit of global science just before he died even while he was withholding atomic information from his partners the Russians. He wanted to unite liberal Democrats and internationalist Republicans in one progressive party but he never did the spadework or took the personal political risks that such a strategy required. He yearned to help Indians and other Asiatic peoples gain their independence, but not at the risk of disrupting his military coalition with Britain and other Atlantic nations with colonial possessions in Asia. He ardently hoped to bring a strong, united, and democratic China into the Big Four, but he refused to apply to Chungking the military resources and political pressure necessary to arrest the dry rot in that country. Above all, he wanted to build a strong postwar international organization, but he dared not surrender his country's substantive veto in the council over peace-keeping, and as a practical matter he seemed more committed to Big Four, great-power peace-keeping than he did to a federation acting for the brotherhood of all mankind.

"I dream dreams but am, at the same time, an intensely practical person," Roosevelt wrote to Smuts during the war. Both his dreams and his practicality were admirable; the problem lay in the relation between the two. He failed to work out the intermediary ends and means necessary to accomplish his purposes. Partly because of his disbelief in planning far ahead, partly because he elevated short-run goals over long-run, and always because of his experience and temperament, he did not fashion the structure of action—the full array of mutually consistent means, political, economic, psychological, military—necessary to realize his paramount ends.

So the more he preached his lofty ends and practiced his limited means, the more he reflected and encouraged the old habit of the American democracy to "praise the Lord—and keep your powder dry" and the more he widened the gap between popular expectations and actual possibilities. Not only did this derangement of ends and means lead to crushed hopes, disillusion, and cynicism at home, but it helped sow the seeds of the cold war during World War II, as the Kremlin contrasted Roosevelt's coalition rhetoric with his Atlantic First strategy and falsely suspected a bourgeois conspiracy to destroy Soviet communism; and Indians and Chinese contrasted Roosevelt's anticolonial words with his military concessions to colonial powers, and falsely inferred that he was an imperialist at heart and a hypocrite to boot.

Roosevelt's critics attacked him as naïve, ignorant, amateurish in foreign affairs, but this man who had bested all his domestic enemies and most of his foreign was no innocent. His supreme difficulty lay not in his view as to what *was*—he had a Shakespearian appreciation of all the failings, vices, cruelties, and complexities of man—but of what *could be.* The last words he ever wrote, on the eve of his death, were the truest words he ever wrote. He had a strong and active faith, a huge and unprovable faith, in the possibilities of human understanding, trust, and love. He could say with Reinhold Niebuhr that love is the law of life even when people do not live by the law of love.

Suggestions for Additional Reading

Since historians have only recently begun to look at the foreign policy of Franklin D. Roosevelt as a single, self-contained package, there is no comprehensive, up-to-date study of his diplomacy. Instead, published works have concentrated upon either the prewar or the wartime phases, although an established Roosevelt scholar is working on a one-volume study of the Roosevelt foreign policy. Given Roosevelt's penchant for personal diplomacy, some understanding of the man is a prerequisite to any examination of his conduct on foreign affairs. Frank Freidel has written three volumes of a biography, *Franklin D. Roosevelt* (Boston, 1952–1959), dealing with the pre-presidential years, and is currently working on a fourth volume. Arthur Schlesinger, Jr. has also published three volumes of his study of the New Deal, *The Age of Roosevelt** (Boston, 1957, 1959, 1960), and has promised a separate volume on foreign affairs. An excellent one-volume study of Roosevelt as President, though it unfortunately ends with his reelection in 1940, is William Leuchtenberg, *Franklin D. Roosevelt and the New Deal, 1932–1940** (New York, 1963). The most recent complete study of Roosevelt's presidency is the two readable and perceptive volumes by James MacGregor Burns: *Roosevelt: The Lion and The Fox** and *Roosevelt: The Soldier of Freedom* (New York, 1956–1970). Burns is particularly adept at illustrating the relationship between domestic politics and Roosevelt's foreign policy.

A substantial body of primary printed sources on the Roosevelt foreign policy has accumulated. The most ambitious and informative collection will be *Franklin D. Roosevelt and Foreign Affairs,* edited by the staff of the Franklin D. Roosevelt Library in Hyde Park, New York. To date the series covers only Roosevelt's first term in office in three volumes edited by Edgar Nixon (Cambridge, Mass., 1969). Although all of the various collections of Roosevelt's speeches, press conferences, and radio talks are incomplete and must be supplemented by research in manuscript materials, the best compilation is Samuel I. Roseman's *The Public Papers and Addresses of Franklin D. Roosevelt* (13 vols.; New York and London, 1938–1950). Other useful collections are *F.D.R.: His Personal Letters, 1928–1945,* ed.

* Indicates paperbound edition available.

Elliott Roosevelt (2 vols.; New York, 1950): and *Roosevelt and Frank-furter: Their Correspondence, 1928–1945,* ed. Max Freedman (Boston, 1968). The indispensable source of documents from State Department files for any phase of American foreign policy since 1861 is the on-going series *Foreign Relations of the United States* (Washington, D. C., 1861–) which includes a special Conference Series cover-ing the major wartime meetings between the Allied leaders. The Soviet Union has published *Correspondence between the Chairman of the Council of Ministers of the U.S.S.R. (Stalin) and the Presidents of the U.S.A. and the Prime Ministers of Great Britain during the Great Patriotic War of 1941–1945** (2 vols.; Moscow, 1957). German diplomacy is fully outlined in Auswärtiges Amt, *Documents on Ger-man Foreign Policy, 1918–1945,* Series D, 1937–1945 (13 vols.; Wash-ington, D.C., 1949–1964). There is no similar publication of British documents, but the recent declassification of British Cabinet records up to 1945 should stimulate publication of some useful collections. Additional information regarding documentary sources on American foreign policy can be found in the current edition of the pamphlet *Publications of the Department of State: An Annotated Bibliography** (Washington, D.C.).

The large number of official governmental histories of the Second World War are characterized by a wealth of information and an avoid-ance of controversy and conclusions. The most useful for data on foreign policy and diplomacy during the war are *The United States Army in World War II,* particularly the volumes subtitled *The War Department,* and *The Western Hemisphere,* all published by the Office of the Chief of Military History; and the British *History of the Second World War,* especially the volume by Sir Llewellyn Woodward, *Brit-ish Foreign Policy in the Second World War* (London, 1962) and two volumes in the *United Kingdom Civil Series:* H. Duncan Hall, *North American Supply* (London, 1955) and R. S. Sayers, *Financial Policy, 1939–1945* (London, 1956).

Published diaries and memoirs from the Roosevelt years abound. Although useful comments on foreign affairs can be found in almost all of them, the following have the most information on the broad scope of the Roosevelt foreign policy: Cordell Hull (Secretary of State), *The Memoirs of Cordell Hull* (2 vols.; New York, 1948); Henry L. Stimson (Secretary of War) and McGeorge Bundy, *On Active Service in Peace and War* (New York, 1948); Robert Sherwood (with the assistance and from the papers of Harry L. Hopkins, Presidential Assistant), *Roosevelt and Hopkins: An Intimate History** (rev. ed., New York, 1950); John M. Blum, *From the Morgenthau Diaries* (Henry Morgenthau, Jr., Secretary of the Treasury) (3 vols.; Boston, 1959, 1965, 1967); Harold L. Ickes (Secretary of the Interior), *The Secret Diary of Harold L. Ickes* (3 vols.; New York, 1954); Henry Morgenthau, Jr., *Morgenthau Diary (China),** ed. Committee on the Judiciary, U.S. Senate (Washington, D.C., 1965) and *Morgenthau Diary (Germany)** (Washington, D.C., 1967); Jay Pierrepont Moffat (State Dept. official), *The Moffat Papers,* ed. Nancy H. Hooker (Cambridge, Mass., 1956); Joseph C. Grew (Ambassador to Japan and Acting Secretary of State), *Ten Years in Japan, 1931–1942* (New York, 1944) and *Turbulent Era: A Diplomatic Record of Forty Years, 1904–1945* (2 vols.; Boston, 1952); Breckinridge Long (State Dept. official), *The War Diary of Breckinridge Long, 1939–1944,* ed. Fred L. Israel (Lincoln, Neb., 1966); George F. Kennan (State Dept. official), *Memoirs, 1925–1950** (Boston, 1967); Dean Acheson (State Dept. official), *Present at the Creation: My Years in the State Department* (New York, 1969); Elliott Roosevelt, *As He Saw It* (New York, 1946); and three quasi-memoirs by Sumner Welles (State Dept. official), *Seven Decisions That Shaped History* (New York, 1950), *The Time For Decision* (New York, 1944), and *Where Are We Heading?* (New York, 1946). Many of the memoirs and diaries of foreign statesmen deal in part with America's conduct of foreign relations, but the only one which consistently provides extensive insights and information on Roosevelt's activities is the monumental memoir by British Prime Minister Winston S. Churchill, *The Second World War** (6 vols.; Boston, 1948–1953). Though memoirs and diaries make fascinating reading and provide detail and atmosphere not otherwise available to readers, students should keep in mind that they are invariably tinged with self-justification and wishful thinking.

A complete bibliography of American foreign relations during the period 1937–1945 would fill a book nearly as long as this one, hence the titles below represent the best and usually most recent studies on the various topics and time periods. For additional reading and research guidance, students should consult the bibliographies in these books. Because of the fast-growing number of books and articles on Roosevelt's policies, particularly during the war, there is no up-to-date, complete bibliographical survey. The Franklin D.

Roosevelt Library has published a comprehensive, annotated bibliography in *The Era of Franklin D. Roosevelt: List of Periodical and Dissertation Literature, 1945–1966** (Hyde Park, New York, 1967). The editor, William Stewart, is currently preparing a new addition which will cover periodicals and dissertations written between 1966 and 1972.

Equally valuable is *The Second World War: A Bibliography—A Select List of Publications Appearing Since 1968** (dissertation and books only), comp., Arthur L. Funk for the American Committee on the History of the Second World War (Gainesville, Fla., June, 1972). John E. Wiltz has written a useful historiographical/bibliographical survey, *From Isolation to War, 1931–1941** (New York, 1968). Robert A. Divine has provided an excellent bibliography as well as a perceptive historiographical essay in his edited collection *Causes and Consequences of World War II** (Chicago, 1969), and both Wayne Cole, "American Entry into World War II: A Historiographical Appraisal," *Mississippi Valley Historical Review,* XLIII (March, 1957), 595–617, and Ernest R. May, *American Intervention: 1917 and 1941** (2nd ed.; Washington, D.C., 1967), analyze the debate over Roosevelt's prewar policies. Louis Morton's *Writings on World War II** (Washington, D.C., 1967), and "World War II: A Survey of Recent Writings," *American Historical Review,* LXXV (December, 1970), 1987–2008, are useful bibliographical/historiographical surveys. Thomas A. Bailey in his text, *A Diplomatic History of the American People* (8th ed.; New York, 1969) provides very complete bibliographies. Somewhat more recent but equally comprehensive in its bibliography is the text by Alexander DeConde, *A History of American Foreign Policy** (2d ed.; New York, 1971). An interesting *Select Bibliography of Revisionist Books Dealing with the Two World Wars and Their Aftermath,** ed. Harry Elmer Barnes (Oxford, California, n.d.) cites most of the important right-revisionist works published before 1959.

For the beginning student, the best place to start an examination of the secondary literature on Roosevelt's foreign policy is the America in Crisis series edited by Robert A. Divine, which includes two general surveys; Robert A. Divine, *The Reluctant Belligerent: American Entry into World War II** (New York, 1965) and Gaddis Smith, *American Diplomacy during the Second World War, 1941–1945** (New York, 1965). Divine's interpretative essays in *Roosevelt and World War*

*II** (Baltimore, 1969) survey the full range of President Roosevelt's foreign policy from 1933 through 1945, and like the two studies just mentioned, reflect a "traditional" point of view. William A. Williams, in the *Tragedy of American Diplomacy** (rev. ed.; New York, 1962), places the Roosevelt diplomacy in the context of Open Door expansionism during the twentieth century, while George F. Kennan's widely read *American Diplomacy, 1900–1950** (Chicago, 1951) briefly treats American foreign policy during World War II as unrealistic and erratic. Willard Range discusses the President's broad views of international relations in *Franklin D. Roosevelt's World Order* (Athens, Ga., 1959). The book is arranged topically and presupposes a solid knowledge of the chronological developments of policy.

There are a number of biographies of important public figures that provide special insights into the making and conduct of foreign policy between 1937 and 1945. In addition to the ones on Franklin D. Roosevelt listed above, see Forrest C. Pogue, *George C. Marshall* (2 vols. to date; New York, 1963–1968); Richard J. Whalen, *The Founding Father: The Story of Joseph P. Kennedy** (U.S. Ambassador to G.B.) (New York, 1964); Rexford G. Tugwell, *The Democratic Roosevelt: A Biography of Franklin Delano Roosevelt** (New York, 1957); Elting S. Morison, *Turmoil and Tradition: A Study of the Life and Times of Henry L. Stimson** (New York, 1964); Richard N. Current, *Secretary Stimson: A Study in Statecraft* (New Brunswick, N.J., 1954); Wayne S. Cole, *Senator Gerald P. Nye and American Foreign Relations* (Minneapolis, 1962); Julius W. Pratt, *Cordell Hull, 1933–1944* (2 vols.; New York, 1964); and Waldo Heinrichs, Jr., *American Ambassador: Joseph C. Grew and the Development of the United States Diplomatic Tradition* (Boston, 1966).

Studies of American foreign policy in the prewar period appeared as soon as the events themselves. Under strong criticism from anti-interventionists, the Roosevelt Administration privately sponsored the publication of two accounts; Joseph Alsop and Robert Kintner, *American White Paper: The Story of American Diplomacy and the Second World War* (New York, 1940) and Forrest Davis and Ernest K. Lindley, *How War Came: An American White Paper; From the Fall of France to Pearl Harbor* (New York, 1942). Relying largely upon the documents and statements brought forth by the U.S. Congress, Joint Committee on the Investigation of the Pearl Harbor Attack, *Hearings* (39 parts; Washington, D.C., 1946), as well as the public statements of administration officials, Charles A. Beard bitterly attacked Roosevelt's disingenuousness in *American Foreign Policy in the Making, 1932–1940* (New Haven, 1946) and the companion volume *President Roosevelt and the Coming of the War, 1941* (New Haven, 1948). The Truman Administration responded to this and other less scholarly attacks on its predecessor by opening official records to William L. Langer and S. Everett Gleason, who, under the aegis of the Council on Foreign Relations, published two volumes dealing with American entry into the war, *The Challenge to Isolation** (New York, 1952) and *The Undeclared War, 1940–1941* (New York, 1953). Although the authors were free to draw their own conclusions, their previous and then existing relationship to the Roosevelt/Truman Administrations virtually guaranteed a basically favorable account, though other historians have drawn more critical conclusions from just the evidence they presented. Similar treatment for Herbert Feis, a long-time State Department official, culminated in a predictably traditional monograph; *The Road to Pearl Harbor** (Princeton, 1950). Loud accusations of favoritism and "court histories" forced the State Department to open its files to a more critical scholar, and the result was Charles C. Tansill's *Back Door to War: The Roosevelt Foreign Policy, 1933–1941* (Chicago, 1952), a vicious, often personal attack on Roosevelt's character and intentions. The most representative piece of "right" revisionist history is a collection of essays edited by Harry Elmer Barnes, *Perpetual War for Perpetual Peace* (Caldwell, Idaho, 1953). Historians dismissed most early revisionist history all too facilely and only recently have begun to reexamine some of the valid questions and criticisms raised by men like Beard, Barnes, and Tansill. Although most of this reevaluation has centered on wartime diplomacy, Bruce M. Russett in *No Clear and Present Danger** (New York, 1972) has looked at the immediate prewar period from a strongly revisionist point of view.

Throughout the late 1950s and 1960s a large body of solidly researched studies of prewar policy appeared, most in the traditional vein of criticism of specifics but general approval for the broad elements of Roosevelt's foreign policy. Domestic influences on policy were the subject of a number of studies. Manfred Jonas tackled a critical and still unsolved question in *Isolationism in America, 1935–1941** (Ithaca, N.Y., 1966), while portions of that topic were studied by Wayne Cole in *America First: The Battle Against Intervention,*

1940–1941 (Madison, Wisc., 1953); Mark L. Chadwin, *Hawks of World War II** (Chapel Hill, N.C., 1968), William M. Tuttle, Jr., "Aid-to-the-Allies-Short-of-War versus American Intervention, 1940: A Reappraisal of William Allen White's Leadership," *Journal of American History*, LVI (March, 1970), 840–58; and Leland V. Bell, "The Failure of Nazism in America: The German American Bund, 1936–1941," *Political Science Quarterly*, LXXXV (December, 1970), 585–99.

The relationship of economics, domestic politics, and foreign policy has been dealt with on a broad scale by Lloyd C. Gardner, *Economic Aspects of New Deal Diplomacy** (Madison, Wisc., 1964), and Robert F. Smith, "American Foreign Relations, 1920–1942," in *Towards a New Past,** ed. Barton J. Bernstein (New York, 1968), both proceeding from a left-revisionist position. Studies which also emphasize the economic facet of foreign policy but which come to somewhat more traditional conclusions are Richard Gardner's *Sterling-Dollar Diplomacy* (exp. ed.; New York, 1969); Raymond Dawson's discussion of *The Decision to Aid Russia, 1941: Foreign Policy and Domestic Politics* (Chapel Hill, N.C., 1959); Warren F. Kimball's treatment of the development of the major American economic/military aid program in *"The Most Unsordid Act": Lend-Lease, 1939–1941* (Baltimore, 1969); Theodore Wilson's treatment of the Atlantic Conference, *The First Summit: Roosevelt and Churchill at Placentia Bay* (Boston, 1969); and John McV. Haight's *American Aid to France, 1938–1940* (New York, 1970).

German-American relations in the prewar period have received considerable scholarly attention in recent years. Earlier studies have largely been replaced by James V. Compton, *The Swastika and the Eagle: Hitler, the United States and the Origins of World War II* (Boston, 1967); Saul Friedlander, *Prelude to Downfall: Hitler and the United States, 1939–1941* (New York, 1967); Alton Frye, *Nazi Germany and the American Hemisphere, 1931–1941* (New Haven, 1967); and Gerhard L. Weinberg, "Hitler's Image of the United States," *American Historical Review*, LXIX (July, 1964), 1006–1021. Gabriel Kolko attacked American corporate leaders for cooperating with Hitler's military and industrial buildup in "American Business and Germany, 1930–1941," *Western Political Quarterly*, XV (1962), 713–728. America's failure to live up to its public ideals on the question of effectively helping European Jews is sensitively discussed in David S. Wyman, *Paper Walls: America and the Refugee Crisis, 1938–1941*

(Amherst, 1968), angrily condemned in Arthur Morse, *While Six Million Died** (New York, 1967), and most recently studied by Henry Feingold, *The Politics of Rescue* (New Brunswick, 1970).

American policy in East Asia requires study on a far more broad canvas than does the reaction of the United States to Nazi actions. Excellent background sources are William Neumann, *America Encounters Japan: From Perry to MacArthur** (Baltimore, 1963); Dorothy Borg, *The United States and the Far Eastern Crisis of 1933–1938* (Cambridge, Mass., 1964); James B. Crowley, *Japan's Quest for Autonomy: National Security and Foreign Policy, 1930–1938* (Princeton, 1966); Warren I. Cohen, *America's Response to China** (New York, 1970); and two books by Akira Iriye, *After Imperialism: The Search for a New Order in the Far East, 1921–1931** (Cambridge, Mass., 1965) and *Across the Pacific** (New York, 1967). A number of studies deal specifically with Japanese-American relations just before the war. Robert J. C. Butow, *Tojo and the Coming of the War* (Princeton, 1961) provided an excellent examination of the motives and methods of Japanese policy, while Paul Schroeder, *The Axis Alliance and Japanese-American Relations, 1941* (Ithaca, New York, 1958) criticized the American government for unrealistic and provocative policies which unwittingly forced Japan into war. Feis' study of the *Road to Pearl Harbor* pictured American policy-makers as having far less freedom of action, but most recent literature views the war in the Pacific as an avoidable tragedy; for example, John Toland's eminently readable *Rising Sun: The Decline and the Fall of the Japanese Empire, 1936–1945** (New York, 1970). The once emotional argument over the Pearl Harbor attack is now essentially a dead issue, having been laid to rest by two persuasive studies: Roberta Wohlstetter, *Pearl Harbor: Warning and Decision** (Stanford, 1962) and Ladislas Farago, *The Broken Seal: The Story of "Operation Magic" and the Pearl Harbor Disaster** (New York, 1967).

Much of the early literature on America's wartime diplomacy came in response to claims that the Roosevelt Administration had either consciously or stupidly sold out to the Communists, particularly during the conferences at Teheran and Yalta. Books like George N. Crocker's *Roosevelt's Road to Russia* (Chicago, 1959) and Hanson Baldwin's *Great Mistakes of the War* (New York, 1950), offered arguments which survived largely in the arena of partisan politics. Scholarly defenses of the Roosevelt Administration came from John

Snell (ed.), *The Meaning of Yalta** (Baton Rouge, 1956), and Herbert Feis *Churchill, Roosevelt, Stalin: The War They Waged and the Peace They Sought** (Princeton, 1957), to mention only two.

The understandably intense scholarly interest in the origins and development of the cold war has provided a set of blinders for most recent studies of American foreign policy during World War II. A few have attempted to study wartime diplomacy for itself, for example, John Snell, *Illusion and Necessity: The Diplomacy of Global War, 1939–1945** (Boston, 1963), but with little success. The substantial changes in the nature of the cold war as well as the intellectual effects of the American war in Vietnam have stimulated a large number of intensive studies of the World War II origins of Soviet-American conflict, through none has fully replaced William H. McNeill's *America, Britain and Russia: Their Cooperation and Conflict, 1941–1946** (London, 1953). Among the important recent general treatments are the early chapters in Lloyd Gardner, *Architects of Illusion: Men and Ideas in American Foreign Policy, 1941–1949** (Chicago, 1970); John L. Gaddis, *The United States and the Origins of the Cold War, 1941–1947** (New York, 1972); William L. Neumann, *After Victory: Churchill, Roosevelt, Stalin and the Making of the Peace** (New York, 1965); and a radical-left critique by Gabriel Kolko, *The Politics of War: The World and United States Foreign Policy, 1943–1945** (New York, 1968). More specific studies of wartime diplomacy and cold war beginnings can be found in George C. Herring, Jr., *Aid to Russia, 1941–1946: Strategy, Diplomacy, and the Origins of the Cold War* (New York, 1973); John Snell, *Wartime Origins of the East-West Dilemma Over Germany* (New Orleans, 1959); Stephen Ambrose, *Eisenhower and Berlin, 1945: The Decision to Halt at the Elbe** (New York, 1967); and Raymond G. O'Connor, *Diplomacy for Victory: FDR and Unconditional Surrender** (New York, 1971); Bruce Kuklick, *American Policy and the Division of Germany: The Clash with Russia over Reparations* (Ithaca, 1972); and Diane S. Clemens, *Yalta** (New York, 1970).

The question of Roosevelt's China policy received much attention following the collapse of the Nationalist government. Herbert Feis in *The China Tangle: The American Effort in China from Pearl Harbor to the Marshall Mission** (Princeton, 1953) placed the essential blame for a Communist take-over on the Chiang Kai-shek regime, while Anthony Kubek in *How the Far East Was Lost* (Chicago, 1963), writing in the tradition of his mentor, Charles Tansill, claimed that Communist agents in the State Department and general naiveté about Russian designs caused Roosevelt and Truman to abandon the Chiang government. Tang Tsou, in *America's Failure in China, 1941–1950** (Chicago, 1963) tended to split the difference. Barbara Tuchman's engrossing biography, *Stilwell and the American Experience in China, 1911–1945* (New York, 1970) provides background and additional detail.

The relationship between military strategy and foreign policy is perceptively studied in Kent R. Greenfield, *American Strategy in World War II: A Reconsideration** (Baltimore, 1963) and Greenfield (ed.), *Command Decisions* (Washington, D.C., 1963). Trumbull Higgins critically examined two controversial aspects of Anglo-American military planning in *Winston Churchill and the Second Front, 1940–1943* (New York, 1957) and *Soft Underbelly: The Anglo-American Controversy over the Italian Campaign, 1939–1945* (New York, 1968); and Michael Howard has also looked at the same questions in *The Mediterranean Strategy in the Second World War* (New York, 1968). The raw material for understanding strategic and tactical decisions is contained in the multivolume series *The United States Army in World War II* (cited above), though the current emphasis on declassification of military records from the Second World War should stimulate a new rash of secondary studies.

American policy toward Latin America and its relationship to the world crisis of 1937–1945 is touched on in many of the general studies of Roosevelt's diplomacy. More detail can be found in Donald Dozer, *Are We Good Neighors? Three Decades of Inter-American Relations, 1930–1960* (Gainesville, Fla., 1959). David Green has perceptively reexamined Roosevelt's policy toward Latin America in *The Containment of Latin America: A History of the Myths and Realities of the Good Neighbor Policy* (Chicago, 1971), finding that American economic goals played the dominant role. Two other studies previously cited, Alton Frye, *Nazi Germany and the American Hemisphere,* and Lloyd Gardner, *Economic Aspects of New Deal Diplomacy** also deal extensively with aspects of the Good Neighbor policy.

Although the actual use of the atomic bomb occurred after Roosevelt's death, the critical political implications as discussed in the Roosevelt Administration have become a battleground between traditional and left-revisionist historians. Gar Alperovitz, *Atomic Diplomacy: Hiroshima and Potsdam** (New York, 1965), accused Truman of changing Roosevelt's policy for one of atomic blackmail against the Soviet Union, while Herbert Feis, *The Atomic Bomb and the End of World War II** (Princeton, 1966), saw the decision as essentially military, though unnecessary. The variety of revisionist history is demonstrated by the fact that most other left revisionists see Truman's decision as the logical extension of Roosevelt's basic commitment to the Open Door and the extension of American hegemony.

There are a number of other useful monographs and memoirs which deal with a wide variety of subjects. Among the more useful are Milton Viorst, *Hostile Allies: F.D.R. and Charles de Gaulle* (New York, 1965); the memoir by presidential envoy in North Africa, Robert Murphy, *Diplomat Among Warriors* (Garden City, New York, 1964); a memoir by Churchill's personal physician Lord Moran, *Churchill: Taken from the Diaries of Lord Moran* (Boston, 1966); Robert Divine's discussion of the pro-United Nations movement, *Second Chance: The Triumph of Internationalism in America during World War II** (New York, 1967); Herbert Feis, *The Spanish Story: Franco and the Nations at War** (New York, 1948); and Stephen Xydis, *Greece and the Great Powers, 1944–1947* (Thessaloniki, 1963). Roosevelt's postwar plans for the Third World were haphazard, usually speculative, and always subordinated to the maintenance of great power cooperation during and after the war. Foster R. Dulles and Gerald Ridinger have written a useful article, "The Anti-Colonial Policies of Franklin D. Roosevelt," *Political Science Quarterly,* LXX (March, 1955), while Gary R. Hess has analyzed the President's shifting attitude toward French Indochina in "Franklin Roosevelt and Indochina," *Journal of American History,* LIX (September, 1972), 353–68.

DATE DUE